DAN-7    DANTES SUBJECT STANDARDIZED TESTS (DSST)

*This is your*
*PASSBOOK for...*

# Business Law (II)

*Test Preparation Study Guide*
*Questions & Answers*

# COPYRIGHT NOTICE

This book is SOLELY intended for, is sold ONLY to, and its use is RESTRICTED to individual, bona fide applicants or candidates who qualify by virtue of having seriously filed applications for appropriate license, certificate, professional and/or promotional advancement, higher school matriculation, scholarship, or other legitimate requirements of education and/or governmental authorities.

This book is NOT intended for use, class instruction, tutoring, training, duplication, copying, reprinting, excerption, or adaptation, etc., by:

1) Other publishers
2) Proprietors and/or Instructors of "Coaching" and/or Preparatory Courses
3) Personnel and/or Training Divisions of commercial, industrial, and governmental organizations
4) Schools, colleges, or universities and/or their departments and staffs, including teachers and other personnel
5) Testing Agencies or Bureaus
6) Study groups which seek by the purchase of a single volume to copy and/or duplicate and/or adapt this material for use by the group as a whole without having purchased individual volumes for each of the members of the group
7) Et al.

Such persons would be in violation of appropriate Federal and State statutes.

PROVISION OF LICENSING AGREEMENTS – Recognized educational, commercial, industrial, and governmental institutions and organizations, and others legitimately engaged in educational pursuits, including training, testing, and measurement activities, may address request for a licensing agreement to the copyright owners, who will determine whether, and under what conditions, including fees and charges, the materials in this book may be used them. In other words, a licensing facility exists for the legitimate use of the material in this book on other than an individual basis. However, it is asseverated and affirmed here that the material in this book CANNOT be used without the receipt of the express permission of such a licensing agreement from the Publishers. Inquiries re licensing should be addressed to the company, attention rights and permissions department.

All rights reserved, including the right of reproduction in whole or in part, in any form or by any means, electronic or mechanical, including photocopying, recording, or by any information storage and retrieval system, without permission in writing from the Publisher.

Copyright © 2025 by
## National Learning Corporation

212 Michael Drive, Syosset, NY 11791
(516) 921-8888 • www.passbooks.com
E-mail: info@passbooks.com

# PASSBOOK® SERIES

THE *PASSBOOK® SERIES* has been created to prepare applicants and candidates for the ultimate academic battlefield – the examination room.

At some time in our lives, each and every one of us may be required to take an examination – for validation, matriculation, admission, qualification, registration, certification, or licensure.

Based on the assumption that every applicant or candidate has met the basic formal educational standards, has taken the required number of courses, and read the necessary texts, the *PASSBOOK® SERIES* furnishes the one special preparation which may assure passing with confidence, instead of failing with insecurity. Examination questions – together with answers – are furnished as the basic vehicle for study so that the mysteries of the examination and its compounding difficulties may be eliminated or diminished by a sure method.

This book is meant to help you pass your examination provided that you qualify and are serious in your objective.

The entire field is reviewed through the huge store of content information which is succinctly presented through a provocative and challenging approach – the question-and-answer method.

A climate of success is established by furnishing the correct answers at the end of each test.

You soon learn to recognize types of questions, forms of questions, and patterns of questioning. You may even begin to anticipate expected outcomes.

You perceive that many questions are repeated or adapted so that you can gain acute insights, which may enable you to score many sure points.

You learn how to confront new questions, or types of questions, and to attack them confidently and work out the correct answers.

You note objectives and emphases, and recognize pitfalls and dangers, so that you may make positive educational adjustments.

Moreover, you are kept fully informed in relation to new concepts, methods, practices, and directions in the field.

You discover that you are actually taking the examination all the time: you are preparing for the examination by "taking" an examination, not by reading extraneous and/or supererogatory textbooks.

In short, this PASSBOOK®, used directedly, should be an important factor in helping you to pass your test.

# NONTRADITIONAL EDUCATION

Students returning to school as adults bring more varied experience to their studies than do the teenagers who begin college shortly after graduating from high school. As a result, there are numerous programs for students with nontraditional learning curves. Hundreds of colleges and universities grant degrees to people who cannot attend classes at a regular campus or have already learned what the college is supposed to teach.

You can earn nontraditional education credits in many ways:
- Passing standardized exams
- Demonstrating knowledge gained through experience
- Completing campus-based coursework, and
- Taking courses off campus

Some methods of assessing learning for credit are objective, such as standardized tests. Others are more subjective, such as a review of life experiences.

With some help from four hypothetical characters – Alice, Vin, Lynette, and Jorge – this article describes nontraditional ways of earning educational credit. It begins by describing programs in which you can earn a high school diploma without spending 4 years in a classroom. The college picture is more complicated, so it is presented in two parts: one on gaining credit for what you know through course work or experience, and a second on college degree programs. The final section lists resources for locating more information.

## Earning High School Credit

People who were prevented from finishing high school as teenagers have several options if they want to do so as adults. Some major cities have back-to-school programs that allow adults to attend high school classes with current students. But the more practical alternatives for most adults are to take the General Educational Development (GED) tests or to earn a high school diploma by demonstrating their skills or taking correspondence classes.

Of course, these options do not match the experience of staying in high school and graduating with one's friends. But they are viable alternatives for adult learners committed to meeting and, often, continuing their educational goals.

### GED Program

Alice quit high school her sophomore year and took a job to help support herself, her younger brother, and their newly widowed mother. Now an adult, she wants to earn her high school diploma – and then go on to college. Because her job as head cook and her family responsibilities keep her busy during the day, she plans to get a high school equivalency diploma. She will study for, and take, the GED tests. Every year, about half a million adults earn their high school credentials this way. A GED diploma is accepted in lieu of a high school one by more than 90 percent of employers, colleges, and universities, so it is a good choice for someone like Alice.

The GED testing program is sponsored by the American Council on Education and State and local education departments. It consists of examinations in five subject areas: Writing, science, mathematics, social studies, and literature and the arts. The tests also measure skills such as analytical ability, problem solving, reading comprehension, and ability to understand and apply information. Most of the questions are multiple choice; the writing test includes an essay section on a topic of general interest.

Eligibility rules for taking the exams vary, but some states require that you must be at least 18. Tests are given in English, Spanish, and French. In addition to standard print, versions in large print, Braille, and audiocassette are also available. Total time allotted for the tests is 7 1/2 hours.

The GED tests are not easy. About one-fourth of those who complete the exams every year do not pass. Passing scores are established by administering the tests to a sample of graduating high school seniors. The minimum standard score is set so that about one-third of graduating seniors would not pass the tests if they took them.

Because of the difficulty of the tests, people need to prepare themselves to take them. Often, they start by taking the Official GED Practice Tests, usually available through a local adult education center. Centers are listed in your phone book's blue pages under "Adult Education," "Continuing Education," or "GED." Adult education centers also have information about GED preparation classes and self-study materials. Classes are generally arranged to accommodate adults' work schedules. National Learning Corporation publishes several study guides that aim to thoroughly prepare test-takers for the GED.

School districts, colleges, adult education centers, and community organizations have information about GED testing schedules and practice tests. For more information, contact them, your nearest GED testing center, or:

GED Testing Service
One Dupont Circle, NW, Suite 250
Washington, DC 20036-1163
1(800) 62-MY GED (626-9433)
(202) 939-9490

**Skills Demonstration**

Adults who have acquired high school level skills through experience might be eligible for the National External Diploma Program. This alternative to the GED does not involve any direct instruction. Instead, adults seeking a high school diploma must demonstrate mastery of 65 competencies in 8 general areas: Communication; computation; occupational preparedness; and self, social, consumer, scientific, and technological awareness.

Mastery is shown through the completion of the tasks. For example, a participant could prove competency in computation by measuring a room for carpeting, figuring out the amount of carpet needed, and computing the cost.

Before being accepted for the program, adults undergo an evaluation. Tests taken at one of the program's offices measure reading, writing, and mathematics abilities. A take-home segment includes a self-assessment of current skills, an individual skill evaluation, and an occupational interest and aptitude test.

Adults accepted for the program have weekly meetings with an assessor. At the meeting, the assessor reviews the participant's work from the previous week. If the task has not been completed properly, the assessor explains the mistake. Participants continue to correct their errors until they master each competency. A high school diploma is awarded upon proven mastery of all 65 competencies.

Fourteen States and the District of Columbia now offer the External Diploma Program. For more information, contact:

External Diploma Program
One Dupont Circle, NW, Suite 250
Washington, DC 20036-1193
(202) 939-9475

## Correspondence and Distance Study

Vin dropped out of high school during his junior year because his family's frequent moves made it difficult for him to continue his studies. He promised himself at the time he dropped out that he would someday finish the courses needed for his diploma. For people like Vin, who prefer to earn a traditional diploma in a nontraditional way, there are about a dozen accredited courses of study for earning a high school diploma by correspondence, or distance study. The programs are either privately run, affiliated with a university, or administered by a State education department.

Distance study diploma programs have no residency requirements, allowing students to continue their studies from almost any location. Depending on the course of study, students need not be enrolled full time and usually have more flexible schedules for finishing their work. Selection of courses ranges from vo-tech to college prep, and some programs place different emphasis on the types of diplomas offered. University affiliated schools, for example, allow qualified students to take college courses along with their high school ones. Students can then apply the college credits toward a degree at that university or transfer them to another institution.

Taking courses by distance study is often more challenging and time consuming than attending classes, especially for adults who have other obligations. Success depends on each student's motivation. Students usually do reading assignments on their own. Written exercises, which they complete and send to an instructor for grading, supplement their reading material.

A list of some accredited high schools that offer diplomas by distance study is available free from the Distance Education and Training Council, formerly known as the National Home Study Council. Request the "DETC Directory of Accredited Institutions" from:

The Distance Education and Training Council
1601 18th Street, NW.
Washington, DC 20009-2529
(202) 234-5100

Some publications profiling nontraditional college programs include addresses and descriptions of several high school correspondence ones. See the Resources section at the end of this article for more information.

## Getting College Credit For What You Know

Adults can receive college credit for prior coursework, by passing examinations, and documenting experiential learning. With help from a college advisor, nontraditional students should assess their skills, establish their educational goals, and determine the number of college credits they might be eligible for.

Even before you meet with a college advisor, you should collect all your school and training records. Then, make a list of all knowledge and abilities acquired through experience, no matter how irrelevant they seem to your chosen field. Next, determine your educational goals: What specific field do you wish to study? What kind of a degree do you want? Finally, determine how your past work fits into the field of study. Later on, you will evaluate educational programs to find one that's right for you.

People who have complex educational or experiential learning histories might want to have their learning evaluated by the Regents Credit Bank. The Credit Bank, operated by Regents College of the University of the State of New York, allows people to consolidate credits earned through college, experience, or other methods. Special assessments are available for Regents College enrollees whose knowledge in a specific field cannot be adequately evaluated by standardized exams. For more information, contact the Regents Credit Bank at:

Regents College
7 Columbia Circle
Albany, NY 12203-5159
(518) 464-8500

**Credit For Prior College Coursework**

When Lynette was in college during the 1970s, she attended several different schools and took a variety of courses. She did well in some classes and poorly in others. Now that she is a successful business owner and has more focus, Lynette thinks she should forget about her previous coursework and start from scratch. Instead, she should start from where she is.

Lynette should have all her transcripts sent to the colleges or universities of her choice and let an admissions officer determine which classes are applicable toward a degree. A few credits here and there may not seem like much, but they add up. Even if the subjects do not seem relevant to any major, they might be counted as elective credits toward a degree. And comparing the cost of transcripts with the cost of college courses, it makes sense to spend a few dollars per transcript for a chance to save hundreds, and perhaps thousands, of dollars in books and tuition.

Rules for transferring credits apply to all prior coursework at accredited colleges and universities, whether done on campus or off. Courses completed off campus, often called extended learning, include those available to students through independent study and correspondence. Many schools have extended learning programs; Brigham Young University, for example, offers more than 300 courses through its Department of Independent Study. One type of extended learning is distance learning, a form of correspondence study by technological means such as television, video and audio, CD-ROM, electronic mail, and computer tutorials. See the Resources section at the end of this article for more information about publications available from the National University Continuing Education Association.

Any previously earned college credits should be considered for transfer, no matter what the subject or the grade received. Many schools do not accept the transfer of courses graded below a C or ones taken more than a designated number of years ago. Some colleges and universities also have limits on the number of credits that can be transferred and applied toward a degree. But not all do. For example, Thomas Edison State College, New Jersey's State college for adults, accepts the transfer of all 120 hours of credit required for a baccalaureate degree – provided all the credits are transferred from regionally accredited schools, no more than 80 are at the junior college level, and the student's grades overall and in the field of study average out to C.

To assign credit for prior coursework, most schools require original transcripts. This means you must complete a form or send a written, signed request to have your transcripts released directly to a college or university. Once you have chosen the schools you want to apply to, contact the schools you attended before. Find out how much each transcript costs, and ask them to send your transcripts to the ones you are applying to. Write a letter that includes your name (and names used during attendance, if different) and dates of attendance, along with the names and addresses of the schools to which your transcripts should be sent. Include payment and mail to the registrar at the schools you have attended. The registrar's office will process your request and send an official transcript of your coursework to the colleges or universities you have designated.

**Credit For Noncollege Courses**

Colleges and universities are not the only ones that offer classes. Volunteer organizations and employers often provide formal training worth college credit. The American Council on Education has two programs that assess thousands of specific courses and make recommendations on the amount of college credit they are worth. Colleges and universities accept the recommendations or use them as guidelines.

One program evaluates educational courses sponsored by government agencies, business and industry, labor unions, and professional and voluntary organizations. It is the Program on Noncollegiate Sponsored Instruction (PONSI). Some of the training seminars Alice has participated in covered topics such as food preparation, kitchen safety, and nutrition. Although she has not yet earned her GED, Alice can earn college credit because of her completion of these formal job-training seminars. The number of credits each seminar is worth does not hinge on Alice's current eligibility for college enrollment.

The other program evaluates courses offered by the Army, Navy, Air Force, Marines, Coast Guard, and Department of Defense. It is the Military Evaluations Program. Jorge has never attended college, but the engineering technology classes he completed as part of his military training are worth college credit. And as an Army veteran, Jorge is eligible for a service that takes the evaluations one step further. The Army/American Council on Education Registry Transcript System (AARTS) will provide Jorge with an individualized transcript of American Council on Education credit recommendations for all courses he completed, the military occupational specialties (MOS's) he held, and examinations he passed while in the Army. All Army and National Guard enlisted personnel and veterans who enlisted after October 1981 are eligible for the transcript. Similar services are being considered by the Navy and Marine Corps.

To obtain a free transcript, see your Army Education Center for a 5454R transcript request form. Include your name, Social Security number, basic active service date, and complete address where you want the transcript sent. Mail your request to:
AARTS Operations Center
415 McPherson Ave.
Fort Leavenworth, KS 66027-1373

Recommendations for PONSI are published in *The National Guide to Educational Credit for Training Programs;* military program recommendations are in *The Guide to the Evaluation of Educational Experiences in the Armed Forces.* See the Resources section at the end of this article for more information about these publications.

Former military personnel who took a foreign language course through the Defense Language Institute may request course transcripts by sending their name, Social Security number, course title, duration of the course, and graduation date to:

    Commandant, Defense Language Institute
    Attn: ATFL-DAA-AR
    Transcripts
    Presidio of Monterey
    Monterey, CA 93944-5006

Not all of Jorge's and Alice's courses have been assessed by the American Council on Education. Training courses that have no Council credit recommendation should still be assessed by an advisor at the schools they want to attend. Course descriptions, class notes, test scores, and other documentation may be helpful for comparing training courses to their college equivalents. An oral examination or other demonstration of competency might also be required.

There is no guarantee you will receive all the credits you are seeking – but you certainly won't if you make no attempt.

**Credit By Examination**

Standardized tests are the best-known method of receiving college credit without taking courses. These exams are often taken by high school students seeking advanced placement for college, but they are also available to adult learners. Testing programs and colleges and universities offer exams in a number of subjects. Two U.S. Government institutes have foreign language exams for employees that also may be worth college credit.

It is important to understand that receiving a passing score on these exams does not mean you get college credit automatically. Each school determines which test results it will accept, minimum scores required, how scores are converted for credit, and the amount of credit, if any, to be assigned. Most colleges and universities accept the American Council on Education credit recommendations, published every other year in the 250-page *Guide to Educational Credit by Examination*. For more information, contact:

    The American Council on Education
    Credit by Examination Program
    One Dupont Circle, Suite 250
    Washington, DC 20036-1193
    (202) 939-9434

*Testing programs:*

You might know some of the five national testing programs by their acronyms or initials: CLEP, ACT PEP: RCE, DANTES, AP, and NOCTI. (The meanings of these initialisms are explained below.) There is some overlap among programs; for example, four of them have introductory accounting exams. Since you will not be awarded credit more than once for a specific subject, you should carefully evaluate each program for the subject exams you wish to take. And before taking an exam, make sure you will be awarded credit by the college or university you plan to attend.

CLEP (College-Level Examination Program), administered by the College Board, is the most widely accepted of the national testing programs; more than 2,800 accredited schools award credit for passing exam scores. Each test covers material taught in basic undergraduate courses. There are five general exams – English composition, humanities, college mathematics, natural sciences, and social sciences and history – and many subject exams. Most exams are entirely multiple-choice, but English composition exams may include an essay section. For more information, contact:

    CLEP
    P.O. Box 6600
    Princeton, NJ 08541-6600
    (609) 771-7865

ACT PEP: RCE (American College Testing Proficiency Exam Program: Regents College Examinations) tests are given in 38 subjects within arts and sciences, business, education, and nursing. Each exam is recommended for either lower- or upper-level credit. Exams contain either objective or extended response questions, and are graded according to a standard score, letter grade, or pass/fail. Fees vary, depending on the subject and type of exam. For more information or to request free study guides, contact:

    ACT PEP: Regents College Examinations
    P.O. Box 4014
    Iowa City, IA 52243
    (319) 337-1387
    (New York State residents must contact Regents College directly.)

DANTES (Defense Activity for Nontraditional Education Support) standardized tests are developed by the Educational Testing Service for the Department of Defense. Originally administered only to military personnel, the exams have been available to the public since 1983. About 50 subject tests cover business, mathematics, social science, physical science, humanities, foreign languages, and applied technology. Most of the tests consist entirely of multiple-choice questions. Schools determine their own administering fees and testing schedules. For more information or to request free study sheets, contact:

    DANTES Program Office
    Mail Stop 31-X
    Educational Testing Service
    Princeton, NJ 08541
    1(800) 257-9484

The AP (Advanced Placement) Program is a cooperative effort between secondary schools and colleges and universities. AP exams are developed each year by committees of college and high school faculty appointed by the College Board and assisted by consultants from the Educational Testing Service. Subjects include arts and languages, natural sciences, computer science, social sciences, history, and mathematics. Most tests are 2 or 3 hours long and include both multiple-choice and essay questions. AP courses are available to help students prepare for exams, which are offered in the spring. For more information about the Advanced Placement Program, contact:

    Advanced Placement Services
    P.O. Box 6671
    Princeton, NJ 08541-6671
    (609) 771-7300

NOCTI (National Occupational Competency Testing Institute) assessments are designed for people like Alice, who have vocational-technical skills that cannot be evaluated by other tests. NOCTI assesses competency at two levels: Student/job ready and teacher/experienced worker. Standardized evaluations are available for occupations such as auto-body repair, electronics, mechanical drafting, quantity food preparation, and upholstering. The tests consist of multiple-choice questions and a performance component. Other services include workshops, customized assessments, and pre-testing. For more information, contact:

NOCTI
500 N. Bronson Ave.
Ferris State University
Big Rapids, MI 49307
(616) 796-4699

### *Colleges and universities:*

Many colleges and universities have credit-by-exam programs, through which students earn credit by passing a comprehensive exam for a course offered by the institution. Among the most widely recognized are the programs at Ohio University, the University of North Carolina, Thomas Edison State College, and New York University.

Ohio University offers about 150 examinations for credit. In addition, you may sometimes arrange to take special examinations in non-laboratory courses offered at Ohio University. To take a test for credit, you must enroll in the course. If you plan to transfer the credit earned, you also need written permission from an official at your school. Books and study materials are available, for a cost, through the university. Exams must be taken within 6 months of the enrollment date; most last 3 hours. You may arrange to take the exam off campus if you do not live near the university.

Ohio University is on the quarter-hour system; most courses are worth 4 quarter hours, the equivalent of 3 semester hours. For more information, contact:

Independent Study
Tupper Hall 302
Ohio University
Athens, OH 45701-2979
1(800) 444-2910
(614) 593-2910

The University of North Carolina offers a credit-by-examination option for 140 independent study (correspondence) courses in foreign languages, humanities, social sciences, mathematics, business administration, education, electrical and computer engineering, health administration, and natural sciences. To take an exam, you must request and receive approval from both the course instructor and the independent studies department. Exams must be taken within six months of enrollment, and you may register for no more than two at a time. If you are not near the University's Chapel Hill campus, you may take your exam under supervision at an accredited college, university, community college, or technical institute. For more information, contact:

Independent Studies
CB #1020, The Friday Center
UNC-Chapel Hill
Chapel Hill, NC 27599-1020
1(800) 862-5669 / (919) 962-1134

The Thomas Edison College Examination Program offers more than 50 exams in liberal arts, business, and professional areas. Thomas Edison State College administers tests twice a month in Trenton, New Jersey; however, students may arrange to take their tests with a proctor at any accredited American college or university or U.S. military base. Most of the tests are multiple choice; some also include short answer or essay questions. Time limits range from 90 minutes to 4 hours, depending on the exam. For more information, contact:

Thomas Edison State College
TECEP, Office of Testing and Assessment
101 W. State Street
Trenton, NJ 08608-1176
(609) 633-2844

New York University's Foreign Language Program offers proficiency exams in more than 40 languages, from Albanian to Yiddish. Two exams are available in each language: The 12-point test is equivalent to 4 undergraduate semesters, and the 16-point exam may lead to upper level credit. The tests are given at the university's Foreign Language Department throughout the year.

Proof of foreign language proficiency does not guarantee college credit. Some colleges and universities accept transcripts only for languages commonly taught, such as French and Spanish. Nontraditional programs are more likely than traditional ones to grant credit for proficiency in other languages.

For an informational brochure and registration form for NYU's foreign language proficiency exams, contact:

New York University
Foreign Language Department
48 Cooper Square, Room 107
New York, NY 10003
(212) 998-7030

### *Government institutes:*

The Defense Language Institute and Foreign Service Institute administer foreign language proficiency exams for personnel stationed abroad. Usually, the tests are given at the end of intensive language courses or upon completion of service overseas. But some people – like Jorge, who knows Spanish – speak another language fluently and may be allowed to take a proficiency exam in that language before completing their tour of duty. Contact one of the offices listed below to obtain transcripts of those scores. Proof of proficiency does not guarantee college credit, however, as discussed above.

To request score reports from the Defense Language Institute for Defense Language Proficiency Tests, send your name, Social Security number, language for which you were tested, and, most importantly, when and where you took the exam to:

Commandant, Defense Language Institute
Attn: ATFL-ES-T
DLPT Score Report Request
Presidio of Monterey
Monterey, CA 93944-5006

To request transcripts of scores for Foreign Service Institute exams, send your name, Social Security number, language for which you were tested, and dates or year of exams to:

Foreign Service Institute
Arlington Hall
4020 Arlington Boulevard
Rosslyn, VA 22204-1500
Attn: Testing Office (Send your request to the attention of the testing office of the foreign language in which you were tested)

**Credit For Experience**

Experiential learning credit may be given for knowledge gained through job responsibilities, personal hobbies, volunteer opportunities, homemaking, and other experiences. Colleges and universities base credit awards on the knowledge you have attained, not for the experience alone. In addition, the knowledge must be college level; not just any learning will do. Throwing horseshoes as a hobby is not likely to be worth college credit. But if you've done research on how and where the sport originated, visited blacksmiths, organized tournaments, and written a column for a trade journal – well, that's a horseshoe of a different color.

Adults attempting to get credit for their experience should be forewarned: Having your experience evaluated for college credit is time-consuming, tedious work – not an easy shortcut for people who want quick-fix college credits. And not all experience, no matter how valuable, is the equivalent of college courses.

Requesting college credit for your experiential learning can be tricky. You should get assistance from a credit evaluations officer at the school you plan to attend, but you should also have a general idea of what your knowledge is worth. A common method for converting knowledge into credit is to use a college catalog. Find course titles and descriptions that match what you have learned through experience, and request the number of credits offered for those courses.

Once you know what credit to ask for, you must usually present your case in writing to officials at the college you plan to attend. The most common form of presenting experiential learning for credit is the portfolio. A portfolio is a written record of your knowledge along with a request for equivalent college credit. It includes an identification and description of the knowledge for which you are requesting credit, an explanatory essay of how the knowledge was gained and how it fits into your educational plans, documentation that you have acquired such knowledge, and a request for college credit. Required elements of a portfolio vary by schools but generally follow those guidelines.

In identifying knowledge you have gained, be specific about exactly what you have learned. For example, it is not enough for Lynette to say she runs a business. She must identify the knowledge she has gained from running it, such as personnel management, tax law, marketing strategy, and inventory review. She must also include brief descriptions about her knowledge of each to support her claims of having those skills.

The essay gives you a chance to relay something about who you are. It should address your educational goals, include relevant autobiographical details, and be well organized, neat, and convey confidence. In his essay, Jorge might first state his goal of becoming an engineer. Then he would explain why he joined the Army, where he got hands-on training and experience in developing and servicing electronic equipment.

This, he would say, led to his hobby of creating remote-controlled model cars, of which he has built 20. His conclusion would highlight his accomplishments and tie them to his desire to become an electronic engineer.

Documentation is evidence that you've learned what you claim to have learned. You can show proof of knowledge in a variety of ways, including audio or video recordings, letters from current or former employers describing your specific duties and job performance, blueprints, photographs or artwork, and transcripts of certifying exams for professional licenses and certification – such as Alice's certification from the American Culinary Federation. Although documentation can take many forms, written proof alone is not always enough. If it is impossible to document your knowledge in writing, find out if your experiential learning can be assessed through supplemental oral exams by a faculty expert.

## Earning a College Degree

Nontraditional students often have work, family, and financial obligations that prevent them from quitting their jobs to attend school full time. Can they still meet their educational goals? Yes.

More than 150 accredited colleges and universities have nontraditional bachelor's degree programs that require students to spend little or no time on campus; over 300 others have nontraditional campus-based degree programs. Some of those schools, as well as most junior and community colleges, offer associate's degrees nontraditionally. Each school with a nontraditional course of study determines its own rules for awarding credit for prior coursework, exams, or experience, as discussed previously. Most have charges on top of tuition for providing these special services.

Several publications profile nontraditional degree programs; see the Resources section at the end of this article for more information. To determine which school best fits your academic profile and educational goals, first list your criteria. Then, evaluate nontraditional programs based on their accreditation, features, residency requirements, and expenses. Once you have chosen several schools to explore further, write to them for more information. Detailed explanations of school policies should help you decide which ones you want to apply to.

Get beyond the printed word – especially the glowing words each school writes about itself. Check out the schools you are considering with higher education authorities, alumni, employers, family members, and friends. If possible, visit the campus to talk to students and instructors and sit in on a few classes, even if you will be completing most or all of your work off campus. Ask school officials questions about such things as enrollment numbers, graduation rate, faculty qualifications, and confusing details about the application process or academic policies. After you have thoroughly investigated each prospective college or university, you can make an informed decision about which is right for you.

**Accreditation**

Accreditation is a process colleges and universities submit to voluntarily for getting their credentials. An accredited school has been investigated and visited by teams of observers and has periodic inspections by a private accrediting agency. The initial review can take two years or more.

Regional agencies accredit entire schools, and professional agencies accredit either specialized schools or departments within schools. Although there are no national accrediting standards, not just any accreditation will do. Countless "accreditation associations" have been invented by schools, many of which have no academic programs and sell phony degrees, to accredit themselves. But 6 regional and about 80 professional accrediting associations in the United States are recognized by the U.S. Department of Education or the Commission on Recognition of Postsecondary Accreditation. When checking accreditation, these are the names to look for. For more information about accreditation and accrediting agencies, contact:

    Institutional Participation Oversight Service Accreditation and State Liaison Division
    U.S. Department of Education
    ROB 3, Room 3915
    600 Independence Ave., SW
    Washington, DC 20202-5244
    (202) 708-7417

Because accreditation is not mandatory, lack of accreditation does not necessarily mean a school or program is bad. Some schools choose not to apply for accreditation, are in the process of applying, or have educational methods too unconventional for an accrediting association's standards. For the nontraditional student, however, earning a degree from a college or university with recognized accreditation is an especially important consideration. Although nontraditional education is becoming more widely accepted, it is not yet mainstream. Employers skeptical of a degree earned in a nontraditional manner are likely to be even less accepting of one from an unaccredited school.

**Program Features**

Because nontraditional students have diverse educational objectives, nontraditional schools are diverse in what they offer. Some programs are geared toward helping students organize their scattered educational credits to get a degree as quickly as possible. Others cater to those who may have specific credits or experience but need assistance in completing requirements. Whatever your educational profile, you should look for a program that works with you in obtaining your educational goals.

A few nontraditional programs have special admissions policies for adult learners like Alice, who plan to earn their GEDs but want to enroll in college in the meantime. Other features of nontraditional programs include individualized learning agreements, intensive academic counseling, cooperative learning and internship placement, and waiver of some prerequisites or other requirements – as well as college credit for prior coursework, examinations, and experiential learning, all discussed previously.

Lynette, whose primary goal is to finish her degree, wants to earn maximum credits for her business experience. She will look for programs that do not limit the number of credits awarded for equivalency exams and experiential learning. And since well-documented proof of knowledge is essential for earning experiential learning credits, Lynette should make sure the program she chooses provides assistance to students submitting a portfolio.

Jorge, on the other hand, has more credits than he needs in certain areas and is willing to forego some. To become an engineer, he must have a bachelor's degree; but because he is accustomed to hands-on learning, Jorge is interested in getting experience as he gains more technical skills. He will concentrate on finding schools with strong cooperative education, supervised fieldwork, or internship programs.

## Residency Requirements

Programs are sometimes deemed nontraditional because of their residency requirements. Many people think of residency for colleges and universities in terms of tuition, with in-state students paying less than out-of-state ones. Residency also may refer to where a student lives, either on or off campus, while attending school.

But in nontraditional education, residency usually refers to how much time students must spend on campus, regardless of whether they attend classes there. In some nontraditional programs, students need not ever step foot on campus. Others require only a very short residency, such as one day or a few weeks. Many schools have standard residency requirements of several semesters but schedule classes for evenings or weekends to accommodate working adults.

Lynette, who previously took courses by independent study, prefers to earn credits by distance study. She will focus on schools that have no residency requirement. Several colleges and universities have nonresident degree completion programs for adults with some college credit. Under the direction of a faculty advisor, students devise a plan for earning their remaining credits. Methods for earning credits include independent study, distance learning, seminars, supervised fieldwork, and group study at arranged sites. Students may have to earn a certain number of credits through the degree-granting institution. But many programs allow students to take courses at accredited schools of their choice for transfer toward their degree.

Alice wants to attend lectures but has an unpredictable schedule. Her best course of action will be to seek out short residency programs that require students to attend seminars once or twice a semester. She can take courses that are televised and videotape them to watch when her schedule permits, with the seminars helping to ensure that she properly completes her coursework. Many colleges and universities with short residency requirements also permit students to earn some credits elsewhere, by whatever means the student chooses.

Some fields of study require classroom instruction. As Jorge will discover, few colleges and universities allow students to earn a bachelor's degree in engineering entirely through independent study. Nontraditional residency programs are designed to accommodate adults' daytime work schedules. Jorge should look for programs offering evening, weekend, summer, and accelerated courses.

## Tuition and Other Expenses

The final decisions about which schools Alice, Jorge, and Lynette attend may hinge in large part on a single issue: Cost. And rising tuition is only part of the equation. Beginning with application fees and continuing through graduation fees, college expenses add up.

Traditional and nontraditional students have some expenses in common, such as the cost of books and other materials. Tuition might even be the same for some courses, especially for colleges and universities offering standard ones at unusual times. But for nontraditional programs, students may also pay fees for services such as credit or transcript review, evaluation, advisement, and portfolio assessment.

Students are also responsible for postage and handling or setup expenses for independent study courses, as well as for all examination and transcript fees for transferring credits. Usually, the more nontraditional the program, the more detailed the fees. Some schools charge a yearly enrollment fee rather than tuition for degree completion candidates who want their files to remain active.

Although tuition and fees might seem expensive, most educators tell you not to let money come between you and your educational goals. Talk to someone in the financial aid department of the school you plan to attend or check your library for publications about financial aid sources. The U.S. Department of Education publishes a guide to Federal aid programs such as Pell Grants, student loans, and work-study. To order the free 74-page booklet, *The Student Guide: Financial Aid from the U.S. Department of Education,* contact:

Federal Student Aid Information Center
P.O. Box 84
Washington, DC 20044
1 (800) 4FED-AID (433-3243)

**Resources**

Information on how to earn a high school diploma or college degree without following the usual routes is available from several organizations and in numerous publications. Information on nontraditional graduate degree programs, available for master's through doctoral level, though not discussed in this article, can usually be obtained from the same resources that detail bachelor's degree programs.

National Learning Corporation publishes study guides for all of these exams, for both general examinations and tests in specific subject areas. To order study guides, or to browse their catalog featuring more than 5,000 titles, visit NLC online at www.passbooks.com, or contact them by phone at (800) 632-8888.

**Organizations**

Adult learners should always contact their local school system, community college, or university to learn about programs that are readily available. The following national organizations can also supply information:

American Council on Education
One Dupont Circle
Washington, DC 20036-1193
(202) 939-9300

Within the American Council on Education, the Center for Adult Learning and Educational Credentials administers the National External Diploma Program, the GED Program, the Program on Noncollegiate Sponsored Instruction, the Credit by Examination Program, and the Military Evaluations Program.

# DANTES Subject Standardized Tests

## INTRODUCTION

The DANTES (Defense Activity for Non-Traditional Education Support) subject standardized tests are comprehensive college and graduate level examinations given by the Armed Forces, colleges and graduate schools as end-of-subject course evaluation final examinations or to obtain college equivalency credits in the various subject areas tested.

The DANTES Examination Program enables students to obtain college credit for what they have learned on the job, through self-study, personal interest, correspondence courses or by any other means. It is used by colleges and universities to award college credit to students who demonstrate that they know as much as students completing an equivalent college course. It is a cost-efficient, time-saving way for students to use their knowledge to accomplish their educational goals.

Most schools accept the American Council on Education (ACE) recommendations for the minimum score required and the amount of credit awarded, but not all schools do. Be sure to check the policy regarding the score level required for credit and the number of credits to be awarded.

Not all tests are accepted by all institutions. Even when a test is accepted by an institution, it may not be acceptable for every program at that institution. Before considering testing, ascertain the acceptability of a specific test for a particular course.

Colleges and universities that administer DANTES tests may administer them to any applicant – or they may administer the tests only to students registered at their institution. Decisions about who will be allowed to test are made by the school. Students should contact the test center to determine current policies and schedules for DANTES testing.

Colleges and universities authorized to administer DANTES tests usually do so throughout the calendar year. Each school sets its own fee for test administration and establishes its own testing schedule. Contact the representative at the administering school directly to make arrangements for testing.

# Checklist For Students

✓ Visit **www.getcollegecredit.com** to obtain a list of tests, fact sheets, test preparation materials, participating colleges and universities, and much more.

✓ Contact your school advisor to confirm that the DSST you selected will fit into your curriculum.

✓ Consult the ***DSST Candidate Information Bulletin*** for answers to specific questions.

✓ Contact the test site to schedule your test.

✓ Prepare for your examination by using the fact sheet as a guide.

✓ Take the test.

*If you would like a score report sent to your college or university, it is a good idea to bring the four-digit code with you. You must write the DSST Test Center Code for that institution on your answer sheet at the time of testing. DSST Test Center Codes are noted in the DSST Participating Colleges and Universities listing on the Web site.*

*If you prefer to send a score report to an institution at a later date, there is a transcript fee of $20 for each transcript ordered.*

Thomson Prometric
DSST Program
2000 Lenox Drive, Third Floor
Lawrenceville, NJ 08648

Toll-free: 877-471-9860
609-895-5011

E-mail: pnj-dsst@thomson.com

parts of this introduction excerpted for educational purposes from the official announcement ©2006 Thompson Prometric

# MAKING A COLLEGE DEGREE WITHIN YOUR REACH

Today, there are many educational alternatives to the classroom—you can learn from your job, your reading, your independent study, and special interests you pursue. You may already have learned the subject matter covered by some college-level courses.

The DSST Program is a nationally recognized testing program that gives you the opportunity to receive college credit for learning acquired outside the traditional college classroom. Colleges and universities throughout the United States administer the program, developed by Thomson Prometric, year-round. Annually, over 90,000 DSSTs are administered to individuals who are interested in continuing their education. Take advantage of the DSST testing program; it speeds the educational process and provides the flexibility adults need, making earning a degree more feasible.

Since requirements differ from college to college, please check with the credit-awarding institution before taking a DSST. More than 1,800 colleges and universities currently award credit for DSSTs, and the number is growing every day. You can choose from 37 test titles in the areas of Social Science, Business, Mathematics, Applied Technology, Humanities, and Physical Science. A brief description of each examination is found on the pages that follow.

**Reach Your Career Goals Through DSSTs**

Use DSSTs to help you earn your degree, get a promotion, or simply demonstrate that you have college-level knowledge in subjects relevant to your work.

*Save Time...*

You don't have to sit through classes when you have previously acquired the knowledge or experience for most of what is being taught and can learn the rest yourself. You might be able to bypass introductory-level courses in subject areas you already know.

*Save Money...*

DSSTs save you money because the classes you bypass by earning credit through the DSST Program are classes you won't have to pay for on your way to earning your degree. You can use the money instead to take more advanced courses that can be more challenging and rewarding.

**Improve Your Chances for Admission to College**

Each college has its own admission policies; however, having passing scores for DSSTs on your transcript can provide strong evidence of how well you can perform at the college level.

**Gain Confidence Performing at a College Level**

Many adults returning to college find that lack of confidence is often the greatest hurdle to overcome. Passing a DSST demonstrates your ability to perform on a college level.

## Make Up for Courses You May Have Missed

You may be ready to graduate from college and find that you are a few credits short of earning your degree. By using semester breaks, vacation time, or leisure time to study independently, you can prepare to take one or more DSSTs, fulfill your academic requirements, and graduate on time.

## If You Cannot Attend Regularly Scheduled Classes...

If your lifestyle or responsibilities prevent you from attending regularly scheduled classes, you can earn your college degree from a college offering an external degree program. The DSST Program allows you to earn your degree by study and experience outside the traditional classroom.

Many colleges and universities offer external degree or distance learning programs. For additional information, contact the college you plan to attend or:

Center for Lifelong Learning
American Council on Education
One DuPont Circle NW, Suite 250
Washington, DC 20036
202-939-9475
www.acenet.edu
(Select "Center for Lifelong Learning" under "Programs & Services"
for more information)

## Fact Sheets

For each test, there is a Fact Sheet that outlines the topics covered by each test and includes a list of sample questions, a list of recommended references of books that would be useful for review, and the number of credits awarded for a passing score as recommended by the American Council on Education (ACE). *Please note that some schools require scores that are higher than the minimum ACE-recommended passing score.* It is suggested that you check with your college or university to determine what score they require in order to earn credit. You can obtain Fact Sheets by:
- Downloading them from www.getcollegecredit.com
- E-mailing a request to pnj-dsst@thomson.com
- Completing a Candidate Publications Order Form

## DSST Online Practice Tests

DSST online practice tests contain items that reflect a *partial range of difficulty* identified in the Content Outline section on each Fact Sheet. There is an online DSST Practice Test in the following categories:
- Mathematics
- Social Science
- Business
- Physical Science
- Applied Technology
- Humanities

Although the online DSST Practice Test questions do not indicate the full range of difficulty you would find in an actual DSST test, they will help you assess your knowledge level. Each online DSST Practice Test can be purchased by visiting www.getcollegecredit.com and clicking on DSST Practice Exams.

# TAKING DSST EXAMINATIONS

### Earning College Credit for DSST Examinations
To find out if the college of your choice awards credit for passing DSST scores, contact the admissions office or counseling and testing office. The college can also provide information on the scores required for awarding credit, the number of credit hours awarded, and any courses that can be bypassed with satisfactory scores.

<u>It is important that you contact the institution of your choice as early as possible since credit-awarding policies differ among colleges and universities.</u>

### Where to Take DSSTs
DSSTs are administered at colleges and universities nationwide. Each location determines the frequency and scheduling of test administrations. To obtain the most current list of participating DSST colleges and universities:
- Visit and download the information from www.getcollegecredit.com
- E-mail pnj-dsst@thomson.com

### Scheduling Your Examination
*Please be aware that some colleges and universities provide DSST testing services to enrolled students only.* After you have selected a college or university that administers DSSTs, you will need to contact them to schedule your test date.

The fee to take a DSST is $60 per test. This fee entitles you to two score reports after the test is scored. One will be sent directly to you and the other will be sent to the college or university that you designate on your answer sheet. You may pay the test fee with a certified check or U.S. money order made payable to Thomson Prometric or you may charge the test fee to your Visa, MasterCard or American Express credit card. Note: The credit card statement will reflect a charge from Thomson Prometric for all DSST examinations. *(Declined credit card charges will be assessed an additional $25 processing fee.)*

In addition, the test site may also require a test administration fee for each examination, to be paid directly to the institution. Contact the test site to determine its administration fee and payment policy.

### Other Testing Arrangements
If you are unable to find a participating DSST college or university in your area, you may want to contact the testing office of a local accredited college or university to determine whether a representative from that office will agree to administer the test(s) for you.

The school's representative should then contact the DSST Program at 866-794-3497 to arrange for this administration. If you are unable to locate a test site, contact Thomson Prometric for assistance at pnj-dsst@thomson.com or 866-794-3497.

### Testing Accommodations for Students with Disabilities
Thomson Prometric is committed to serving test takers with disabilities by providing services and reasonable testing accommodations as set forth in the provisions of the *Americans with Disabilities Act* (ADA). If you have a disability, as prescribed by the ADA, and require special testing services or arrangements, please contact the test administrator at the test site. You will be asked to submit to the test administrator documentation of your disability and your request for special accommodations. The test

administrator will then forward your documentation along with your request for testing accommodations to Thomson Prometric for approval.

Please submit your request as far in advance of your test date as possible so that the necessary accommodations can be made. Only test takers with documented disabilities are eligible for special accommodations.

**On the Day of the Examination**

It is important to review this information and to have the correct identification present on the day of the examination:
- Arrive on time as a courtesy to the test administrator.
- Bring a valid form of government-issued identification that includes a current photo and your signature (acceptable documents include a driver's license, passport, state-issued identification card or military identification). *Anyone who fails to present valid identification will not be allowed to test.*
- Bring several No. 2 (soft-lead) sharpened pencils with good erasers, a watch, and a black pen if you will be writing an essay.
- Do not bring books or papers.
- Do not bring an alarm watch that beeps, a telephone, or a phone beeper into the testing room.
- The use of nonprogrammable calculators, slide rules, scratch paper and/or other materials is permitted for some of the tests.

## DSST SCORING POLICIES

Your DSST examination scores are reported only to you, unless you request that they be sent elsewhere. If you want your scores sent to your college, you must provide the correct DSST code number of the school on your answer sheet at the time you take the test. See the *DSST Directory of Colleges and Universities* on the Web site www.getcollegecredit.com.

If your institution is not listed, contact Thomson Prometric at 866-794-3497 to establish a code number. (Some schools may require a student to be enrolled prior to receiving a score report.)

**Receiving Your Score Report**

Allow approximately four weeks after testing to receive your score report.

Calling DSST Customer Service before the required four-week score processing time has elapsed will not expedite the processing of your scores. Due to privacy and security requirements, scores will not be reported to students over the telephone under any circumstance.

**Scoring of Principles of Public Speaking Speeches**

The speech portion of the *Principles of Public Speaking* examination will be sent to speech raters who are faculty members at accredited colleges that currently teach or have previously taught the course. Scores for the *Principles of Public Speaking* examination are available six to eight weeks from receipt by Thomson Prometric. If you take the *Principles of Public Speaking* examination and fail (either the objective, speech portion, or both), you must follow the retesting policy waiting period of six months (180 days) before retaking the entire exam.

**Essays**

The essays for *Ethics in America* and *Technical Writing* are <u>optional</u> and thus are not scored by raters. The essays are forwarded to the college or university that you designate, along with your score report, for their use in determining the award of credit. <u>Before taking the *Ethics in America* or *Technical Writing* examinations, check with your college or university to determine whether the essay is required.</u>

**NOTE:** *Principles of Public Speaking* speech topic cassette tapes and essays are kept on file at Thomson Prometric for one year from the date of administration.

**How to Get Transcripts**

There is a $20 fee for each transcript you request. Payment must be in the form of a certified check, U.S. money order payable to Thomson Prometric, or credit card. Personal checks and debit cards are NOT an acceptable method of payment. One transcript may include scores for one or more examinations taken. To request a transcript, download the Transcript Order Form from www.getcollegecredit.com.

## DESCRIPTION OF THE DSST EXAMINATIONS

**Mathematics**

- **Fundamentals of College Algebra** covers mathematical concepts such as fundamental algebraic operations; linear, absolute value; quadratic equations, inequalities, radials, exponents and logarithms, factoring polynomials and graphing. The use of a nonprogrammable, handheld calculator is permitted.

- **Principles of Statistics** tests the understanding of the various topics of statistics, both qualitatively and quantitatively, and the ability to apply statistical methods to solve a variety of problems. The topics included in this test are descriptive statistics; correlation and regression; probability; chance models and sampling and tests of significance. The use of a nonprogrammable, handheld calculator is permitted.

**Social Science**

- **Art of the Western World** deals with the history of art during the following periods: classical; Romanesque and Gothic; early Renaissance; high Renaissance, Baroque; rococo; neoclassicism and romanticism; realism, impressionism and post-impressionism; early twentieth century; and post-World War II.

- **Western Europe Since 1945** tests the knowledge of basic facts and terms and the understanding of concepts and principles related to the areas of the historical background of the aftermath of the Second World War and rebuilding of Europe; national political systems; issues and policies in Western European societies; European institutions and processes; and Europe's relations with the rest of the world.

- **An Introduction to the Modern Middle East** emphasizes core knowledge (including geography, Judaism, Christianity, Islam, ethnicity); nineteenth-century European impact; twentieth-century Western influences; World Wars I and II; new nations; social and cultural changes (1900-1960) and the Middle East from 1960 to present.

- **Human/Cultural Geography** includes the Earth and basic facts (coordinate systems, maps, physiography, atmosphere, soils and vegetation, water); culture and environment, spatial processes (social processes, modern economic systems, settlement patterns, political geography); and regional geography.

- **Rise and Fall of the Soviet Union** covers Russia under the Old Regime; the Revolutionary Period; New Economic Policy; Pre-war Stalinism; The Second World War; Post-war Stalinism; The Khrushchev Years; The Brezhnev Era; and reform and collapse.

- **A History of the Vietnam War** covers the history of the roots of the Vietnam War; the First Vietnam War (1946-1954); pre-war developments (1954-1963); American involvement in the Vietnam War; Tet (1968); Vietnamizing the War (1968-1973); Cambodia and Laos; peace; legacies and lessons.

- **The Civil War and Reconstruction** covers the Civil War from presecession (1861) through Reconstruction. It includes causes of the war; secession; Fort Sumter; the war in the east and in the west; major battles; the political situation; assassination of Lincoln; end of the Confederacy; and Reconstruction.

- **Foundations of Education** includes topics such as contemporary issues in education; past and current influences on education (philosophies, democratic ideals, social/economic influences); and the interrelationships between contemporary issues and influences.

- **Life-span Developmental Psychology** covers models and theories; methods of study; ethical issues; biological development; perception, learning and memory; cognition and language; social, emotional, and personality development; social behaviors, family life cycle, extrafamilial settings; singlehood and cohabitation; occupational development and retirement; adjustment to life stresses; and bereavement and loss.

- **Drug and Alcohol Abuse** includes such topics as drug use in society; classification of drugs; pharmacological principles; alcohol (types, effects of, alcoholism); general principles and use of sedative hypnotics, narcotic analgesics, stimulants, and hallucinogens; other drugs (inhalants, steroids); and prevention/treatment.

- **General Anthropology** deals with anthropology as a discipline; theoretical perspectives; physical anthropology; archaeology; social organization; economic organization; political organization; religion; and modernization and application of anthropology.

- **Introduction to Law Enforcement** includes topics such as history and professional movement of law enforcement; overview of the U.S. criminal justice system; police systems in the U.S.; police organization, management, and issues; and U.S. law and precedents.

- **Criminal Justice** deals with criminal behavior (crime in the U.S., theories of crime, types of crime); the criminal justice system (historical origins, legal foundations, due process); police; the court system (history and organization, adult court system, juvenile court, pre-trial and post-trial processes); and corrections.

- **Fundamentals of Counseling** covers historical development (significant influences and people); counselor roles and functions; the counseling relationship; and theoretical approaches to counseling.

## Business
- **Principles of Finance** deals with financial statements and planning; time value of money; working capital management; valuation and characteristics; capital budgeting; cost of capital; risk and return; and international financial management. The use of a nonprogrammable, handheld calculator is permitted.

- **Principles of Financial Accounting** includes topics such as general concepts and principles, accounting cycle and classification; transaction analysis; accruals and deferrals; cash and internal control; current accounts; long- and short-term liabilities; capital stock; and financial statements. The use of a nonprogrammable, handheld calculator is permitted.

- **Human Resource Management** covers general employment issues; job analysis; training and development; performance appraisals; compensation issues; security issues; personnel legislation and regulation; labor relations and current issues; an overview of the Human Resource Management Field; Human Resource Planning; Staffing; training and development; compensation issues; safety and health; employee rights and discipline; employment law; labor relations and current issues and trends.

- **Organizational Behavior** deals with the study of organizational behavior (scientific approaches, research designs, data collection methods); individual processes and characteristics; interpersonal and group processes and characteristics; organizational processes and characteristics; and change and development processes.

- **Principles of Supervision** deals with the roles and responsibilities of the supervisor; management functions (planning, organization and staffing, directing at the supervisory level); and other topics (legal issues, stress management, union environments, quality concerns).

- **Business Law II** covers topics such as sales of goods; debtor and creditor relations; business organizations; property; and commercial paper.

- **Introduction to Computing** includes topics such as history and technological generations; hardware/software; applications to information technology; program development; data management; communications and connectivity; and computing and society. The use of a nonprogrammable, handheld calculator is permitted.

- **Management Information Systems** covers systems theory, analysis and design of systems, hardware and software; database management; telecommunications; management of the MIS functional area and informational support.

- **Introduction to Business** deals with economic issues affecting business; international business; government and business; forms of business ownership; small business, entrepreneurship and franchise; management process; human resource management; production and operations; marketing management; financial management; risk management and insurance; and management and information systems.

- **Money and Banking** covers the role and kinds of money; commercial banks and other financial intermediaries; central banking and the Federal Reserve system; money and macroeconomics activity; monetary policy in the U.S.; and the international monetary system.

- **Personal Finance** includes topics such as financial goals and values; budgeting; credit and debt; major purchases; taxes; insurance; investments; and retirement and estate planning. The use of auxiliary materials, such as calculators and slide rules, is NOT permitted.

- **Business Mathematics** deals with basic operations with integers, fractions, and decimals; round numbers; ratios; averages; business graphs; simple interest; compound interest and annuities; net pay and deductions; discounts and markups; depreciation and net worth; corporate securities; distribution of ownership; and stock and asset turnover.

**Physical Science**
• **Astronomy** covers the history of astronomy, celestial mechanics; celestial systems; astronomical instruments; the solar system; nature and evolution; the galaxy; the universe; determining astronomical distances; and life in the universe.

• **Here's to Your Health** covers mental health and behavior; human development and relationships; substance abuse; fitness and nutrition; risk factors, disease, and disease prevention; and safety, consumer awareness, and environmental concerns.

• **Environment and Humanity** deals with topics such as ecological concepts (ecosystems, global ecology, food chains and webs); environmental impacts; environmental management and conservation; and political processes and the future.

• **Principles of Physical Science I** includes physics: Newton's Laws of Motion; energy and momentum; thermodynamics; wave and optics; electricity and magnetism; chemistry: properties of matter; atomic theory and structure; and chemical reactions.

• **Physical Geology** covers Earth materials; igneous, sedimentary, and metamorphic rocks; surface processes (weathering, groundwater, glaciers, oceanic systems, deserts and winds, hydrologic cycle); internal Earth processes; and applications (mineral and energy resources, environmental geology).

**Applied Technology**
• **Technical Writing** covers topics such as theory and practice of technical writing; purpose, content, and organizational patterns of common types of technical documents; elements of various technical reports; and technical editing. Students have the option to write a short essay on one of the technical topics provided. Thomson Prometric will not score the essay; however, for determining the award of credit, a copy of the essay will be forwarded to the college or university you've designated along with the score report or transcript.

**Humanities**
• **Ethics in America** deals with ethical traditions (Greek views, Biblical traditions, moral law, consequential ethics, feminist ethics); ethical analysis of issues arising in interpersonal and personal-societal relationships and in professional and occupational roles; and relationships between ethical traditions and the ethical analysis of situations. Students have the option to write an essay to analyze a morally problematic situation in terms of issues relevant to a decision and arguments for alternative positions. Thomson Prometric will not score the essay; however, for determining the award of credit, a copy of the essay will be forwarded to the college or university you've designated along with the score report or transcript.

• **Introduction to World Religions** covers topics such as dimensions and approaches to religion; primal religions; Hinduism; Buddhism; Confucianism; Taoism; Judaism; Christianity; and Islam.

• **Principles of Public Speaking** consists of two parts: Part One consists of multiple-choice questions covering considerations of Principles of Public Speaking; audience analysis; purposes of speeches; structure/organization; content/supporting materials; research; language and style; delivery; communication apprehension; listening and feedback; and criticism and evaluation. Part Two requires the student to record an impromptu persuasive speech that will be scored.

# FREQUENTLY ASKED QUESTIONS ABOUT DSSTs

*In order to pass the test, must I study from one of the recommended references?*

The recommended references are a listing of books that were being used as textbooks in college courses of the same or similar title at the time the test was developed. Appropriate textbooks for study are not limited to those listed in the fact sheet. If you wish to obtain study resources to prepare for the examination, you may reference either the current edition of the listed titles or textbooks currently used at a local college or university for the same class title. It is recommended that you reference more than one textbook on the topics outlined in the fact sheet. You should begin by checking textbook content against the content outline included on the front page of the DSST fact sheet before selecting textbooks that cover the text content from which to study. Textbooks may be found at the campus bookstore of a local college or university offering a course on the subject.

*Is there a penalty for guessing on the tests?*

There is no penalty for guessing on DSSTs, so you should mark an answer for each question.

*How much time will I have to complete the test?*

Many DSSTs can be completed within 90 minutes; however, additional time can be allowed if necessary.

*What should I do if I find a test question irregularity?*

Continue testing and then report the irregularity to the test administrator after the test. This may be done by asking that the test administrator note the irregularity on the Supervisor's Irregularity Report or you can write to Thomson Prometric, DSST Program, 2000 Lenox Drive, Third Floor, Lawrenceville, NJ 08648, and indicate the form and question number(s) or circumstances as well as your name and address.

*When will I receive my score report?*

Allow approximately four weeks from the date of testing to receive your score report. Allow six to eight weeks to receive a score report for the *Principles of Public Speaking* examination.

*Will my test scores be released without my permission?*

Your test score will not be released to anyone other than the school you designate on your answer sheet unless you write to us and ask us to send a transcript elsewhere. Instructions about how to do this can be found on your score report. Your scores may be used for research purposes, but individual scores are never made public nor are individuals identified if research findings are made public.

*If I do not achieve a passing score on the test, how long must I wait until I can take the test again?*

If you do not receive a score on the test that will enable you to obtain credit for the course, you may take the test again after six months (180 days). Please do not attempt to take the test before six months (180 days) have passed because you will receive a score report marked *invalid* and your test fee will not be refunded.

*Can my test scores be canceled?*

The test administrator is required to report any irregularities to Thomson Prometric. <u>The consequence of bringing unauthorized materials into the testing room, or giving or receiving help, will be the forfeiture of your test fee and the invalidation of test scores.</u> The DSST Program reserves the right to cancel scores and not issue score reports in such situations.

*What can I do if I feel that my test scores were not accurately reported?*

Thomson Prometric recognizes the extreme importance of test results to candidates and has a multi-step quality-control procedure to help ensure that reported scores are accurate. If you have reason to believe that your score(s) were not accurately reported, you may request to have your answer sheet reviewed and hand scored.

The fees for this service are:
- $20 fee if requested within six months of the test date
- $30 fee if requested more than six months from the test date
- $30 fee if a re-evaluation of the *Principles of Public Speaking* speech is requested

The fee for this service can be paid by credit card or by certified check or U.S. money order payable to Thomson Prometric. Submit your request for score verification along with the appropriate fee or credit card information (credit card number and expiration date) to Thomson Prometric, DSST Program, 2000 Lenox Drive, Third Floor, Lawrenceville, NJ 08648. Include your full name, the test title, the date you took the test, and your Social Security number. Candidates will be notified if a scoring discrepancy is discovered within four weeks of receipt of the request.

*What does ACE recommendation mean?*

The ACE recommendation is the minimum passing score recommended by the American Council on Education for any given test. It is equivalent to the average score of students in the DSST norming sample who received a grade of C for the course. Some schools require a score higher than the ACE recommendation.

*Who is NLC?*

National Learning Corporation (NLC) has been successfully preparing candidates for 40 years for over 5,000 exams. NLC publishes Passbook® study guides to help candidates prepare for all DANTES and CLEP exams and almost every other type of exam from high school through adult career.

Go to our website — www.passbooks.com — or call (800) 632-8888 for information about ordering our Passbooks.

---

To get detailed information on the DSST program and DSST preparation materials, visit www.getcollegecredit.com.

If you are interested in taking the DSST exams, call 877-471-9860 or e-mail pnj-dsst@thomson.com.

# HOW TO TAKE A TEST

You have studied long, hard and conscientiously.

With your official admission card in hand, and your heart pounding, you have been admitted to the examination room.

You note that there are several hundred other applicants in the examination room waiting to take the same test.

They all appear to be equally well prepared.

You know that nothing but your best effort will suffice. The "moment of truth" is at hand: you now have to demonstrate objectively, in writing, your knowledge of content and your understanding of subject matter.

You are fighting the most important battle of your life—to pass and/or score high on an examination which will determine your career and provide the economic basis for your livelihood.

What extra, special things should you know and should you do in taking the examination?

I. YOU MUST PASS AN EXAMINATION

A. WHAT EVERY CANDIDATE SHOULD KNOW
Examination applicants often ask us for help in preparing for the written test. What can I study in advance? What kinds of questions will be asked? How will the test be given? How will the papers be graded?

B. HOW ARE EXAMS DEVELOPED?
Examinations are carefully written by trained technicians who are specialists in the field known as "psychological measurement," in consultation with recognized authorities in the field of work that the test will cover. These experts recommend the subject matter areas or skills to be tested; only those knowledges or skills important to your success on the job are included. The most reliable books and source materials available are used as references. Together, the experts and technicians judge the difficulty level of the questions.
Test technicians know how to phrase questions so that the problem is clearly stated. Their ethics do not permit "trick" or "catch" questions. Questions may have been tried out on sample groups, or subjected to statistical analysis, to determine their usefulness.
Written tests are often used in combination with performance tests, ratings of training and experience, and oral interviews. All of these measures combine to form the best-known means of finding the right person for the right job.

## II. HOW TO PASS THE WRITTEN TEST

### A. BASIC STEPS

**1) Study the announcement**

How, then, can you know what subjects to study? Our best answer is: "Learn as much as possible about the class of positions for which you've applied." The exam will test the knowledge, skills and abilities needed to do the work.

Your most valuable source of information about the position you want is the official exam announcement. This announcement lists the training and experience qualifications. Check these standards and apply only if you come reasonably close to meeting them. Many jurisdictions preview the written test in the exam announcement by including a section called "Knowledge and Abilities Required," "Scope of the Examination," or some similar heading. Here you will find out specifically what fields will be tested.

**2) Choose appropriate study materials**

If the position for which you are applying is technical or advanced, you will read more advanced, specialized material. If you are already familiar with the basic principles of your field, elementary textbooks would waste your time. Concentrate on advanced textbooks and technical periodicals. Think through the concepts and review difficult problems in your field.

These are all general sources. You can get more ideas on your own initiative, following these leads. For example, training manuals and publications of the government agency which employs workers in your field can be useful, particularly for technical and professional positions. A letter or visit to the government department involved may result in more specific study suggestions, and certainly will provide you with a more definite idea of the exact nature of the position you are seeking.

**3) Study this book!**

## III. KINDS OF TESTS

Tests are used for purposes other than measuring knowledge and ability to perform specified duties. For some positions, it is equally important to test ability to make adjustments to new situations or to profit from training. In others, basic mental abilities not dependent on information are essential. Questions which test these things may not appear as pertinent to the duties of the position as those which test for knowledge and information. Yet they are often highly important parts of a fair examination. For very general questions, it is almost impossible to help you direct your study efforts. What we can do is to point out some of the more common of these general abilities needed in public service positions and describe some typical questions.

**1) General information**

Broad, general information has been found useful for predicting job success in some kinds of work. This is tested in a variety of ways, from vocabulary lists to questions about current events. Basic background in some field of work, such as sociology or economics, may be sampled in a group of questions. Often these are principles which have become familiar to most persons through exposure rather than through formal training. It is difficult to advise you how to study for these questions; being alert to the world around you is our best suggestion.

2) Verbal ability

An example of an ability needed in many positions is verbal or language ability. Verbal ability is, in brief, the ability to use and understand words. Vocabulary and grammar tests are typical measures of this ability. Reading comprehension or paragraph interpretation questions are common in many kinds of civil service tests. You are given a paragraph of written material and asked to find its central meaning.

## IV. KINDS OF QUESTIONS

1. Multiple-choice Questions

Most popular of the short-answer questions is the "multiple choice" or "best answer" question. It can be used, for example, to test for factual knowledge, ability to solve problems or judgment in meeting situations found at work.

A multiple-choice question is normally one of three types:
- It can begin with an incomplete statement followed by several possible endings. You are to find the one ending which best completes the statement, although some of the others may not be entirely wrong.
- It can also be a complete statement in the form of a question which is answered by choosing one of the statements listed.
- It can be in the form of a problem – again you select the best answer.

Here is an example of a multiple-choice question with a discussion which should give you some clues as to the method for choosing the right answer:

When an employee has a complaint about his assignment, the action which will best help him overcome his difficulty is to
  A. discuss his difficulty with his coworkers
  B. take the problem to the head of the organization
  C. take the problem to the person who gave him the assignment
  D. say nothing to anyone about his complaint

In answering this question, you should study each of the choices to find which is best. Consider choice "A" – Certainly an employee may discuss his complaint with fellow employees, but no change or improvement can result, and the complaint remains unresolved. Choice "B" is a poor choice since the head of the organization probably does not know what assignment you have been given, and taking your problem to him is known as "going over the head" of the supervisor. The supervisor, or person who made the assignment, is the person who can clarify it or correct any injustice. Choice "C" is, therefore, correct. To say nothing, as in choice "D," is unwise. Supervisors have and interest in knowing the problems employees are facing, and the employee is seeking a solution to his problem.

2. True/False

3. Matching Questions
Matching an answer from a column of choices within another column.

## V. RECORDING YOUR ANSWERS

Computer terminals are used more and more today for many different kinds of exams.

For an examination with very few applicants, you may be told to record your answers in the test booklet itself. Separate answer sheets are much more common. If this separate answer sheet is to be scored by machine – and this is often the case – it is highly important that you mark your answers correctly in order to get credit.

## VI. BEFORE THE TEST

### YOUR PHYSICAL CONDITION IS IMPORTANT

If you are not well, you can't do your best work on tests. If you are half asleep, you can't do your best either. Here are some tips:

1) Get about the same amount of sleep you usually get. Don't stay up all night before the test, either partying or worrying—DON'T DO IT!
2) If you wear glasses, be sure to wear them when you go to take the test. This goes for hearing aids, too.
3) If you have any physical problems that may keep you from doing your best, be sure to tell the person giving the test. If you are sick or in poor health, you relay cannot do your best on any test. You can always come back and take the test some other time.

Common sense will help you find procedures to follow to get ready for an examination. Too many of us, however, overlook these sensible measures. Indeed, nervousness and fatigue have been found to be the most serious reasons why applicants fail to do their best on civil service tests. Here is a list of reminders:

- Begin your preparation early – Don't wait until the last minute to go scurrying around for books and materials or to find out what the position is all about.
- Prepare continuously – An hour a night for a week is better than an all-night cram session. This has been definitely established. What is more, a night a week for a month will return better dividends than crowding your study into a shorter period of time.
- Locate the place of the exam – You have been sent a notice telling you when and where to report for the examination. If the location is in a different town or otherwise unfamiliar to you, it would be well to inquire the best route and learn something about the building.
- Relax the night before the test – Allow your mind to rest. Do not study at all that night. Plan some mild recreation or diversion; then go to bed early and get a good night's sleep.
- Get up early enough to make a leisurely trip to the place for the test – This way unforeseen events, traffic snarls, unfamiliar buildings, etc. will not upset you.
- Dress comfortably – A written test is not a fashion show. You will be known by number and not by name, so wear something comfortable.
- Leave excess paraphernalia at home – Shopping bags and odd bundles will get in your way. You need bring only the items mentioned in the official notice you received; usually everything you need is provided. Do not bring reference books to the exam. They will only confuse those last minutes and be taken away from you when in the test room.

- Arrive somewhat ahead of time – If because of transportation schedules you must get there very early, bring a newspaper or magazine to take your mind off yourself while waiting.
- Locate the examination room – When you have found the proper room, you will be directed to the seat or part of the room where you will sit. Sometimes you are given a sheet of instructions to read while you are waiting. Do not fill out any forms until you are told to do so; just read them and be prepared.
- Relax and prepare to listen to the instructions
- If you have any physical problem that may keep you from doing your best, be sure to tell the test administrator. If you are sick or in poor health, you really cannot do your best on the exam. You can come back and take the test some other time.

## VII. AT THE TEST

The day of the test is here and you have the test booklet in your hand. The temptation to get going is very strong. Caution! There is more to success than knowing the right answers. You must know how to identify your papers and understand variations in the type of short-answer question used in this particular examination. Follow these suggestions for maximum results from your efforts:

1) Cooperate with the monitor

The test administrator has a duty to create a situation in which you can be as much at ease as possible. He will give instructions, tell you when to begin, check to see that you are marking your answer sheet correctly, and so on. He is not there to guard you, although he will see that your competitors do not take unfair advantage. He wants to help you do your best.

2) Listen to all instructions

Don't jump the gun! Wait until you understand all directions. In most civil service tests you get more time than you need to answer the questions. So don't be in a hurry. Read each word of instructions until you clearly understand the meaning. Study the examples, listen to all announcements and follow directions. Ask questions if you do not understand what to do.

3) Identify your papers

Civil service exams are usually identified by number only. You will be assigned a number; you must not put your name on your test papers. Be sure to copy your number correctly. Since more than one exam may be given, copy your exact examination title.

4) Plan your time

Unless you are told that a test is a "speed" or "rate of work" test, speed itself is usually not important. Time enough to answer all the questions will be provided, but this does not mean that you have all day. An overall time limit has been set. Divide the total time (in minutes) by the number of questions to determine the approximate time you have for each question.

5) Do not linger over difficult questions

If you come across a difficult question, mark it with a paper clip (useful to have along) and come back to it when you have been through the booklet. One caution if you do this – be sure to skip a number on your answer sheet as well. Check often to be sure that you have not lost your place and that you are marking in the row numbered the same as the question you are answering.

6) Read the questions
Be sure you know what the question asks! Many capable people are unsuccessful because they failed to read the questions correctly.

7) Answer all questions
Unless you have been instructed that a penalty will be deducted for incorrect answers, it is better to guess than to omit a question.

8) Speed tests
It is often better NOT to guess on speed tests. It has been found that on timed tests people are tempted to spend the last few seconds before time is called in marking answers at random – without even reading them – in the hope of picking up a few extra points. To discourage this practice, the instructions may warn you that your score will be "corrected" for guessing. That is, a penalty will be applied. The incorrect answers will be deducted from the correct ones, or some other penalty formula will be used.

9) Review your answers
If you finish before time is called, go back to the questions you guessed or omitted to give them further thought. Review other answers if you have time.

10) Return your test materials
If you are ready to leave before others have finished or time is called, take ALL your materials to the monitor and leave quietly. Never take any test material with you. The monitor can discover whose papers are not complete, and taking a test booklet may be grounds for disqualification.

## VIII. EXAMINATION TECHNIQUES

1) Read the general instructions carefully. These are usually printed on the first page of the exam booklet. As a rule, these instructions refer to the timing of the examination; the fact that you should not start work until the signal and must stop work at a signal, etc. If there are any special instructions, such as a choice of questions to be answered, make sure that you note this instruction carefully.

2) When you are ready to start work on the examination, that is as soon as the signal has been given, read the instructions to each question booklet, underline any key words or phrases, such as least, best, outline, describe and the like. In this way you will tend to answer as requested rather than discover on reviewing your paper that you listed without describing, that you selected the worst choice rather than the best choice, etc.

3) If the examination is of the objective or multiple-choice type – that is, each question will also give a series of possible answers: A, B, C or D, and you are called upon to select the best answer and write the letter next to that answer on your answer paper – it is advisable to start answering each question in turn. There may be anywhere from 50 to 100 such questions in the three or four hours allotted and you can see how much time would be taken if you read through all the questions before beginning to answer any. Furthermore, if you

come across a question or group of questions which you know would be difficult to answer, it would undoubtedly affect your handling of all the other questions.

4) If the examination is of the essay type and contains but a few questions, it is a moot point as to whether you should read all the questions before starting to answer any one. Of course, if you are given a choice – say five out of seven and the like – then it is essential to read all the questions so you can eliminate the two that are most difficult. If, however, you are asked to answer all the questions, there may be danger in trying to answer the easiest one first because you may find that you will spend too much time on it. The best technique is to answer the first question, then proceed to the second, etc.

5) Time your answers. Before the exam begins, write down the time it started, then add the time allowed for the examination and write down the time it must be completed, then divide the time available somewhat as follows:
    - If 3-1/2 hours are allowed, that would be 210 minutes. If you have 80 objective-type questions, that would be an average of 2-1/2 minutes per question. Allow yourself no more than 2 minutes per question, or a total of 160 minutes, which will permit about 50 minutes to review.
    - If for the time allotment of 210 minutes there are 7 essay questions to answer, that would average about 30 minutes a question. Give yourself only 25 minutes per question so that you have about 35 minutes to review.

6) The most important instruction is to read each question and make sure you know what is wanted. The second most important instruction is to time yourself properly so that you answer every question. The third most important instruction is to answer every question. Guess if you have to but include something for each question. Remember that you will receive no credit for a blank and will probably receive some credit if you write something in answer to an essay question. If you guess a letter – say "B" for a multiple-choice question – you may have guessed right. If you leave a blank as an answer to a multiple-choice question, the examiners may respect your feelings but it will not add a point to your score. Some exams may penalize you for wrong answers, so in such cases only, you may not want to guess unless you have some basis for your answer.

7) Suggestions
    a. Objective-type questions
        1. Examine the question booklet for proper sequence of pages and questions
        2. Read all instructions carefully
        3. Skip any question which seems too difficult; return to it after all other questions have been answered
        4. Apportion your time properly; do not spend too much time on any single question or group of questions
        5. Note and underline key words – all, most, fewest, least, best, worst, same, opposite, etc.
        6. Pay particular attention to negatives
        7. Note unusual option, e.g., unduly long, short, complex, different or similar in content to the body of the question
        8. Observe the use of "hedging" words – probably, may, most likely, etc.

9. Make sure that your answer is put next to the same number as the question
10. Do not second-guess unless you have good reason to believe the second answer is definitely more correct
11. Cross out original answer if you decide another answer is more accurate; do not erase until you are ready to hand your paper in
12. Answer all questions; guess unless instructed otherwise
13. Leave time for review

b. Essay questions
1. Read each question carefully
2. Determine exactly what is wanted. Underline key words or phrases.
3. Decide on outline or paragraph answer
4. Include many different points and elements unless asked to develop any one or two points or elements
5. Show impartiality by giving pros and cons unless directed to select one side only
6. Make and write down any assumptions you find necessary to answer the questions
7. Watch your English, grammar, punctuation and choice of words
8. Time your answers; don't crowd material

8) Answering the essay question

Most essay questions can be answered by framing the specific response around several key words or ideas. Here are a few such key words or ideas:

M's: manpower, materials, methods, money, management
P's: purpose, program, policy, plan, procedure, practice, problems, pitfalls, personnel, public relations

a. Six basic steps in handling problems:
1. Preliminary plan and background development
2. Collect information, data and facts
3. Analyze and interpret information, data and facts
4. Analyze and develop solutions as well as make recommendations
5. Prepare report and sell recommendations
6. Install recommendations and follow up effectiveness

b. Pitfalls to avoid
1. Taking things for granted – A statement of the situation does not necessarily imply that each of the elements is necessarily true; for example, a complaint may be invalid and biased so that all that can be taken for granted is that a complaint has been registered
2. Considering only one side of a situation – Wherever possible, indicate several alternatives and then point out the reasons you selected the best one
3. Failing to indicate follow up – Whenever your answer indicates action on your part, make certain that you will take proper follow-up action to see how successful your recommendations, procedures or actions turn out to be
4. Taking too long in answering any single question – Remember to time your answers properly

# EXAMINATION SECTION

# EXAMINATION SECTION
# TEST 1

DIRECTIONS: Each question or incomplete statement is followed by several suggested answers or completions. Select the one that BEST answers the question or completes the statement. *PRINT THE LETTER OF THE CORRECT ANSWER IN THE SPACE AT THE RIGHT.*

1. In payment for a television set, C gave D a $400 note dated January 15, and payable in 30 days. D discounted the note at the S Bank.
   On the date of maturity, C may legally refuse to pay the note if

   A. D used duress in obtaining C's signature
   B. D misrepresented the merchandise he sold to C
   C. C was an infant
   D. D took the completed note from C's desk without C's permission

   1.____

2. A, a general partner in the firm of A and B, died. He left a will leaving all his business and personal property to his wife.
   His wife should then be

   A. legally entitled to become a general partner of the firm immediately
   B. entitled to her husband's share of the firm's net worth
   C. required to carry out, personally or otherwise, the partnership duties formerly carried out by her husband
   D. expected to serve as a general partner until the end of the firm's fiscal year

   2.____

3. A television set was sold to E by the G Appliance Co. for $250 terms 30 days.
   Title to the television set passed to E when

   A. the sale was made             B. the set was delivered
   C. the set was paid for          D. 30 days have passed

   3.____

4. A fire insurance contract becomes effective when the

   A. insurance company issues the policy
   B. insured receives the policy
   C. insured pays his first premium
   D. agent agrees to insure the property

   4.____

5. I bought a radio on the installment plan from the H Appliance Co. After the set had been delivered to I, but before he had fully paid for it, vandals broke into I's apartment and stole the radio.
   The loss would be borne by

   A. H Appliance Co.
   B. I
   C. I – only to the extent of what he had already paid
   D. H Appliance Co. and I equally

   5.____

1

6. K sold $500 merchandise to J, terms n/30. K immediately assigned his $500 claim against J to L. After the assignment was made, J returned $100 defective merchandise to K.
   L can collect

   A. $500 from J. J must settle with K.
   B. $500 from K. J must settle with K.
   C. $400 from J and $100 from K.
   D. $500 from J after J has settled with K.

7. A refusal by a creditor to accept a debtor's offer to pay cash in settlement of his debt

   A. discharges the debt
   B. excuses the debtor from interest payments
   C. renews the debt for six years
   D. bars legal action by the creditor on the debt

8. S, the buyer for the dress department of F Stores, was instructed by R, the proprietor, to pay for all merchandise with sixty-day notes. S signed one note given in full payment of a bill of goods, F Stores, by S, Agent; a second was signed, S, Agent for F Stores; and a third was signed, S, Agent.
   The principal could be held liable on

   A. all the notes
   B. none of the notes
   C. the first note only
   D. the first and second notes only

9. M asked B, his bookkeeper, to purchase a fan for the office for not more than $40. B bought a fan for $24 as well as a desk lamp for $16 from the Q Appliance Company.
   The Q Appliance Company legally can collect

   A. $24 from M and $16 from B
   B. $40 from M and compel him to take the lamp
   C. $24 from M and accept the return of the lamp
   D. $40 from M and ask M to collect $16 from B

10. D and F were partners engaged in the wholesale grocery business. Without the knowledge or consent of his partner, D executed and delivered to M a promissory note in payment of a partnership debt. He signed the firm's name on the note.
    On the promissory note, M can legally hold

    A. D only
    B. D and F
    C. neither D nor F
    D. D to the extent of his investment, and F for the balance, if any

11. W, in order to meet the claims of his creditors, borrowed $2500 from P. In order to protect his interest, P insured W's life for $2500. Later, W paid $1500 to P, on account. P continued paying the premiums on W's life insurance policy.
    On W's death, P could collect _____ from the insurance company and $1000 from P's estate.

    A. nothing   B. $1000   C. $1500   D. $2500

12. A principal will ordinarily be held liable for the acts of his agent *only* of these acts are    12.____

    A. to the principal's advantage
    B. to the agent's advantage
    C. within the principal's express instructions
    D. within the actual or apparent scope of the agent's authority

13. A dealer sold and delivered a record player to F. Later, discovering that F was a minor, the dealer sought to avoid the contract and recover the record player.    13.____
    Which statement BEST explains why the dealer cannot recover the record player?

    A. Ordinarily a contract between an adult and an infant is voidable at the option of the infant
    B. Infancy is an absolute defense good against all parties
    C. The dealer should have determined F's age before entering into this agreement
    D. An infant is bound only on his contracts for necessaries

14. K, a holder in due course, failed to make proper presentment of a negotiable instrument on the due date. K's failure to present the paper to the party primarily liable, discharged    14.____

    A. the maker only
    B. both the maker and the indorsers
    C. all indorsers
    D. K's immediate indorser only

15. If an ultra vires contract has been fully performed by both parties,    15.____

    A. neither party can rescind the contract
    B. the stockholders of the corporation may compel the Board of Directors to rescind the contract
    C. the Board of Directors may rescind the contract without a stockholder's vote
    D. only the other party (not the corporation) may rescind the contract

---

# KEY (CORRECT ANSWERS)

1. C          6. C
2. B          7. B
3. A          8. C
4. D          9. A
5. B         10. B

11. D
12. D
13. A
14. C
15. A

# TEST 2

DIRECTIONS: Each question or incomplete statement is followed by several suggested answers or completions. Select the one that BEST answers the question or completes the statement. *PRINT THE LETTER OF THE CORRECT ANSWER IN THE SPACE AT THE RIGHT.*

1. In a C.O.D. sale, title

   A. passes at the date of the sale
   B. is retained by the seller until delivered to the buyer
   C. passes when the goods are delivered to the carrier
   D. passes when the purchaser receives and pays for the item

2. A, and insane person, before so officially adjudged, entered into a contract with B. This contract is

   A. an aleatory contract
   B. voidable at option of A
   C. void
   D. voidable at option of B

3. A bill of lading serves four distinct functions as
   I. a receipt
   II. a contract
   III. evidence of the kind, quality, and the quantity of good shipped, *and*
   IV. ....................

   A. an invoice
   B. evidence of liability
   C. evidence of title
   D. a purchase order

4. Liquidated damages

   A. constitute compensation which parties have agreed upon to be paid which will follow a breach of contract
   B. are damages which result from particular circumstances in a case
   C. are damages resulting when a wrong is established but no real damage is shown, or proven
   D. are synonymous with *mitigated damages*

5. An executory contract is

   A. an implied contract
   B. a contract used in wills
   C. one fully performed
   D. one not yet performed

6. Champerty is

   A. encouragement of liquidation by contract
   B. an unlicensed transaction
   C. in restraint of trade
   D. a form of price-fixing

7. Contracts made on Sundays and legal holidays, including checks and promissory notes, not consummated or calling for performance on such days, are

   A. void
   B. voidable
   C. valid
   D. contrary to public policy

8. The substitution of a new contract, or a new debtor, for an existing one, is called

   A. a *condition precedent*  B. a *quasi contract*
   C. unenforceable  D. a *novation*

9. The right of *stoppage-in-transitu* arises only when an unpaid seller has

   A. made a mistake in price
   B. defaulted in paying creditors
   C. shipped goods to a buyer who is insolvent
   D. admitted a fourth partner

10. Design patents are good for _____ years.

    A. 7  B. 17  C. 28  D. no time limit

11. When a seller has a voidable title to goods because of fraud, a *bona fide* purchaser for value acquires _____ title.

    A. voidable  B. valid  C. defective  D. no

12. In this state, a contract for the sale of goods comes under the Statute of Frauds if the value is _____ or upward.

    A. $50  B. $200  C. $250  D. $500

13. An insurance company receives its right to seek payment from a third party who was negligent and caused the loss from the _____ clause.

    A. subrogation  B. contributions
    C. co-insurance  D. general average

14. An addition to a will is known as a(n)

    A. amendment  B. allonge
    C. continuance  D. codicil

15. On July 14, W in New York, shipped goods to C, in Rochester. The goods were sent *F.O.B. Rochester* as directed in the written order of July 8. The goods arrived at the station in Rochester on July 18 and C was notified. On July 21, C picked up the goods at the station.
    The title to the goods passed to C on July _____ .

    A. 18  B. 8  C. 21  D. 14

## KEY (CORRECT ANSWERS)

1. C
2. B
3. C
4. A
5. D

6. A
7. C
8. D
9. D
10. A

11. B
12. D
13. A
14. D
15. A

---

# EXAMINATION SECTION
# TEST 1

DIRECTIONS: Each question or incomplete statement is followed by several suggested answers or completions. Select the one that BEST answers the question or completes the statement. *PRINT THE LETTER OF THE CORRECT ANSWER IN THE SPACE AT THE RIGHT.*

1. The questioning of a plaintiff's witness by the defendant's attorney is legally known as
   A. an objection
   B. an accusation
   C. direct examination
   D. cross-examination

2. Fisher was indicted by a grand jury on a charge of armed robbery. The charges brought against Fisher will be prosecuted by the
   A. presiding justice
   B. public defender
   C. district attorney
   D. court bailiff

3. The document which orders a witness to appear in court to testify is known as a(n)
   A. subpoena
   B. affidavit
   C. writ of habeas corpus
   D. summons

4. Stacey completely ignored a formal notice to serve on the grand jury. The court could charge Stacey with
   A. conversion
   B. contempt of court
   C. negligence
   D. perjury

5. The Novelty Manufacturing Company is required by a court order to deduct part of an employee's weekly paycheck and send it to the Super Furniture Store until the employee's debt to the store is paid.
   This deduction is legally known as a(n)
   A. attachment    B. injunction    C. lien    D. garnishment

6. Advertisements of merchandise in a newspaper generally create a(n)
   A. binding offer
   B. binding counteroffer
   C. invitation to make an offer
   D. voidable agreement

7. Roth sold his car to Mills for $2,000. Later, Roth discovered the car was worth $3,000.
   Roth would be legally entitled to collect
   A. $1,000 only
   B. $1,000 plus court fees
   C. $3,000
   D. nothing

8. A right that is NOT assignable is the right to receive
   A. money
   B. professional services
   C. unskilled, purely mechanical services
   D. a shipment of merchandise

9. Romano sold her pizza shop, located in Boston, to Zilli. Romano agreed never to open another pizza shop in that city.
   This agreement represents a(n)
   A. unreasonable restraint of trade
   B. reasonable restraint of trade
   C. illegal lobbying contract
   D. monopoly

10. Goodfellow was declared an involuntary bankrupt.
    This involuntary bankrupt would probably have been brought by
    A. himself
    B. his creditors
    C. his debtors
    D. his employer

11. Robbins orally promised to buy his 15-year-old daughter a stereo if she went to school every day.
    Robbins is NOT legally bound to his promise because
    A. his daughter is a minor
    B. the promise was oral
    C. his daughter's consideration is already required by law
    D. a minor's contracts for luxury items are voidable

12. The voluntary surrender of a person's contractual rights is known as a
    A. satisfaction    B. breach    C. tender    D. waiver

13. Thomas paid Rogers $100 to hold an offer open for two weeks.
    This is known as a(n)
    A. bid    B. option    C. firm offer    D. implied offer

14. Which type of agreement does NOT need to be evidenced by a writing in order to be enforceable? A
    A. promise to make a suit specifically designed for one customer and not resellable to another customer
    B. promise by an executor to pay the debts of the estate out of his own funds
    C. promise to marry in return for a monetary consideration
    D. title transfer to a home

15. The Statute of Frauds provides that a contract for the sale of goods for $500 or more does NOT have to be evidenced by a writing to be enforceable if the
    A. agreement is an executory agreement
    B. buyer makes a deposit of at least $50 on the goods
    C. goods have been received and accepted
    D. goods are sold on the installment plan

16. Nixon agreed to sell a racehorse to Krupa for $1,000. Unknown to either party, the horse had been killed one hour prior to the signing of the contract.
As a result of this event, the contract is
    A. valid because of a unilateral mistake
    B. void because of a mutual mistake
    C. illegal
    D. unenforceable because of fraud

17. Which is an example of a contract for work and material?
    A. Buying furniture in a department store
    B. Having a suit drycleaned
    C. Selling 50 shares of stock
    D. Building and installing a kitchen cabinet

18. If no definite time limit is stated by the offeror, an offer would normally continue
    A. for a reasonable time, depending upon the circumstances
    B. for the time limited by the statute of limitations
    C. for the time necessary to receive a letter, usually 7 days
    D. until the offer is definitely accepted or rejected by the offeree

19. A change made in the terms of an executory contract by one party without the knowledge and consent of the other party is called a(n)
    A. novation    B. substitution    C. accord    D. alteration

20. Jackson was induced by fraud to enter into a contract with Simms. What is the legal result? Jackson
    A. is bound to this contract
    B. is guilty of contributory negligence
    C. may avoid the contract and sue for any damages
    D. may be brought to court for being part of a fraudulent contract

21. In a contract, Adams promises to paint Burr's house for a sum of $1,500. The $1,500 Burr may pay Adams is known as Burr's
    A. grant    B. right    C. obligation    D. response

22. A minor makes an agreement to purchase a luxury item from an adult for a given price. This agreement would be enforceable by
    A. the adult only                B. the minor only
    C. either the adult or the minor    D. neither the adult nor the minor

23. Donaldson, a contractor, built a house for Simmons and complete all work except for installing the carpet. The carpet was to be installed the following week.
This contract is an example of a(n) _____ contract.
    A. formal    B. unilateral    C. executed    D. executory

24. Moreau contracted to install aluminum siding on Wood's house for $4,500 during the first two weeks of August. When Moreau arrived on August 2 to install the siding, Wood informed him that the job would have to be postponed to a later date.
Moreau's obligation to perform the contract was discharged by
   A. tender of performance
   B. operation of law
   C. agreement
   D. delegation of duty

25. A rate of interest higher than that allowed by law is called a _____ rate.
   A. contract    B. usurious    C. legal    D. maximum

# KEY (CORRECT ANSWERS)

| | | | |
|---|---|---|---|
| 1. | D | 11. | C |
| 2. | C | 12. | D |
| 3. | A | 13. | B |
| 4. | B | 14. | A |
| 5. | D | 15. | C |
| 6. | C | 16. | B |
| 7. | D | 17. | D |
| 8. | B | 18. | A |
| 9. | A | 19. | D |
| 10. | B | 20. | C |

| | |
|---|---|
| 21. | C |
| 22. | B |
| 23. | D |
| 24. | A |
| 25. | B |

# TEST 2

DIRECTIONS: Each question or incomplete statement is followed by several suggested answers or completions. Select the one that BEST answers the question or completes the statement. *PRINT THE LETTER OF THE CORRECT ANSWER IN THE SPACE AT THE RIGHT.*

1. A partnership agreement MUST be evidenced by a writing to be enforceable if the partnership is
    A. expected to last for more than one year
    B. engaged in the retail drug business
    C. using an assumed or fictitious name
    D. made up of more than two partners

    1.____

2. Saxon became seriously ill as a result of eating contaminated food in a restaurant.
Saxon has a right to sue for damages because of
    A. the rule of caveat venditor
    B. the rule of caveat emptor
    C. breach of implied warranty
    D. breach of express warranty

    2.____

3. Thayer found a watch belonging to Layne.
Thayer obtained rights to the watch that are good against
    A. the original owner
    B. no one
    C. anyone, including Layne
    D. anyone except Layne

    3.____

4. Flynn in Mastic, New York, ordered goods F.O.B. destination from Sunrise House in Philadelphia, Pennsylvania.
Risk of loss passed to Flynn when the goods
    A. were delivered to the common carrier in Philadelphia
    B. were in transit to Flynn
    C. arrived in Mastic, New York
    D. were paid for

    4.____

5. An innkeeper would be liable for the loss of a guest's baggage if the loss was caused by
    A. an act of a public enemy
    B. an act of God
    C. the carelessness of the guest
    D. the carelessness of a hotel employee

    5.____

6. Winkler loaned her lawnmower to Johnson for the day.
This transaction is classified as a(n)
    A. bailment for the sole benefit of the bailee
    B. bailment for the sole benefit of the bailor
    C. mutual benefit bailment
    D. extraordinary bailment

    6.____

7. As a favor, Phillips agreed to store his friend's golf clubs in his garage for the winter.
   During the period that the clubs were in storage, Phillips had the right to
   A. place them outdoors in his yard for the winter if he needed the garage for his own possessions
   B. move them into the basement if he felt the garage had become unsafe
   C. use them as long as he exercised ordinary skill and care
   D. lend them to another friend

   7.____

8. Which is TRUE of unordered goods received through the mail? They
   A. must be returned to the sender
   B. must be returned to the post office
   C. may be used or discarded by the person receiving them
   D. may be kept by the person receiving the goods but may not be used or discarded

   8.____

9. Burford applied for a loan of $5000 from the Friendly Finance Company. Since her credit rating was very poor, Burford was required to sign a contract transferring conditional rights to her automobile to the finance company.
   The legal document used in this transaction is known as a
   A. chattel mortgage          B. real estate mortgage
   C. bailee's lien              D. property attachment

   9.____

10. In an effort to induce Mango to purchase a used car, Hawk, the saleswoman, stated, *This is the best deal on the lot*.
    Hawk's statement is BEST described as
    A. an express warranty       B. an implied warranty
    C. false representation      D. sales talk

    10.____

11. Which clause in a life insurance policy would keep the policy in force if the insured made the quarterly payment 15 days after its due date?
    A. Incontestability          B. Lapse and reinstatement
    C. Days of grace             D. Nonforfeiture options

    11.____

12. Winfield had a $250 deductible collision policy on her car.
    If she caused an accident resulting in damage in the amount of $550 to her car, how much would the insurance company have to pay?
    A. $50      B. $300      C. $350      D. $400

    12.____

13. Gervais lost control of his motor bike and crashed into a store.
    What kind of insurance coverage would pay for the damages to the building?
    A. Uninsured motorist        B. Collision
    C. Comprehensive             D. Property damage

    13.____

14. The type of life insurance policy affording the GREATEST amount of monetary protection to the insured for the lowest cost is called _____ life.
    A. whole                     B. term
    C. endowment                 D. limited-payment

    14.____

15. Williams obtained insurance on her home.
    The consideration given to the insurance company for this coverage is called
    A. a premium
    B. a dividend
    C. coinsurance
    D. cash surrender value

16. Snyder bought furniture for $1,200 and had it insured for $1,000 under a three-year life insurance policy. Two years later, when its value was only $900, a fire caused damage to the furniture amounting to $450.
    What amount did Snyder receive from the insurance company?
    A. $1,200   B. $1,000   C. $900   D. $450

17. Which part of a promissory note is absolutely essential to the negotiability of the instrument?
    A. I promise to pay to the order of
    B. Sixty days after sale of my house
    C. Payable at Farmers Bank, Burke, Ohio
    D. In consideration of

18. Gomez wants to deposit his entire paycheck in his checking account by mailing it to the bank.
    In order to provide the BEST safeguard, he should use _____ endorsement.
    A. blank
    B. special or full
    C. restrictive
    D. qualified

19. A personal check returned to the payee for lack of sufficient funds is said to be
    A. disaffirmed   B. dishonored   C. rescinded   D. voidable

20. Lee hired Wertman to repair some plumbing in his home. Wertman was a licensed plumber who furnished all his own tools and services.
    In this relationship, Wertman is legally known as an
    A. agent
    B. independent contractor
    C. employee
    D. employer

21. Swift, an agent, mixed his own money with money belonging to his principal so that it could not be separated.
    Under these conditions, the money belongs
    A. entirely to the principal
    B. entirely to the agent
    C. to both the principal and agent, equally
    D. to a trust fund

22. An agent is given written authority to sign checks for his principal.
    This written authorization is known as a(n)
    A. affidavit
    B. allonge
    C. certification
    D. power of attorney

23. Miles works as a clerk-typist for the All Star Modeling Agency. Her legal relationship with the agency is one of
    A. agent-principal
    B. grantor-grantee
    C. employer-employee
    D. bailor-bailee

24. A general partner ORDINARILY has the
    A. power to sell the entire business
    B. power to act as general agent for the firm within the scope of the business
    C. right to sell his interest in the business without the consent of the other partners
    D. right to receive compensation for extra services rendered to the business

25. Which act performed by a partner would cause the partnership to be dissolved?
    The partner
    A. hires employees for the conduct of the business
    B. borrows money in the firm's name for partnership purposes
    C. endorses checks payable to the partnership
    D. petitions the court for bankruptcy and the petition is accepted

## KEY (CORRECT ANSWERS)

| | | | | |
|---|---|---|---|---|
| 1. | A | | 11. | C |
| 2. | C | | 12. | B |
| 3. | D | | 13. | D |
| 4. | C | | 14. | B |
| 5. | D | | 15. | A |
| 6. | A | | 16. | D |
| 7. | B | | 17. | A |
| 8. | C | | 18. | C |
| 9. | A | | 19. | B |
| 10. | D | | 20. | B |

21. A
22. D
23. C
24. B
25. D

# TEST 3

DIRECTIONS: Each question or incomplete statement is followed by several suggested answers or completions. Select the one that BEST answers the question or completes the statement. *PRINT THE LETTER OF THE CORRECT ANSWER IN THE SPACE AT THE RIGHT.*

1. Orlick is admitted to an existing partnership. 1.____
 What is his liability, if any, for debts incurred by the firm before his admission?
 A. Unlimited liability
 B. Liability limited to his business assets
 C. Liability limited to his investment in the partnership
 D. No liability

2. One requirement for making a valid will is that the will 2.____
 A. be signed by the testator
 B. include a codicil
 C. be written on a printed legal form
 D. name an executor

3. Wills are probated in the _____ Court. 3.____
 A. United States District          B. Appellate Division of the State
 C. Municipal                       D. Surrogate

4. Generally, an administrator is required to distribute the property of an estate 4.____
 in accordance with
 A. the will                        B. the intestate law
 C. his own wishes                  D. the heirs' wishes

5. In order to make a valid will, the testator MUST 5.____
 A. inform witnesses of the content of the will
 B. handwrite the will
 C. be of sound mind
 D. be at least 21 years of age

Questions 6-10.

DIRECTIONS: Questions 6 through 10 are to be answered on the basis of the following information.

> **REAL ESTATE EXCLUSIVE SALE AND LISTING AGREEMENT**
>
> In consideration of the services to be performed by the undersigned broker, the undersigned seller does hereby grant to said broker, for a term of three months from date hereof, the sole and exclusive right to submit offers for the sale of the property located at <u>1680 Hamilton</u> Avenue, situated in the city of <u>Chicago, Cook County</u>.
>     Selling Price <u>$600,000</u>
>     Terms <u>$120,000 cash, balance a 20-year 12% mortgage</u>
> When the broker obtains an offer to purchase on the terms set forth in this Agreement, seller agrees to pay the broker a commission of 6% of selling price of said property.
>
> June 15, 2016                      *Arnold Miller*   Seller
>                                           Arnold Miller
>
>                                         *Harry Burke*   Broker
>                                           Harry Burke

6. The legal relationship between the seller and the broker is one of _____ and _____.
   - A. employer; employee
   - B. vendor; vendee
   - C. bailor; bailee
   - D. principal; agent

7. If Burke sells Miller's property at the stated price, Burke will be entitled to
   - A. the deed
   - B. the mortgage
   - C. a commission
   - D. $120,000 in cash

8. If Burke is not a licensed broker, the agreement between Miller and Burke would be
   - A. valid
   - B. void
   - C. voidable at the option of Burke
   - D. voidable at the option of Miller

9. According to the terms of the broker's agreement, Burke has the exclusive right to sell Miller's property until _____ 15, 2016.
   - A. June
   - B. July
   - C. August
   - D. September

10. Burke spends money out of his own personal funds to have the lawn mowed around the property.
    Miller owes Burke
    - A. reimbursement
    - B. compensation
    - C. indemnification
    - D. accounting

Questions 1-15.

DIRECTIONS: Questions 11 through 15 are to be answered on the basis of the following information.

3 (#3)

```
                    CONDITIONAL SALES AGREEMENT
Date: April 15, 2016
To:   Stereo Shanty                  Buyer's Name: Weldon Galloway
      (seller)
      Rt. 25A                        Residence Address: South Count Road
      (street)                                          (street)
      Rocky Point, NY                                   Patchogue, NY
      (city)    (state)                                 (city)    (state)
I (meaning the undersigned buyer or buyers, jointly and severally) hereby purchase the
following goods from you.
```

Article: Stereo Hi-Fi   Model: 515H   Serial No. FM-324167

| | | |
|---|---|---|
| Cash Price | $274.39 | Downpayment |
| Sales Tax | 14.36 | (a) Cash $25.00 |
| Total Cash Price | $288.75 | (b) Trade-in None |
| | | Balance (Amount Financed) $263.75 |
| | | Finance Charge 40.88 |
| | | $304.63 |

ANNUAL PERCENTAGE RATE: 12%

Purchaser hereby agrees to pay the TOTAL OF PAYMENTS shown above in 24 monthly installments of $12.75 (final payment to be $11.38), the first installment being payable May 15, 2016 and all subsequent installments on the same day of each consecutive month until paid in full.

Stereo Shanty
*Kray F. Eddee*                                      *Weldon Calloway*
Seller's Signature                                   Buyer's Signature

11. This document is legally referred to as a                                    11._____
    A. warehouse receipt            B. bill of lading
    C. retail installment contract  D. purchase offer

12. In this agreement, Calloway is called the                                    12._____
    A. vendor      B. vendee      C. agent      D. consignee

13. If Calloway fails to make his payments, how long does Stereo Shanty have     13._____
    to bring an action against him? _____ year(s)
    A. 1           B. 10          C. 20         D. 4

14. The filing of a financing statement (UCC-1) would be the responsibility of   14._____
    A. Weldon Calloway             B. Stereo Shanty
    C. city of Rocky Point         D. city of Patchogue

15. On April 30, Stereo Shanty transferred this agreement to a local bank.       15._____
    This created a(n)
    A. assignment                  B. bailment
    C. sales contract              D. agency

Questions 16-20.

DIRECTIONS: Questions 16 through 20 are to be answered on the basis of the following information.

Richards, while hunting without permission on land belonging to Wells, accidentally shot and killed Wells' horse. Richards realized his guilt and offered Wells $10 for the loss. Wells refused the $10 because it was not sufficient, and sought court action to satisfy her claim for damages.

16. In this situation, Richards is MOST likely guilty of 16.____
  A. the tort of assault
  B. the tort of conversion
  C. the tort of trespass
  D. breach of moral law

17. In this court action, Wells is known as the 17.____
  A. public defender
  B. defendant
  C. victim
  D. plaintiff

18. Which type of law is involved in this court action? 18.____
  A. Criminal  B. Civil  C. Moral  D. Administrative

19. During the trial, Richards' interruptions hindered the proceedings and his behavior insulted the court. 19.____
Richard could be found guilty of
  A. contempt
  B. perjury
  C. condemnation
  D. libel

20. The official determination of the court is known as the 20.____
  A. complaint  B. judgment  C. injunction  D. summation

Questions 21-25.

DIRECTIONS: Questions 21 through 25 are to be answered on the basis of the following information.

Davis mailed Stevens a letter on March 10 stating, *I will sell you my original Jamie Wyeth landscape painting for $500,000. Please reply within ten days.*

21. Stevens was out of town on a business trip and did not receive the offer until March 20. 21.____
If he mailed a letter of acceptance at the post office at noon on March 20 and Davis did not receive it until March 23, what effect would the acceptance have?
It would
  A. result in a binding contract
  B. have no effect on the offer because it was mailed too late
  C. have no effect on the offer because it was received too late
  D. have the effect of a counteroffer

5 (#3)

22. If Stevens had replied, *I am willing to buy the painting for $450,000 cash,* this reply would represent a
    A. valid contract
    B. bilateral contract
    C. voidable contract
    D. counteroffer

23. If Stevens accepts the offer as made within ten days and Davis refuses to deliver the painting, Stevens could bring suit in a court of law for
    A. liquidated damages
    B. specific performance
    C. writ of mandamus
    D. breach of warranty

24. If Stevens brings a civil action against Davis, the court with legal jurisdiction to decide the issue would be the
    A. State Supreme Court
    B. State Court of Appeals
    C. family court
    D. criminal court

25. If Davis accepts Stevens' offer of $450,000 and delivers the painting to him upon receipt of the money, the contract would be discharged by
    A. accord and satisfaction
    B. alteration
    C. performance
    D. substantial performance

## KEY (CORRECT ANSWERS)

| | | | | |
|---|---|---|---|---|
| 1. | C | | 11. | C |
| 2. | A | | 12. | B |
| 3. | D | | 13. | D |
| 4. | B | | 14. | B |
| 5. | C | | 15. | A |
| 6. | D | | 16. | C |
| 7. | C | | 17. | D |
| 8. | B | | 18. | B |
| 9. | D | | 19. | A |
| 10. | A | | 20. | B |

| | |
|---|---|
| 21. | A |
| 22. | D |
| 23. | B |
| 24. | A |
| 25. | C |

# TEST 4

DIRECTIONS: Each question or incomplete statement is followed by several suggested answers or completions. Select the one that BEST answers the question or completes the statement. *PRINT THE LETTER OF THE CORRECT ANSWER IN THE SPACE AT THE RIGHT.*

1. If Johnson dumped trash on land owned by Swift, Johnson could be held liable for
   A. negligence  B. arson  C. trespass  D. fraud

   1.____

2. An employee unlawfully takes for his own use money entrusted to his care. Which crime has he committed?
   A. Embezzlement  B. Robbery  C. Conversion  D. Forgery

   2.____

3. While playing ball in an empty lot, Bruce hit a baseball which broke a picture window in a house across the street.
   This is an example of a(n)
   A. felony
   B. tort
   C. misdemeanor
   D. infraction

   3.____

4. Which agreement constitutes a legally enforceable contract?
   A. Hart orally agreed to pay his aunt's fuel bill if she was unable to pay.
   B. Kirby agreed to pay his daughter $10,000 if she would stay single and take care of him.
   C. Ross made an oral agreement to sell Kelley ten acres of timberland.
   D. Carlin, age 16, purchased a $10,000 term insurance policy on his own life.

   4.____

5. Harrington provided lodging for Adams, who was stranded by a snowstorm. Following the snowstorm, Adams promised to pay Harrington $25 for his kindness.
   Adams is NOT legally bound to this promise because the consideration is
   A. past  B. future  C. present  D. nominal

   5.____

6. Barney agreed to sell Shelby an antique desk. When Shelby brought his truck to pick it up the next day, Barney said he had changed his mind and refused to deliver the antique desk to Shelby.
   If Shelby seeks court action to get possession of the desk, the court will MOST likely grant the remedy of
   A. specific performance
   B. nominal damages
   C. replevin
   D. liquidated damages

   6.____

7. Gonyea sent a letter to Mayne offering to sell Mayne his house.
   A binding contract was created when
   A. Mayne wrote a letter accepting Gonyea's offer
   B. Mayne mailed a letter accepting Gonyea's offer
   C. Gonyea received Mayne's letter of acceptance
   D. Gonyea and Mayne met at the bank for the closing

   7.____

8. When ordering two dozen chainsaws from Acme Supply Co., Marlowe entered the wrong catalog number on the purchase order. Upon receipt of the chainsaws, Marlowe realized his error.
What effect, if any, did this mistake have on the contract? The
   A. contract was voidable by Marlowe only
   B. contract was voidable either by Marlowe or Acme Supply Company
   C. mistake did not affect the validity of the contract
   D. contract was void

8.____

9. Morris was considering Brand's offer to sell her a used dirt bike for $695. Brand agreed that if Morris would pay him $50, he would give Morris one week to consider the offer before arriving at a decision.
This $50 paid by Morris to keep the offer open is known as a(n)
   A. conditional acceptance	B. firm offer
   C. counteroffer	D. option

9.____

10. Reilly was appointed as administrator of his father's estate. He orally promised Fisher, a creditor of the estate, that if there were inadequate funds in the estate, Reilly would pay the debt from his personal funds.
To be enforceable, the agreement MUST be
   A. in writing
   B. for debts over $500
   C. for debts for personal property only
   D. for a period of less than one year

10.____

11. When a valid offer is made to an offeree and no time limit is stated by the offeror, the offer normally terminates within
   A. a period of 30 days
   B. a reasonable time, depending upon the circumstances
   C. the time stated in the Statute of Frauds
   D. the time stated in the Statute of Limitations

11.____

12. If the performance of the terms of a contract becomes illegal, the contract is discharged by
   A. mutual agreement	B. breach
   C. operation of the law	D. performance

12.____

13. Ordinarily, 6the Statute of Frauds applies only to
   A. executory contracts	B. executed contracts
   C. contracts for labor and materials	D. oral contracts

13.____

14. Which agreement is void?
An
   A. agreement in reasonable restraint of trade
   B. agreement in unreasonable restraint of trade
   C. agreement with a minor
   D. oral agreement to sell real property

14.____

15. Caldwell offered to sell his automobile to Jones for $1,800. Jones refused. The offer is terminated by
    A. performance
    B. mutual agreement
    C. revocation
    D. rejection

16. Which is TRUE of an individual who has been declared bankrupt? He
    A. is prohibited by law from ever being given any more credit
    B. may never again own any real property
    C. is, in effect, given a chance to start over
    D. may never serve as a juror or vote

17. A newspaper advertisement that offers a reward for the return of a lost dog is an example of a(n)
    A. counteroffer
    B. firm offer
    C. invitation to offer
    D. general offer

18. Sara Matthews rented a boat from Hill.
    Matthews is liable for any damages to the boat if she
    A. did not use great care in operating the boat
    B. did not use ordinary care in operating the boat
    C. was in a boating accident caused by the negligence of another boater
    D. was not aware that the boat had a defect

19. Which is an example of a mutual benefit bailment?
    A. Borrowing a pound of coffee from a neighbor
    B. Depositing money in a bank account
    C. Renting an apartment
    D. Selling goods on consignment

20. A complaint concerning misleading advertising by a business firm should be referred to the
    A. Federal Trade Commission
    B. Federal Communications Commission
    C. Food and Drug Administration
    D. U.S. Chamber of Commerce

21. When a pharmacy sells a prescription drug, it ALWAYS gives the buyer
    A. an implied warranty of fitness for purpose
    B. an implied warranty of fitness for consumption only
    C. an implied warranty of title only
    D. implied warranties of title and fitness for consumption

22. The teachers of Oliver Central School threatened to go on strike.
    A court order forbidding this strike is called a(n)
    A. injunction    B. indictment    C. verdict    D. mandamus

23. Borrowing a neighbor's ladder is an example of a(n)  23._____
    A. bailment for the sole benefit of the bailor
    B. bailment for the sole benefit of the bailee
    C. mutual benefit bailment
    D. extraordinary bailment

24. Highland purchased a saxophone on the installment plan. After the  24._____
    security agreement had been partially carried out, Highland defaulted on
    several payments. The dealer told Highland that the instrument was going to
    be repossessed, and Highland refused to give up possession of it.
    Which course of action should the dealer now follow?
    A. Send two of his employees to Highland's place and physically take the
       instrument from Highland.
    B. Get a court order directing Highland to surrender the instrument.
    C. Wait until Highland leaves his house and then enter it and take the
       instrument.
    D. Continue to ask Highland to surrender the instrument and hope that he
       will.

25. A saleswoman in a furniture store told a customer, *This table is solid cherry*  25._____
    *wood.*
    This statement by the saleswomen could legally be looked upon as a(n)
    A. seller's opinion or *puff*
    B. implied warranty of merchantability
    C. implied warranty of fitness for purpose
    D. express warranty

26. Brockway purchased a portable color television set under a security  26._____
    agreement and agreed to make a downpayment of $125 and to pay the
    balance in twelve equal installments.
    Brockway received title to the set when the
    A. security agreement was signed     B. downpayment was made
    C. last installment was paid          D. set was delivered

27. In which type of transaction involving personal property do title and  27._____
    possession ordinarily pass immediately upon delivery to the buyer?
    A. Sale or return                     B. Sale on approval
    C. Contract to sell                   D. Conditional sale

28. Coleman found a valuable watch.  28._____
    What is Coleman's right to the title to this watch? He
    A. acquires title to the watch by accession
    B. acquires title to the watch by adverse possession
    C. acquires title to the watch by finding it
    D. does not acquire title to the watch, even though he has possession

29. Martin had to surrender her property to the government under the right of eminent domain.
Ordinarily, Martin would be entitled to _____ the property.
   A. the original purchase price of
   B. 90% of the assessed value of
   C. fair compensation for
   D. a promise to consider paying for

30. Flynn bought a portable microwave oven for his apartment. Before using it, the landlord said that Flynn would have to pay for electricians to install a new electrical outlet to meet the energy needs of the oven. Flynn agreed, had the work done, and used the oven. When Flynn's lease expired, he planned to move out and take the microwave oven with him. The landlord told him that the microwave oven had to remain with the apartment.
Which statement BEST applies to this situation? The
   A. microwave oven is Flynn's personal property and he may take it
   B. microwave oven is a fixture and has to remain
   C. microwave oven is a trade fixture and has to remain
   D. landlord now owns the microwave oven, but must pay Flynn a fair price for it

## KEY (CORRECT ANSWERS)

| | | | | | |
|---|---|---|---|---|---|
| 1. | C | 11. | B | 21. | D |
| 2. | A | 12. | C | 22. | A |
| 3. | B | 13. | A | 23. | B |
| 4. | D | 14. | B | 24. | B |
| 5. | A | 15. | D | 25. | D |
| 6. | A | 16. | C | 26. | C |
| 7. | B | 17. | D | 27. | A |
| 8. | C | 18. | B | 28. | D |
| 9. | D | 19. | D | 29. | C |
| 10. | A | 20. | A | 30. | A |

# TEST 5

DIRECTIONS: Each question or incomplete statement is followed by several suggested answers or completions. Select the one that BEST answers the question or completes the statement. *PRINT THE LETTER OF THE CORRECT ANSWER IN THE SPACE AT THE RIGHT.*

1. What type of automobile insurance would cover losses due to vandalism?
   A. Collision
   B. Comprehensive
   C. No-fault
   D. Property damage

2. As he approached his home, Browning lost control of his truck and accidentally damaged a cedar hedge on his neighbor's property.
   Which type of coverage must Browning carry to be insured for this loss?
   A. Collision
   B. Comprehensive
   C. Uninsured motorists
   D. Property damage

3. Nancy Wilkes purchased a $270,000 standard fire insurance policy on her house, valued at $330,000. A year later, a fire caused damage to the house amounting to $96,000.
   How much would Wilkes be entitled to collect from her insurance company? The
   A. face value of the insurance policy
   B. amount of the damages sustained
   C. original purchase price of the house
   D. depreciated value of the house

4. At age 35, Bernhoft took out a life insurance policy and stated her age as 29. Bernhoft died five years later.
   What effect, if any, does the misrepresentation have on the payment to the beneficiary?
   The insurer will pay the beneficiary
   A. nothing, because the policy is void
   B. only half the face value of the policy
   C. the amount which is determined by using the insured's correct age
   D. the face value, because the misrepresentation has no effect on the performance of the contract

5. Which clause in a life insurance policy provides that the insurance company may not void a policy after lapses of a specific period of time because of false statements made in the insurance application?
   A. Incontestability
   B. Suicide
   C. Settlement option
   D. Grace period

6. Young people reach majority on _____ birthday.
   A. their eighteenth
   B. the day before their eighteenth
   C. the day after their eighteenth
   D. their twenty-first

7. A valid will must be signed in the presence of
   A. a justice of the peace
   B. a notary public
   C. an attorney
   D. two witnesses

8. Changes in the terms of a valid will may be made by the testator if the testator prepares a(n)
   A. attachment
   B. endorsement
   C. codicil
   D. rider

9. LeDuc died suddenly and did not leave a will.
   LeDuc's estate must be probated by the _____ court.
   A. district
   B. family
   C. supreme
   D. surrogate

10. Upstate Storage Company plans to sell two lots of furniture because the owners owe over six months storage charges.
    Upstate Storage Company may sell these goods because it has a
    A. lien on the goods
    B. mortgage on the goods
    C. right to liquidated damages
    D. right of replevin

11. Which is NOT a requirement of a negotiable instrument?
    It must
    A. be payable in money
    B. be payable at a specified or determinable time
    C. be payable at a specified place
    D. contain an unconditional promise to pay

12. A check made payable to the order of Marcia Smith may be transferred by
    A. novation
    B. endorsement only
    C. delivery only
    D. endorsement and delivery

13. When a check is sent through the mail, _____ endorsement offers the LEAST protection.
    A. restrictive
    B. qualified
    C. special
    D. blank

14. Hutchins received a check from Andrews drawn on the City National Bank.
    The City National Bank would be known as the
    A. accommodation party
    B. drawer
    C. drawee
    D. payee

15. The right of an agent to require the principal to pay for losses incurred by the agent while the agent is performing business for the principal is called
    A. reimbursement
    B. indemnification
    C. recovery
    D. rebate

16. Jacobs was hired for July and August to fill in for employees who were on vacation.
    On September 1, this contract was terminated by
    A. agreement
    B. operation of law
    C. breach of contract
    D. impossibility of performance

17. Rowley hired Melius to paint his house for the sum of $850.
    For tax purposes, Melius would be classified as a(n)
    A. independent contractor
    B. employee
    C. general agent
    D. special agent

    17.____

18. Which Federal legislation regulates the minimum wages and maximum hours which can be worked?
    The _____ Act.
    A. Social Security
    B. Labor-Management Relations
    C. Fair Labor Standards
    D. Civil Rights

    18.____

19. Corporate dividends are declared by the corporation's
    A. stockholders
    B. officers
    C. treasurer
    D. board of directors

    19.____

20. To become a shareholder of record, one who purchases stock must
    A. pay cash for the stock
    B. have his name registered on the books of the corporation
    C. buy only stock listed by the stock exchange
    D. attend shareholders' meetings

    20.____

21. Jonathan received a judgment of $5,000 as the result of a court action against Watson.
    If Watson failed to pay the $5,000, could Jonathan get assistance from the court in collecting the amount?
    A. *Yes*; the court could issue a writ of execution.
    B. *Yes*; the court could issue a writ of habeas corpus.
    C. *No*; the court does not have jurisdiction over debt collection.
    D. *No*; this would be considered double jeopardy.

    21.____

22. Routh read the following advertisement in the daily newspaper: *Lost, solitaire diamond ring, vicinity of Main Road and Broadway. Reward for prompt return. 483-9784.* Two weeks later, Routh found and returned the diamond ring to its owner.
    Was Routh entitled to the reward?
    A. *Yes*; an offer of a reward creates a binding agreement when acted upon by a person with knowledge of the offer.
    B. *Yes*; all finders of lost property are legally entitled to a reward for the return of the goods to their rightful owner.
    C. *No*; finders of lost property have a legal and moral duty to return lost property without expecting a reward.
    D. *No*; newspaper advertisements cannot create a legally binding contract even if acted upon.

    22.____

23. Rogers borrowed a chainsaw from his friend, Collier. While he was using the chainsaw to cut timber, Rogers was seriously injured because of a defective chain. Collier knew the chain was defective, but had neglected to warn Rogers.
    Was Collier liable for Rogers' injuries?

    23.____

4 (#5)

24. Collins, a licensed real estate agent, decided to open a real estate office in his home. His house was on a street zoned as residential. When the zoning board learned that Collins had opened an office in his home, they notified him that he was in violation of the law and must move his business office elsewhere.
Does Collins have the right to use his home for a small business office?
    A. *Yes*; as long as a homeowner does not disturb the peace of his neighbors, he may use his property in any way that he sees fit.
    B. *Yes*; if a homeowner has clear title to his property, there are no legal restrictions that may be made against the use of the property.
    C. *No*; real property cannot be used for any purpose without first obtaining a state permit.
    D. *No*; zoning laws regulate the use of real property and may be enforced by a court injunction.

24.____

25. A freight train of the B&A Railroad had a serious derailment caused by soil erosion due to several days of extremely heavy rains. Defending an action for damages, the B&A Railroad denied all liability because of the nature of the loss.
Must the railroad pay for the damage?
    A. *Yes*; common carriers have insurer-like liability for all damages to goods in their possession, regardless of the cause.
    B. *Yes*; common carriers may be held liable for all damages to goods except those damages caused by faulty packing by the shipper.
    C. *No*; common carriers are not liable for damages caused by an act of God.
    D. *No*; common carriers are only liable for damages to goods when the damage is caused by their own employee's negligence.

25.____

26. Fleck was employed by the Crescent Motor Company as a mechanic. His working hours were 8 A.M. to 5 P.M. with an hour for lunch. After many warnings, Fleck continued to take much more than an hour for lunch.
Would his employer be justified in discharging Fleck?
    A. *Yes*; an employee must obey all rules and regulations of his employer.
    B. *Yes*; an employee must obey all reasonable rules and regulations of his employer.
    C. *No*; an employee may not be dismissed for his failure to abide by just one rule or regulation.
    D. *No*; an employee may only be legally dismissed with union permission.

26.____

27. Thompson was hired by the Babb Co., a plumbing contractor located in Amsterdam, Virginia. After he had worked for the company three weeks, he was informed that he must join the union, as Babb Co. was a union shop. Thompson claimed that he had a right to work for Babb Co. and could not be forced to join their union.
Was Thompson correct?
    A. *Yes*; an employee cannot be forced to join a union because the union shop is illegal in Virginia.
    B. *Yes*; an employee cannot be forced to join a union in any type of union shop against his personal wishes.

27.____

29

C. *No*; in the union shop, all employees must hold union membership before they can be hired.
D. *No*; in the union shop, nonunion employees may be hired, but they must join the union within a certain period of time.

28. Smith bought a used car from Wiley and gave Wiley a promissory note in payment for $600. At the time of the sale, Wiley assured Smith that the odometer reading of 52,148 miles was correct. Later, Smith learned that Wiley had set the odometer back 20,000 miles. Meanwhile, the note was transferred to Morton, a holder in due course. Smith refused to pay the note.
Will Morton be able to collect from Smith?
    A. *Yes*; fraud in the inducement does not bar recovery by a holder in due course.
    B. *Yes*; undue influence does not bar recovery by a holder in due course.
    C. *No*; fraud in the inducement bars recovery by a holder in due course.
    D. *No*; illegality that renders a contract void bars recovery by a holder in due course.

28.____

29. Doyle hired Cameron, a real estate agent, to sell his house. After Doyle was killed in an auto accident, Cameron sold the house to Brooks. Upon learning of Doyle's death, Cameron claimed that the contract was binding on Doyle's estate.
Was Cameron correct?
    A. *Yes*; all contracts made by an agent are binding on the principal or on the principal's estate.
    B. *Yes*; until the agent received legal notice of the principal's death, any contract made by the agent was binding on the principal's estate.
    C. *No*; death terminates an agency and any contract made after the death of the principal is void.
    D. *No*; contracts made by an agent after the death of the principal are only binding on the agent.

29.____

30. Brooker was a secret partner in the Brown and Smith Tire Shop. He took no active part in the business.
Would Brooker have the right to inspect the books of the partnership at reasonable times?
    A. *Yes*; all partners who invest in the business may inspect the books at any time as an ultra vires act.
    B. *Yes*; all partners have the right to inspect the books of the business at reasonable times.
    C. *No*; a secret partner who takes no active part in the business does not have the right to inspect the books of the business.
    D. *No*; the partnership accountant is the only person who has the right to inspect the books of the business.

30.____

## KEY (CORRECT ANSWERS)

| | | | | | |
|---|---|---|---|---|---|
| 1. | B | 11. | C | 21. | A |
| 2. | D | 12. | D | 22. | A |
| 3. | B | 13. | D | 23. | B |
| 4. | C | 14. | C | 24. | D |
| 5. | A | 15. | B | 25. | C |
| 6. | B | 16. | A | 26. | B |
| 7. | D | 17. | A | 27. | D |
| 8. | C | 18. | C | 28. | A |
| 9. | D | 19. | D | 29. | C |
| 10. | A | 20. | B | 30. | B |

# EXAMINATION SECTION
## TEST 1

DIRECTIONS: Each question or incomplete statement is followed by several suggested answers or completions. Select the one that BEST answers the question or completes the statement. *PRINT THE LETTER OF THE CORRECT ANSWER IN THE SPACE AT THE RIGHT.*

Questions 1-5.

DIRECTIONS: Questions 1 through 5 are to be answered on the basis of the document below.

Barney was convicted of DWI (driving while intoxicated). Six months later, following an automobile accident, Barney was arrested and charged again with DWI.

1. If the grand jury issued a formal charge against Barney, it would be known as a(n)

    A. injunction
    B. indictment
    C. summons
    D. subpoena

2. If the grand jury charges Barney with DWI, the charge would be classified as a(n)

    A. felony
    B. misdemeanor
    C. infraction
    D. tort

3. At the trial, the charges against Barney would be presented to the court by the

    A. arresting officer
    B. court clerk
    C. district attorney
    D. public defender

4. Witnesses to the accident could be ordered to appear to give testimony by means of a(n)

    A. complaint
    B. judgment
    C. injunction
    D. subpoena

5. Should it be proved that a witness gave false testimony in the court trial, the witness could be charged with the crime of

    A. alteration
    B. conspiracy
    C. contempt of court
    D. perjury

Questions 6-10.

DIRECTIONS: Questions 6 through 10 are to be answered on the basis of the information below.

Bridges mailed a letter to Johnson on April 10 offering to sell a boat, motor, and trailer for $6,200. Johnson mailed acceptance of the offer on April 16. Johnson received a letter on April 17, mailed by Bridges on April 15, revoking the offer. However, Johnson claimed that his acceptance mailed on April 16 created a binding contract.

6. The above offer was legally communicated when

    A. Bridges wrote the letter
    B. Bridges mailed the letter

C. Johnson received the letter
D. Johnson wrote his acceptance

7. The fact that this agreement must be in writing in order to be binding is a provision of

   A. English common law
   B. Roman civil law
   C. the Statute of Limitations
   D. the Statute of Frauds

8. To cancel or revoke an offer, the revocation must be communicated

   A. in the same manner as the offer was communicated
   B. in any suitable manner before acceptance is made
   C. only by telegram before acceptance is mailed
   D. only by telephone before acceptance is received

9. Johnson's acceptance resulted in a binding agreement because

   A. it was mailed prior to receiving notice of revocation
   B. it was mailed within seven days after receipt of the offer
   C. once a firm offer has been made, it cannot be withdrawn
   D. the revocation was made in an improper manner

10. If Bridges had not revoked the offer and Johnson had never replied to the offer, the offer would have been terminated by

    A. acceptance
    B. counteroffer
    C. lapse
    D. rejection

Questions 11-15.

DIRECTIONS: Questions 11 through 15 are to be answered on the basis of the information below.

> This agreement, made on June 8, 1989, is between John Weider of Shelby, New Jersey, and Adam Varley of Ridgeway, New Jersey.
>
> Varley agrees to furnish all materials and to perform all labor that is needed to make Weider a fur coat. In return Weider agrees to pay Varley the sum of six hundred dollars ($650.00).
>
> This agreement is reached for making a fur coat for Weider.
>
> (Signed) *Adam Varley*
> (Signed) *John Weider*

11. What type of contract is this agreement?
    A(n)

    A. contract in joint tenancy

B. option contract
C. quasi contract
D. contract for labor and materials

12. This agreement does NOT have to be in writing to be binding because it is

   A. for work and services
   B. for the sale of personal property over $500
   C. for real property
   D. a contract of guarantee

13. If there is a question as to the amount of money that Weider owes Varley, the CORRECT amount is

   A. $650 because written figures prevail over written words when there is a conflict
   B. $600 because written words prevail over written figures when there is a conflict
   C. $625 because a compromise on a disputed debt is binding
   D. nothing because a mutual mistake makes an agreement void

14. If Varley furnishes the materials and completes the labor and Weider pays the amount owed, the agreement would be discharged by

   A. agreement
   B. breach
   C. performance
   D. operation of the law

15. If Weider is unable to pay the amount owed and offers to give Varley his stamp collection instead and Varley accepts his offer, the agreement to pay the amount owed is discharged by

   A. impossibility of performance
   B. waiver
   C. anticipatory breach
   D. accord and satisfaction

Questions 16-20.

DIRECTIONS: Questions 16 through 20 are to be answered on the basis of the information below.

Dumas signed a buy and sell agreement to convey a farm and 50 acres of land to Reardon. Reardon gave Dumas a deposit of $500 and made application to the First National Bank to finance 70% of the purchase price.

16. After the bank approves the loan, the document that Reardon will receive to prove that he is the new owner of the farm is known as a(n)

   A. abstract of title
   B. bill of sale
   C. real mortgage
   D. warranty deed

17. After moving into his new home, Reardon found that Turner, a neighbor, had a permanent right-of-way over his land to reach adjoining fields that belonged to Turner. This right-of-way is known as

   A. adverse possession
   B. easement
   C. eminent domain
   D. joint tenancy

18. Reardon engaged Carr to install new plumbing in the farm. If Reardon fails to pay him, Carr could file a(n)

    A. bailee's lien
    B. mortgage lien
    C. mechanic's lien
    D. unpaid seller's lien

19. Under the usual terms of a mortgage, which court action does the First National Bank have the right to institute if Reardon defaults in his mortgage payments?

    A. Foreclosure proceedings
    B. Condemnation proceedings
    C. Adverse possession
    D. Specific performance

20. The mortgage on the property would NORMALLY be recorded in the proper office by

    A. Reardon
    B. Reardon's lawyer
    C. Dumas
    D. the First National Bank

Questions 21-25.

DIRECTIONS: Questions 21 through 25 are to be answered on the basis of the instrument below.

Bruce Jackson, an independent trucker, contracted to haul a trailer load of oranges from the Ace Fruit Company of Ocala, Florida, to Brown's Fruit Market in Hartford, Connecticut. The goods were shipped F.O.B. Ocala, Florida.

21. The freight rates that Jackson may charge for the shipment of oranges are regulated or determined by the

    A. Federal Trade Commission
    B. Interstate Commerce Commission
    C. Public Service Commission
    D. Congress of the United States

22. As an independent trucker, Jackson is classified as a

    A. consignor
    B. consignee
    C. contract carrier
    D. public carrier

23. The speed limit of 55 miles per hour which was set by Congress and which Jackson must obey is an example of _____ law.

    A. common
    B. constitutional
    C. administrative
    D. statute

24. Title to this shipment of oranges would ordinarily pass to Brown's Fruit Market when the goods are

    A. delivered to the carrier
    B. delivered at their destination
    C. received and accepted by the buyer
    D. set aside and identified to the contract

25. While these goods are in Jackson's possession, he has the liability of a(n) _____ bailee.

    A. extraordinary
    B. gratuitous
    C. mutual benefit
    D. involuntary

Questions 26-30.

DIRECTIONS: Questions 26 through 30 are to be answered on the basis of the information below.

---

PARTNERSHIP AGREEMENT

This AGREEMENT is made between Daniel Albright and Francine Volls on August 8 in the City of Syracuse, Pennsylvania.

It is mutually agreed as follows:
1. That the parties shall be partners and engage in the business of selling sporting goods.
2. That the legal place of business shall be 921 Gwinn St., Syracuse, Pennsylvania.
3. That the name of the business shall be VARSITY SPORTING GOODS.
4. That the capital in the partnership shall be $50,000, with Albright contributing $30,000 and Volls contributing $20,000.
5. That each partner shall share equally in the management of the partnership.
6. That at the end of the year profits and losses will be divided in proportion to the partners' investments.

*Daniel Albright*
*Francine Volls*

Signatures to the above witnessed by:

---

26. At the end of the first year of business, the partnership lost $5,000. Volls' share of this loss was

    A. $2,000    B. $2,500    C. $3,000    D. $5,000

27. The partnership operated at a loss again during the second year. Pierce was added in the third year as a new partner with an investment of $10,000.
    What, if any, would be Pierce's liability for the debts of the partnership incurred during the second year?

    A. Unlimited liability
    B. Limited to his investment of $10,000
    C. Limited to $1,000
    D. No liability

28. During the first year of the partnership, Albright purchased some sporting goods for $400 in the name of the partnership. When they were unable to sell these goods, Volls refused to allow the partnership to pay for them.
    Which statement BEST describes this situation?

A. Albright lacked the authority to buy these goods and, therefore, the partnership is not liable for this debt.
B. The partnership is liable for this debt only if both partners agreed that the debt should be paid.
C. The partnership is liable for this debt because Albright was acting within the actual scope of his authority.
D. The partnership is liable for this debt because the purchase price was less than $500.

29. During the third year of the partnership, Pierce suggested a fundamental change in the partnership agreement. He wanted the partnership to switch from the sale of sporting goods to the sale of books.
Whose consent would such a change require?
The consent of

   A. 2 of the partners *only*
   B. all 3 partners
   C. 2 of the partners, with the permission of the state
   D. all 3 partners, with the permission of the state

30. According to this partnership agreement, what kind of partners are Volls and Albright? _____ partners.

   A. Silent    B. Secret    C. Limited    D. General

## KEY (CORRECT ANSWERS)

| | | | |
|---|---|---|---|
| 1. | B | 16. | D |
| 2. | A | 17. | B |
| 3. | C | 18. | C |
| 4. | D | 19. | A |
| 5. | D | 20. | D |
| 6. | C | 21. | B |
| 7. | D | 22. | C |
| 8. | B | 23. | D |
| 9. | A | 24. | A |
| 10. | C | 25. | C |
| 11. | D | 26. | A |
| 12. | A | 27. | B |
| 13. | B | 28. | C |
| 14. | C | 29. | B |
| 15. | D | 30. | D |

# TEST 2

DIRECTIONS: Each question or incomplete statement is followed by several suggested answers or completions. Select the one that BEST answers the question or completes the statement. *PRINT THE LETTER OF THE CORRECT ANSWER IN THE SPACE AT THE RIGHT.*

1. Which is an example of a felony?   1.____

   A. Slander   B. Trespass   C. Nuisance   D. Perjury

2. If a person feels that he has been injured by the actions of someone else, he may start a court action against that person to obtain relief by filing a   2.____

   A. complaint   B. judgment
   C. subpoena   D. summons

3. Brady contracted to paint Carlin's house. Upon completion of the job, Carlin paid Brady the contracted price.   3.____
   This contract was discharged by

   A. accord and satisfaction   B. operation of the law
   C. performance   D. tender of performance

4. Young people reach majority on _____ birthday.   4.____

   A. their eighteenth
   B. the day before their eighteenth
   C. the day after their eighteenth
   D. their twenty-first

5. Failure of one party to perform in accordance with the terms of the contract is known as   5.____

   A. tender of performance   B. breach
   C. specific performance   D. the right of rescission

6. Brayton's $150 debt to Porter was due on May 10. On April 15, Porter accepted $125 from Brayton and orally promised to discharge the full debt.   6.____
   Which statement provides the BEST basis for determining whether the debt was legally discharged?

   A. A part payment before a debt is due can be consideration for the release of the remainder of the debt.
   B. The payment of a smaller sum of money will not cancel a larger debt that is already due.
   C. A promise to pay another's debt must be in writing to be valid.
   D. The payment of a smaller amount than is due will not discharge the debtor's liability for the balance of a debt.

7. Which promise made by a debtor concerning an outlawed debt will renew the obligation?   7.____

   A. An oral promise to pay
   B. A written promise to pay
   C. The promise to accept a garnishment
   D. The promise to accept an injunction.

8. Which statement concerning an assignment is NOT true?

   A. Most rights to a contract may be assigned to a third person.
   B. No particular form is needed to transfer rights to a contract.
   C. Contracts for personal services are assignable without consent of the other party to the original agreement.
   D. Notice must be given to the third party before the assignment is binding.

9. Which offer would be considered a general or public offer?
   June Lawrence

   A. said to Premo, *I will sell you my car for $1,200 cash*
   B. placed an advertisement in a local newspaper to rent her apartment
   C. advertised an auction and engaged a local auctioneer to sell her collection of antiques
   D. placed an advertisement in a local newspaper offering a $50 reward for the return of her lost dog

10. Smith agreed to repair Mason's car in one week. Mason paid Smith $25 in advance. On the day that the car was to be repaired, Mason needed the car and told Smith to forget the repair work and keep the $25.
    Smith's obligation to repair the car is discharged by

    A. performance             B. waiver
    C. lapse of time           D. tender of performance

11. Dumas, who was an insolvent debtor, lost his job and could not find work. Dumas may get relief from his debts by filing an action for voluntary bankruptcy.
    The _____ court would have jurisdiction over this action.

    A. city family             B. county surrogate
    C. Federal district        D. supreme

12. Harold entered into an oral contract to purchase a series of ten different power tools at an average cost of $59 each. The terms called for the purchase of one each month. After he received and accepted an electric skill saw priced at $49, he decided the quality and features were not what he had expected, so he canceled the contract.
    To what extent, if any, is Harold liable on the contract?
    He is liable for

    A. the full contract price
    B. none of the contract price
    C. the $49 saw *only*
    D. the saw and one more item

13. Bell gave Rhondo $50 as consideration to give him ten days to decide whether or not he would buy Rhondo's used car. The payment of $50 is considered to be a(n)

    A. downpayment             B. option
    C. novation                D. retainer fee

14. Walbridge was unable to pay his fuel bill when it became due because his debts were greater than his assets.
    Walbridge's financial condition would make him a(n)

A. insolvent debtor
B. solvent debtor
C. involuntary bankrupt
D. voluntary bankrupt

15. Coryea called a close friend in the installment loan department of his bank and said, *If my son does not meet all of the payments on his car, I will personally pay them.* Which statement concerning Coryea's promise is CORRECT?
It is

    A. valid because oral contracts are generally enforceable
    B. voidable because Coryea was using undue influence
    C. void because it was against public policy
    D. unenforceable because it was not made in writing

16. Implied contracts are

    A. written and under seal
    B. expressed in written words
    C. understood from conduct or action
    D. used only for real estate transactions

17. Browning owed Taylor $500 on a promissory note. When the note matured, Browning had lost his job and offered Taylor his car in payment of the note. Taylor accepted the vehicle.
This contract was discharged by

    A. accord and satisfaction
    B. alteration
    C. substantial performance
    D. specific performance

18. Wilson developed a process by which used motor oil could be reconditioned and made as good as new oil.
His exclusive rights to this process would BEST be protected if he obtained a

    A. registered trademark
    B. company logo
    C. copyright
    D. patent

19. The finder of a lost article acquires

    A. a valid title
    B. no rights to the article
    C. rights against everyone but the true owner
    D. rights against everyone

20. Under the provisions of the Uniform Commercial Code, a statement by the seller that the goods sold shall conform to a sample or model is called

    A. an express warranty
    B. an implied warranty
    C. mere *sales talk*
    D. consideration for the contract

21. Carter contracted with Ace Galleries to purchase an original painting for his personal art collection. When Carter returned to pay the agreed price, Ace Galleries refused to deliver the painting to Carter.
Carter's BEST course of action for this breach of sales contract is to sue for

A. specific performance  B. compensatory damages
C. liquidated damages  D. nominal damages

22. Webber temporarily stored his furniture in a storage warehouse until his new home could be completed.
    This is an example of a(n) _____ bailment.

    A. extraordinary  B. constructive
    C. gratuitous  D. mutual benefit

23. Which legal form is issued by a carrier to a person who temporarily places his personal property in the custody of the carrier?

    A. Bill of lading  B. Bill of sale
    C. Chattel mortgage  D. Warranty deed

24. According to the Uniform Commercial Code, a _____ is NOT classified as a merchant.

    A. proprietor of a retail hardware store
    B. manufacturer of toys
    C. wholesale distributor of furniture
    D. customer in a supermarket

25. If the seller refuses to surrender possession of goods to which the buyer has title, the buyer may recover the goods by

    A. force  B. replevin
    C. trover  D. garnishment

26. Zukowski purchased an air conditioner on an installment sales contract from the A-to-Z Appliance Company. After making the downpayment and eight monthly payments, Zukowski defaulted on the contract.
    The appliance company would be legally entitled to repossess the air conditioner and

    A. retain all the money received from Zukowski on the contract
    B. refund to Zukowski the money paid on the contract
    C. resell it at private auction with no refund to Zukowski
    D. resell it at public auction with a refund to Zukowski of the auction proceeds minus the unpaid balance and costs

27. When goods are shipped from Albany, New York to Columbus, Georgia, terms F.O.B. Albany, title to the goods passes to the buyer when the

    A. contract is made
    B. goods are delivered to the common carrier
    C. goods reach their destination
    D. goods are received by the consignee

28. Which statement made by a salesclerk at the time of a sale is an express warranty?

    A. This cabinet is made of California mahogany.
    B. The finish on this cabinet will last for a lifetime.
    C. The price of this cabinet makes it an unusual bargain.
    D. The mahogany finish on this cabinet will match any mahogany furniture.

29. A contract whereby one person acquires the right of possession and use of real property that belongs to another is known as a

    A. lease
    B. sale
    C. bailment
    D. mortgage

29.____

30. When a person actually owns an apartment in a large apartment building and possesses a deed for it, such property is called a(n)

    A. escrow arrangement
    B. easement
    C. condominium
    D. cooperative

30.____

# KEY (CORRECT ANSWERS)

| | | | |
|---|---|---|---|
| 1. | D | 16. | C |
| 2. | A | 17. | A |
| 3. | C | 18. | D |
| 4. | B | 19. | C |
| 5. | B | 20. | A |
| 6. | A | 21. | A |
| 7. | B | 22. | D |
| 8. | C | 23. | A |
| 9. | D | 24. | D |
| 10. | B | 25. | B |
| 11. | C | 26. | D |
| 12. | C | 27. | B |
| 13. | B | 28. | A |
| 14. | A | 29. | A |
| 15. | D | 30. | C |

# TEST 3

DIRECTIONS: Each question or incomplete statement is followed by several suggested answers or completions. Select the one that BEST answers the question or completes the statement. *PRINT THE LETTER OF THE CORRECT ANSWER IN THE SPACE AT THE RIGHT.*

1. If Marvin loses his bank credit card while traveling to Europe, Federal law limits his liability for unauthorized charges made on his lost credit card to  1.___

    A. $25   B. $50   C. $100   D. $150

2. An order bill of lading is made out to the order of the  2.___

    A. carrier
    B. consignee
    C. consignor
    D. finance company

3. Horton seriously damaged his car when a blowout caused the car to overturn and hit an embankment.  3.___
   Under which type of insurance could Horton collect for this loss?

    A. Bodily injury
    B. Property damage
    C. Collision
    D. Comprehensive

4. A common carrier of goods would be liable for damages due to  4.___

    A. seizure of the goods by a government agency
    B. loss of the goods due to an earthquake
    C. natural evaporation
    D. a collision damaging the goods

5. Morton was injured by a car driven by Morrissey. Morrissey carries bodily injury insurance with *10/20 limits*.  5.___
   In an action by Morton, Morrissey is protected by this policy up to what amount?

    A. $5,000   B. $10,000   C. $20,000   D. $30,000

6. In a sale of goods, the words *as is* will ordinarily exclude all warranties except the warranty of  6.___

    A. title
    B. fitness for a particular purpose
    C. merchantability
    D. conformity to description

7. The tariff rates charged by a common carrier of freight operating in more than one state are regulated by the  7.___

    A. Federal Trade Commission
    B. Public Service Commission
    C. Better Business Bureau
    D. Interstate Commerce Commission

8. Probating a will by the surrogate's court refers to the legal process of

   A. altering or revoking all unnecessary provisions in a will
   B. collecting the assets of the deceased for proper distribution
   C. establishing the validity of the will
   D. distributing the assets of the deceased to creditors and beneficiaries

9. The sum of money which the insured collects when he cancels his 20-payment life insurance policy is known as

   A. indemnity
   B. maturity value
   C. net proceeds
   D. cash surrender value

10. Jane Stanley transferred a promissory note to Hall when the note was past due. This transfer

    A. did not make Hall a holder in due course
    B. relieved the maker from liability
    C. limited the maker's liability
    D. gave Hall better title than Stanley held

11. The item which must appear on a check to make the instrument negotiable is the

    A. date
    B. check number
    C. sum of money
    D. name of the payee

12. Which instrument is NOT negotiable?

    A. Trade acceptance
    B. Draft
    C. Check
    D. IOU

13. The party who becomes the first endorser of a note is GENERALLY the

    A. payee    B. maker    C. drawer    D. drawee

14. Martin showed approval of an unauthorized act of an employee who had purchased some supplies for Martin.
    Martin created an agency by

    A. appointment
    B. necessity
    C. ratification
    D. power of attorney

15. An employee of a travel agency dealt part time with clients and their travel needs and worked the remainder of the time at routine office typing and filing duties.
    This employee should PROPERLY be classified as a(n)

    A. employee *only*
    B. agent *only*
    C. combination employee and agent
    D. del credere agent

16. Helen Schnitzer hired the Paula Real Estate Agency to sell her home.
    Which of the following duties does the Paula Real Estate Agency owe Schnitzer?

    A. Prudence and skill
    B. Reimbursement
    C. Compensation
    D. Indemnity

17. Which is NOT a requirement for a worker to receive unemployment compensation benefits?
    The worker must

    A. accept any job which is offered to him
    B. have worked at a job covered by unemployment insurance
    C. be ready, willing, and physically able to work
    D. register for a job with the public employment office and make a claim for the benefits

18. If the seller of a house refuses to pay the real estate broker a commission, as per terms of the contract, the broker may

    A. void the sale
    B. file a lien against the real estate sold
    C. bring court action against the buyer
    D. bring court action against the seller

19. Suits for or against a corporation must be brought in the name of the

    A. officers
    B. corporation
    C. stockholders
    D. directors

20. Which is a disadvantage of the partnership form of business organization?

    A. Availability of capital
    B. Distribution of responsibilities among the owners
    C. Full personal liability for partnership debts
    D. Sharing of losses with the other owners

21. Beth Sloan owned common stock in a corporation. Since she was unable to attend the annual stockholders' meeting, she gave James written authorization to vote for her.
    Did James have the right to vote?

    A. Yes; common or preferred stockholders or their proxies may vote at any corporate meetings.
    B. Yes; common stockholders may vote in person at the annual stockholders' meeting or may vote through a proxy of their choice.
    C. No; stockholders must be present in person at a stockholders' meeting in order to cast a vote.
    D. No; stockholders who are unable to personally attend a stockholders' meeting must turn their votes over to the corporation management who may vote it as they so desire.

22. Webber's Hardware Store carried a standard fire insurance policy on their stock of merchandise. Smoke and black soot escaping from a defective oil furnace damaged merchandise stored in the basement, although no actual fire resulted.
    Would Webber's insurance policy cover this loss?

    A. Yes; smoke and soot damage are covered under the standard fire insurance policy.
    B. Yes; the standard fire insurance policy protects against all direct and proximate losses caused by friendly or hostile fires.

C. No; the standard fire insurance policy does not cover damage resulting from smoke or soot unless caused by a hostile fire.
D. No; the standard fire insurance policy does not protect against losses caused by the insured's own negligence.

23. Martha Erikson erected a fence on what she thought was the border between her property and her neighbor's property. Later, she found out that the fence was entirely on her neighbor's property.
Could the neighbor hold Erikson liable through a civil action?

   A. Yes; she could be held liable for nuisance.
   B. Yes; she could be held liable for trespass.
   C. No; she could be held liable for a criminal wrong.
   D. No; she could not be held liable because her act was unintentional.

24. Moore signed a promissory note to pay Jones $500 in 90 days. Ten days before the maturity date, Moore was killed in an accident. Jones presented the note to Moore's wife on the due date and insisted that she must pay it. Was Jones CORRECT?

   A. Yes; all debts of a decedent must be paid by the decedent's spouse.
   B. Yes; the maker's spouse is always liable for a promissory note if the maker fails to pay it.
   C. No; death discharges all unsecured debts of a decedent.
   D. No; a decedent's debts must be paid by the decedent's estate.

25. Tucker, a minor, lied about his age when purchasing a stereo record player. Six months later, Tucker attempted to return the machine.
Can he legally do so?

   A. Yes; all contracts made by minors are voidable by the minor because of incompetency.
   B. Yes; contracts made by minors for goods that are not necessaries are ordinarily voidable by the minor.
   C. No; a minor who deliberately lies about his age cannot avoid his contracts because of incompetency.
   D. No; minors cannot use goods for six months and then avoid the contract on the basis of incompetency.

26. Warren purchased a watch from a pawn shop. Several months later, he was informed that the watch was stolen property and must be turned over to the police.
Does Warren have to turn the watch over to the police?

   A. Yes; an innocent purchaser of stolen goods never gets legal title to the goods.
   B. Yes; any property must be turned over to the police if they request it to be used for evidence.
   C. No; a good faith purchaser does not have to surrender goods if he did not know that they were stolen.
   D. No; an innocent purchaser of stolen goods gets title to the goods if he paid a fair price for the goods.

27. Kimberly wrote out a check to pay for groceries at Day's Supermarket and forgot to fill in the date on the check. Would omission of the date affect the negotiability of this instrument?

    A. Yes; a check must be dated by the drawer or it is not negotiable to other parties.
    B. Yes; a check that is not dated by the drawer would be considered to be forged if dated by any other party.
    C. No; a check's negotiability is not affected by the omission of the date.
    D. No; if a check is undated by the drawer, it must be taken to the drawee to have it dated.

28. Lowell left his truck with Weston for repairs. When Lowell went to pick up the truck, Weston refused to let Lowell take it until the repair bill was paid. Lowell brought suit in replevin to recover the truck.
    Would Lowell succeed in his suit?

    A. Yes; the owner of property may bring a suit of replevin and recover any property wrongfully held by a bailee.
    B. Yes; a bailee must surrender property to the rightful owner, but may bring suit for damages if the repair charges are not paid.
    C. No; the bailee may hold the bailor's property until repair charges are paid under the right of bailee's lien.
    D. No; the bailee may hold the bailor's property and bring suit for conversion if repair charges are not paid.

29. Watkins ships glassware by a common carrier but declares that he is shipping books.
    If the glassware is damaged, can Watkins collect for the loss?

    A. Yes; a common carrier is an insurer of the goods which it carries.
    B. Yes; a carrier is liable for all losses.
    C. No; a carrier is not liable for the acts of its employees if they are carrying out their regular duties.
    D. No; a common carrier is not liable for losses to property which it transports when the shipper misrepresents the goods being shipped.

30. Stone gave Carley authority to sell a jeep for him for $1,650. Carley was able through clever bargaining to get $1,795 and kept the extra $145 for himself.
    May Stone recover the extra $145 from Carley?

    A. Yes; an agent is always liable to his principal for acting beyond the scope of his express authority.
    B. Yes; an agent must always account for all funds received in transactions for the agency.
    C. No; any excess profit made over and above what the principal asks rightfully belongs to the agent.
    D. No; agents are always entitled to a commission when selling goods for their principal.

## KEY (CORRECT ANSWERS)

| | | | |
|---|---|---|---|
| 1. | B | 16. | A |
| 2. | B | 17. | A |
| 3. | C | 18. | D |
| 4. | D | 19. | B |
| 5. | B | 20. | C |
| 6. | A | 21. | B |
| 7. | D | 22. | C |
| 8. | C | 23. | B |
| 9. | D | 24. | D |
| 10. | A | 25. | B |
| 11. | C | 26. | A |
| 12. | D | 27. | C |
| 13. | A | 28. | C |
| 14. | C | 29. | D |
| 15. | C | 30. | B |

---

# TEST 4

DIRECTIONS: Each question or incomplete statement is followed by several suggested answers or completions. Select the one that BEST answers the question or completes the statement. *PRINT THE LETTER OF THE CORRECT ANSWER IN THE SPACE AT THE RIGHT.*

Questions 1-5.

DIRECTIONS: Questions 1 through 5 are to be answered on the basis of the document below.

---

Weston Appliance Store
196 West Avenue
Barker, South Dakota

Date: July 12
Sold To: Frank Schultz
42 Main Street
Barker, South Dakota

| Article | RCA Color TV | Total Purchase Price | $380.00 |
| Model No. | F-208 | Downpayment | 80.00 |
| Serial No. | 817-2654-2961 | Balance | $300.00 |

Payments to be made on the 10th day of the month commencing on August 10 in installments of $100.00 per month for 3 months. Title to these goods is retained by the seller until the full purchase price is paid.

Buyer's Signature *Frank Schultz*

---

1. This document is an example of a

   A. chattel mortgage
   B. lease
   C. deed
   D. security agreement

2. Title to the television set passes to Frank Schultz when the

   A. full purchase price is paid
   B. set is delivered to him
   C. agreement was made
   D. downpayment is made

3. A copy of this agreement should be filed in the proper public office by

   A. both Schultz and Weston Appliance Store
   B. Weston Appliance Store *only*
   C. Schultz *only*
   D. neither Schultz nor Weston Appliance Store

4. If a fire damages the television set after it has been delivered to Schultz, but before he has completed making the payments, who bears the loss?

   A. Both Schultz and Weston Appliance Store
   B. Schultz *only*
   C. Weston Appliance Store *only*
   D. The finance company

5. In this sale, Schultz can NORMALLY rely on the implied warranty that the

   A. purchase price will be refunded if the goods are returned
   B. purchase price is reasonable for those particular goods
   C. goods are free of all liens or encumbrances
   D. goods meet all standards of quality

Questions 6-10.

DIRECTIONS: Questions 6 through 10 are to be answered on the basis of the information below.

Ellis conveyed title to three acres of land and a house to Chatland. Chatland financed the purchase through the Federal Savings and Loan Association. Ellis had previously granted to the Central Light and Power Company the right to run its powerlines over this property.

6. The equity of the Federal Savings and Loan Association in this property will be secured by a

   A. promissory note        B. security agreement
   C. chattel mortgage       D. mortgage

7. The right granted by Ellis to the Central Light and Power Company to run its powerlines over this property is known as a(n)

   A. license                B. easement
   C. abstract of title      D. lien

8. The BEST proof of ownership to this real property that Chatland can obtain is known as a(n)

   A. abstract of title      B. quitclaim deed
   C. warranty deed          D. deed of trust

9. Title to this real property will be conveyed to Chatland when the

   A. abstract of title is completed
   B. contract to convey title is signed
   C. deed is completed
   D. deed is delivered and accepted

10. In conveying title to this property to Chatland, Ellis is known as the

    A. grantor    B. grantee    C. mortgagor    D. mortgagee

Questions 11-15.

DIRECTIONS: Questions 11 through 15 are to be answered on the basis of the information below.

---

**MEDINA MEMORIAL HOSPITAL**

To provide for an additional wing to our hospital and for other needed medical facilities, I pledge the sum of $50.00 dollars less $10.00 dollars paid at this time, resulting in a balance of $40.00 dollars.

Balance to be paid at $5.00 per month.

June 16, 2006
Date

*William Tierney Esq.*
Signature

---

11. The pledge would become binding upon Tierney when

    A. he telephoned the hospital to tell them he would contribute
    B. he signed the pledge
    C. he deposited the signed pledge in a mailbox to be mailed to the hospital
    D. the hospital received the signed pledge

12. This pledge is

    A. not binding because it lacks consideration
    B. not binding because it lacks required form
    C. binding only if Tierney wants it to be
    D. binding even though it lacks consideration

13. The Medina Memorial Hospital would have to make any attempts to collect this pledge within a time period specified by

    A. the Statute of Limitations
    B. the Statute of Frauds
    C. small-loan laws
    D. common law

14. William Tierney is called a

    A. grantor    B. creditor    C. donor    D. drawer

15. Courts GENERALLY consider pledges for charitable contributions to be

    A. gifts            B. quasi-contracts
    C. subsidies        D. grants

Questions 16-20.

DIRECTIONS: Questions 16 through 20 are to be answered on the basis of the information below.

Fleury, Jones, and Murphy each invested $20,000 to form a partnership to manufacture machinery. Profits were to be shared equally. Two years later, the partnership filed with the state to incorporate the business as Pic-Pac, Inc. and asked for authorization to issue common stock in the amount of $200,000.

16. Without the knowledge of Fleury or Jones, Murphy signed a promissory note in the partnership name to pay for an excessive amount of merchandise he had ordered.
What was the legal effect of Murphy's action?

    A. All partners were bound on the note.
    B. The note would be declared void since all the partners did not sign the note.
    C. Murphy must personally pay the total amount of the note.
    D. Murphy's action would dissolve the partnership.

16._____

17. During the second year, Jones was injured in an auto accident and did not return to work for nine months.
Unless otherwise agreed, Jones would be entitled to

    A. no share from that year's profits
    B. one-third of that year's profits
    C. three months' salary plus interest on his investment
    D. three months' salary plus unemployment benefits

17._____

18. If Fleury died six months after the partnership was formed and left all of his business and personal property to his wife by will, Mrs. Fleury would be

    A. expected to serve as a silent partner in the partnership
    B. immediately entitled to become a general partner in the business
    C. legally entitled to her husband's share of the firm's net worth
    D. required to carry on her husband's duties as a secret partner

18._____

19. Which is TRUE regarding Pic-Pac, Inc., the name chosen for the new corporation?
It

    A. may be the sole choice of the incorporators
    B. must be submitted for approval, so as not to conflict with an existing corporation having the same or a similar name
    C. is an unessential factor in incorporating
    D. is left to the vote of the stockholders after incorporating

19._____

20. Which is an advantage of organizing a business as a corporation rather than a partnership?

    A. Control of management decisions
    B. Unlimited liability
    C. Right to determine dividends
    D. Perpetual succession

20._____

Questions 21-25.

DIRECTIONS: Questions 21 through 25 are to be answered on the basis of the instrument below

The foregoing instrument was signed, published, and declared by the said Raymond W. Lewis as and for his Last Will and Testament, in our presence and at his request, and in our presence, and in the presence of each other, we hereunto subscribe our names as attesting witnesses.

| _Frank Drebben_ | ADDRESS _Main St., Homestead, H._ |
| _O. J. Nordberg_ | ADDRESS _Spruce St., Miami, H._ |

21. This statement signed by the witnesses is called a(n) 21.____

    A. codicil                                     B. attestation
    C. devise                                     D. legacy

22. In this document, Raymond W. Lewis is the 22.____

    A. testator      B. devisee      C. legatee      D. executor

23. What would any written addition placed after this statement be called? 23.____
A(n)

    A. ultra vires act                      B. postscript
    C. allonge                                 D. codicil

24. The _____ would determine the validity of this document in its entirety. 24.____

    A. court of appeals                B. surrogate court
    C. small claims court            D. police court

25. When Lewis dies, his will would be sent to the proper court for 25.____

    A. jurisdiction                          B. probate
    C. protest                                 D. intestacy

Questions 26-30.

DIRECTIONS: Questions 26 through 30 are to be answered on the basis of the information below.

    Bill McKay was walking into Midtown Plaza, Rochester, Minnesota when he was attacked by Frank Garba, who hit McKay, knocked him down, and took his wallet containing fifty dollars. McKay was seriously injured. Garba was apprehended by police about twenty minutes later in the Monroe Toy Shop, arrested, taken to police headquarters, and charged with certain crimes.

26. Which crimes is Garba MOST likely to be charged with? 26.____

    A. Assault and burglary          B. Assault and robbery
    C. Burglary and robbery          D. Robbery and fraud

27. If McKay decides to press charges, Garba must formally be accused of the crimes by the 27.____
grand jury before the case comes to trial.
The formal accusation charging Garba with the crimes takes the form of an

    A. indictment                          B. adjudication
    C. allegation                          D. injunction

28. The investigation, preparation, and presentation to the grand jury of Garba's case will be done by the

    A. chief of police
    B. public defender
    C. district attorney
    D. criminal court judge

29. If Garba is formally accused of the crimes by the grand jury and he pleads not guilty, his case is then scheduled for trial in court.
    The plaintiff in this criminal action will be

    A. Midtown Plaza
    B. Monroe Toy Shop
    C. The State of Minnesota
    D. Bill McKay

30. Garba's trial will take place in a court of

    A. appeals
    B. claims
    C. appellate jurisdiction
    D. original jurisdiction

---

# KEY (CORRECT ANSWERS)

| | | | |
|---|---|---|---|
| 1. | D | 16. | A |
| 2. | A | 17. | B |
| 3. | B | 18. | C |
| 4. | B | 19. | B |
| 5. | C | 20. | D |
| 6. | D | 21. | B |
| 7. | B | 22. | A |
| 8. | C | 23. | D |
| 9. | D | 24. | B |
| 10. | A | 25. | B |
| 11. | D | 26. | B |
| 12. | D | 27. | A |
| 13. | A | 28. | C |
| 14. | C | 29. | C |
| 15. | B | 30. | D |

# TEST 5

DIRECTIONS: Each question or incomplete statement is followed by several suggested answers or completions. Select the one that BEST answers the question or completes the statement. *PRINT THE LETTER OF THE CORRECT ANSWER IN THE SPACE AT THE RIGHT.*

1. The Supreme Court of the United States derives its judicial power from the      1.___

    A. United States Constitution
    B. United States President
    C. United States Congress
    D. state courts

2. If bail is set in a criminal case, it means that the      2.___

    A. accused is fined a certain amount by the judge
    B. accused is asked to deposit a sum of money to insure his presence at a later date
    C. district attorney determines what the damages should be
    D. district attorney sets the amount of the fine

3. Brice, who innocently purchased a used television which was stolen by the seller, was requested to surrender the television. Brice would not surrender the set until he was reimbursed the money he paid.      3.___
    Brice is guilty of the tort of

    A. fraud                B. trespass
    C. negligence           D. conversion

4. Common law may be thought of as a system of law that developed      4.___

    A. in England with precedents established from prior disputes
    B. in the early American colonies
    C. after the formation of the United States
    D. after the 18th century

5. An effort to make laws similar between states has been done through      5.___

    A. the Uniform Commercial Code
    B. an amendment to the state constitutions
    C. an amendment to the Federal Constitution
    D. local ordinances within each state

6. A subpoena is an order by the court served on      6.___

    A. the attorney to produce the defendant in court
    B. a person to appear and testify in a legal action
    C. the warden of a jail to produce the prisoner in court
    D. a person to be examined for possible jury duty

7. Regis, who was charged with committing a felony in Albany, New York, was arrested in Lake Placid, N.Y. in Essex County. Regis was then returned to Albany to stand trial in the Albany County Court.      7.___
    The right to have Regis returned to Albany to stand trial is known as

A. indictment  B. jurisdiction
C. subpoena  D. summons

8. For several weeks, Barney used his power lawnmower every Sunday morning at sunrise. Several neighbors asked him to mow his lawn at another time; Barney refused.
The NEXT legal course of action for the neighbors would be to

   A. sue Barney for money damages
   B. swear out a warrant for Barney's arrest
   C. seek a court injunction against the continuation of the act
   D. present a signed petition to the mayor of the city

9. A recent type of law restricts smokers to certain areas of restaurants and theaters. Such laws restricting the freedom of some are thought to be necessary because

   A. freedom of action also includes some restrictions to protect the rights of others
   B. the law must always prohibit actions that are not acceptable to the public
   C. the law never permits an action that is objectionable to any member of that society
   D. any practice that is a health hazard is always declared illegal

10. To create a legally binding contract, both parties to the agreement must be

    A. able to read and write
    B. able to speak and understand English
    C. financially responsible people
    D. of sound mind

11. Thomas said to Wemette, *I'll sell you my car for $2,500.* Wemette replied, *I'll take it if you will put on two new tires.*
Wemette's reply legally resulted in a

    A. binding contract  B. counteroffer
    C. revocation  D. substitution

12. Brockway contracted with Gokey Construction Company to build an office building on a lot that Brockway owned. Before the contractor started the job, the local zoning board rezoned the street where Brockway owned his lot to residential one-family dwellings only. What effect did this change in ordinance have upon the contract between Brockway and Gokey?

    A. Brockway became liable to Gokey for breach of contract.
    B. The city became liable to Brockway for damages.
    C. The change in ordinance did not affect any existing contracts.
    D. The contract was discharged by impossibility of performance.

13. Jake's Auto Center advertised in the local newspaper that all stock was reduced 40% below regular price.
This advertisement legally constituted a(n)

    A. valid offer
    B. voidable offer
    C. invitation to make an offer
    D. binding contract

14. Rose Gilman offered to sell to Rogers, a neighbor, a strip of land 20 feet wide between their two lots so that Rogers would have room to build a garage. Rogers accepted the offer.
    This agreement would be binding on Gilman if

    A. Rogers paid Gilman $100 for an option to buy
    B. it was made in the presence of two witnesses
    C. it was made in writing
    D. it was supported by a memorandum signed by Rogers

15. After a minor reaches the legal age of majority, he may disaffirm an executed contract for a luxury, made while a minor, ONLY if he

    A. accurately represented his age when the item was purchased
    B. acts within a reasonable length of time
    C. disaffirms in writing
    D. returns the luxury item in new or unused condition

16. Bowen, a building contractor, contracted to build kitchen cabinets for Martin's new house. Which event would NORMALLY discharge the contract by impossibility of performance? A(n)

    A. fire that destroyed Bowen's shop
    B. strike at the mill where Bowen purchased his supplies
    C. shortage of hardware available for the cabinets
    D. accident that seriously and permanently injured Bowen

17. Jarvis found and returned Martin's lost wallet. Martin promised to give Jarvis a reward the next day.
    Martin is not legally bound to pay a reward as he promised because the consideration for the promise was

    A. past   B. present   C. future   D. nominal

18. When Charlotte Bruce was 16, she purchased a combination radio and tape player and signed a contract to pay $40 down and the balance in 12 equal monthly payments.
    This contract was

    A. binding on Bruce if the merchant so desired
    B. binding on the merchant if Bruce so desired
    C. void because it was against public policy
    D. voidable on the part of the merchant only

19. Jacobson Wholesale Company and Kutner, the owner of a retail men's store, signed a written contract under which Jacobson was to sell 300 boxes of hosiery to Kutner at $5 per box. Jacobson sent the hosiery, and Kutner paid the $1,500. Jacobson sued Kutner for an additional $900; and at the trial offered evidence that after signing the contract, Kutner orally agreed to pay an additional $3 per box. The court held the evidence inadmissible. Which principle BEST justifies the legal decision in this case?

    A. All contracts must be in writing to be enforceable.
    B. Written contracts may not be modified at the will of the parties.

C. Generally, evidence of an oral agreement contradicting a written contract is inadmissible.
D. A contract of guaranty must be in writing to be enforceable.

20. Which agreement would ORDINARILY be considered illegal? A(n)

   A. agreement made between two men that one would pay the other $20, depending on the outcome of a football game
   B. contract made by a married woman who is a minor
   C. store owner's oral agreement to sell kitchen equipment for $600
   D. contract made on a Sunday to be performed on a weekday

21. Which statement is CORRECT regarding the transfer of contractual rights? The _____ has under the contract.

   A. assignor acquires only such rights as the assignee
   B. assignee acquires only such rights as the assignor
   C. assignee acquires rights greater than the assignor
   D. assignor acquires rights greater than the assignee

22. Mitchell orally agreed to sell Sylvia Sherwin his used car for $850. The car was valued at $1,250 in the NADA used-car guide. When Sherwin came back with the money to pick up the car, Mitchell refused to give it to her or accept the payment.
Sherwin CANNOT enforce this contract because the

   A. contract was not in writing
   B. contract was fraudulent in the making
   C. contract involved a mutual mistake as to value
   D. consideration was grossly inadequate

23. The law that states that contracts of minors for luxuries are voidable by the minor was enacted to

   A. discourage adults from making contracts with minors
   B. discourage minors from making contracts for luxuries
   C. protect minors in their dealings with adults
   D. protect adults in their dealings with minors

24. Peters agreed to sell a painting to Darlene Reynolds for $80. When Reynolds went to take delivery of the painting, Peters refused to deliver it to her. Peters claimed that the painting was easily worth $150; therefore, $80 was insufficient.
The contract is

   A. valid but Reynolds must pay the additional $70
   B. valid because the courts generally will not question the adequacy of consideration
   C. voidable at the option of Peters
   D. void because the consideration is not adequate

25. Jenkins orally contracted to purchase 100 tons of coal from the Jameson Coal & Oil Company at $30 per ton. After the Jameson Company had delivered 10 tons, Jenkins refused to accept any further deliveries.
Under the Uniform Commercial Code, Jenkins must pay for

A. 10 tons *only*　　　　　　　　　B. 90 tons *only*
C. 100 tons *only*　　　　　　　　 D. 0 tons

26. Hall pawned a camera with a pawnbroker.
    The pawnbroker may

    A. demand a receipt before returning the camera
    B. sell the camera at any time
    C. use the pledged property
    D. assign the property to a third party

27. Which bailment relationship is created by a consignment?
    A

    A. bailment for the sole benefit of the bailor
    B. bailment for the sole benefit of the bailee
    C. gratuitous bailment
    D. mutual benefit bailment

28. Audrey Robinson, a grocery store owner, agreed in writing in January to buy all the sweet corn that Davenport would have from his fields the coming summer.
    This agreement is BEST described as a

    A. contract for labor and materials
    B. mutual benefit bailment
    C. sale
    D. contract to sell

29. Which United States government agency helps protect the consumer from false and misleading advertising and unfair trade practices?

    A. Federal Trade Commission
    B. Interstate Commerce Commission
    C. Department of Labor
    D. Department of Agriculture

30. Marlene Tree allowed Becket to use her camera on a crosscountry trip. This transaction is a bailment because it

    A. transfers possession and temporary ownership
    B. involves the transfer of possession of personal property
    C. does not involve consideration
    D. involves a loan of goods for services

## KEY (CORRECT ANSWERS)

1. A
2. B
3. D
4. A
5. A

6. B
7. B
8. C
9. A
10. D

11. B
12. D
13. C
14. C
15. B

16. D
17. A
18. B
19. C
20. A

21. B
22. A
23. C
24. B
25. A

26. A
27. D
28. D
29. A
30. B

# EXAMINATION SECTION
# TEST 1

DIRECTIONS: Each question or incomplete statement is followed by several suggested answers or completions. Select the one that BEST answers the question or completes the statement. *PRINT THE LETTER OF THE CORRECT ANSWER IN THE SPACE AT THE RIGHT.*

1.
```
CIVIL COURT: MONROE COUNTY

Robert N. Fake, Plaintiff
       - against -                          INDEX NO.
Juliet C. Stone, Defendant

PLEASE TAKE NOTICE that you are in default because of your failure to appear or
answer the summons and complaint herein. A judgment will be submitted to the Court
at least 7 days from the date of the mailing of this default, which date will be August 8,
2008.
                                            WILCOX AND NAUM
                                            Attorney for Plaintiff herein
                                            232 Main Street
                                            Rochester, N.H. 03867
                                            589-5375
```
1.____

Issuance of the above document in connection with a civil lawsuit indicates that
   A. Stone requested her attorney to enter a judgment in the court records against Fake
   B. Stone failed to make some reply to Fake's summons and complaint
   C. Fake directed his attorney to seize Stone's property until August 8, 2008
   D. Fake failed to make some reply to Stone's summons and complaint

2. What type of action is indicated by the case title *Harvey Lund v. Dorothy King?*   2.____

   A. Civil                               B. Criminal
   C. Punitive                            D. Bankruptcy

3. On September 1, Porter, aged 17, agreed to purchase a piece of land from Sedam for   3.____
   $750, payment to be made in 30 days.
   This agreement must be in writing because

   A. the purchase price is over $500
   B. one of the parties involved is under 18 years of age
   C. it is a credit sale
   D. it concerns the sale of real property

4. Hall leased an apartment at the Highview Manor apartment complex. At the termination   4.____
   of his lease, the landlord inspected the premises, and upon finding no damage to the
   apartment above wear and tear caused by ordinary use, informed Hall that he would
   return his security deposit of $250 within a week. Hall, after several unsuccessful
   attempts to obtain the security deposit, considered taking legal action.
   In order to get inexpensive, quick, fair justice, Hall should

A. ask the public defender to represent him at state expense in a town justice court having jurisdiction to hear his case
B. take his case to small claims court where a lawyer is not required but where rulings are as legally binding as those of any other court
C. take his case to the court of final authority in the state
D. ask his lawyer to obtain a writ of execution commanding the sheriff to seize and sell the landlord's property, and to apply the proceeds against the $250

5. Unless otherwise specified in an offer, its revocation is effective when notice of revocation is

    A. made by the offerer
    B. received by the offerer
    C. made by the offeree
    D. received by the offeree

6. Which agreement could be binding even though it is NOT in writing?
   A contract

    A. to borrow an automobile
    B. to sell real property
    C. having marriage as consideration
    D. to answer for the obligations of others

7. If money damages would not be an adequate remedy for breach of contract, a court may grant the remedy of

    A. specific performance
    B. replevin
    C. nominal damages
    D. liquidated damages

8. Which would be considered an offer?

    A. Mimeographed letters mailed to all inhabitants of a small village, quoting list prices on furniture
    B. Newspaper advertisements listing dates and prices of a large department store anniversary sale.
    C. A personal letter sent by Davis to Carman listing a 1981 Chevrolet for sale at $1,250 cash
    D. A personal letter sent by Houck to Berra inviting Berra to attend a special auction sale of antiques

9. A person appointed by a court to take possession of the property of a bankrupt person is legally called a(n)

    A. administrator
    B. executor
    C. guardian
    D. trustee

10. Benware said to Riley, *I'll sell you my Volkswagen for $1,000 cash today.* Riley replied, *I'll take it. I can give you $500 today and the other $500 in 60 days.*
    Riley's reply legally resulted in a(n)

    A. accord and satisfaction
    B. binding acceptance
    C. counteroffer
    D. novation

11. Xavier published in the local newspaper an offer of a reward of $250 to anyone who would give information concerning his stolen automobile. The following day, Xavier decided to revoke his offer.
What would be the BEST action for Xavier to take at this time to avoid being legally bound on his published offer?

    A. Publish a withdrawal of the offer through a notice in the local newspaper in which the offer of the reward was made.
    B. Telephone all friends and acquaintances who subscribe to the local newspaper and notify them of the withdrawal of the reward.
    C. Publish a withdrawal of the offer in the newspaper of the neighboring city where the stolen automobile is thought to have been stolen.
    D. Notify the local police department of the withdrawal of the reward since it is their responsibility to apprehend criminals.

12. Blake, a minor, entered into an agreement to purchase a used car. At the time of the agreement, Blake stated that he was 21 years of age. Three months later, Blake attempted to disaffirm the contract.
Which statement BEST describes the above situation?

    A. Misstating his age will bar Blake from disaffirming the contract.
    B. Misstating his age will not bar Blake from disaffirming the contract.
    C. Blake cannot be held liable for fraud.
    D. Blake's act of ratification makes the contract enforceable.

13. The Uniform Commercial Code aims to standardize

    A. state laws relating to the sale of goods and the transfer of negotiable paper
    B. state laws which conflict with Federal laws
    C. state laws relating to realty transactions
    D. Federal and state income tax laws

14. The County Bank held a chattel mortgage with a balance of $600 on Osborne's automobile. Osborne defaulted on the mortgage and the automobile was sold at public auction for $1,400, with the expenses of the auction amounting to $70.
The excess money from the sale must go to

    A. the auctioneer
    B. Osborne
    C. the County Bank
    D. the county in which the sale took place

15. What is a purpose of a statute requiring notice to the creditors when a bulk sale is about to be made?
To

    A. prevent dishonest sellers from defrauding their creditors
    B. prevent dishonest sellers from defrauding the general public
    C. comply with the provisions of the Sherman Anti-Trust Act
    D. comply with the state fair trade laws

16. Which constitutes a bailment relationship?  
    A(n)

    A. exchange of personal property for personal property  
    B. temporary transfer of title to personal property  
    C. temporary transfer of personal property without transfer of title  
    D. transfer of title to personal property for a price

17. The instrument conveying title to real property is known as a

    A. deed  
    B. bill of sale  
    C. mortgage  
    D. contract of sale

18. The rule of caveat emptor is applicable when

    A. there is an implied warranty  
    B. the buyer fails to observe an obvious defect in the goods  
    C. the buyer fails to observe a hidden defect in the goods  
    D. the seller gives the buyer an express warranty as to the character of the goods

19. Which type of sale would offer the MOST advantages to a consumer who is considering buying a television for use in an area where reception is not always entirely satisfactory?

    A. Cash sale  
    B. Sale on approval  
    C. Retail installment contract  
    D. Sale with the privilege of return

20. Which governmental agency has the power to eliminate unfair methods of business competition such as false advertising of food and drugs?  
    _____ Commission.

    A. Federal Trade  
    B. Public Service  
    C. Interstate  
    D. Intrastate Commerce

21. Which is an example of personal property rights?  
    The right to

    A. collect royalty fees on a play you have written  
    B. sell a small summer cottage you own  
    C. sell a stand of timber (trees) you own  
    D. pick the fruit from an orchard you own

22. A certain area of a city has been set aside for the erection of private homes only.  
    This legal principle is known as

    A. eminent domain  
    B. license  
    C. zoning  
    D. easement

23. Martha Highland had a two-year lease on her apartment.  
    She decided to rent it furnished for three months, with the understanding that she would reoccupy it at the end of that time.  
    Such an agreement is known as a(n)

    A. assignment  
    B. subletting  
    C. conveyance  
    D. bailment

24. Haroldson purchased a summer camp for himself and his son, who was living at home with him. If either of them died, Haroldson wished the survivor to become the sole owner of the camp.
    The type of ownership that they should have would be

    A. tenancy in common
    B. tenancy in severalty
    C. joint tenancy
    D. community property

25. The terms that are CORRECTLY associated with the two different parties in a rental agreement are

    A. lessor and lessee
    B. tenant and lessee
    C. landlord and lessor
    D. landlord and owner

26. When property is insured against loss by more than one company, any loss is

    A. shared equally by each company
    B. shared proportionately by each company
    C. forfeited by the insured
    D. limited by the companies

27. In order to insure his house against fire, Feldman had to pay $60 a year.
    This payment by Feldman is called the

    A. dividend    B. premium    C. policy    D. risk

28. A company that transports goods for all who apply is known as a

    A. private carrier
    B. public utility
    C. general carrier
    D. common carrier

29. Which type of automobile insurance allows the insured to collect from his company medical expenses that result from an accident, no matter who is responsible? _____ insurance.

    A. Comprehensive
    B. Collision
    C. No-fault
    D. Liability

30. A common carrier would be relieved of liability due to damages to the goods of a consignor which it carries if the damage was due to a(n)

    A. strike of its employees
    B. earthquake
    C. faulty rail
    D. collision

## KEY (CORRECT ANSWERS)

| | | | |
|---|---|---|---|
| 1. | B | 16. | C |
| 2. | A | 17. | A |
| 3. | D | 18. | B |
| 4. | B | 19. | B |
| 5. | D | 20. | A |
| 6. | A | 21. | A |
| 7. | A | 22. | C |
| 8. | C | 23. | B |
| 9. | D | 24. | C |
| 10. | C | 25. | A |
| 11. | A | 26. | B |
| 12. | B | 27. | B |
| 13. | A | 28. | D |
| 14. | B | 29. | C |
| 15. | A | 30. | B |

# TEST 2

DIRECTIONS: Each question or incomplete statement is followed by several suggested answers or completions. Select the one that BEST answers the question or completes the statement. *PRINT THE LETTER OF THE CORRECT ANSWER IN THE SPACE AT THE RIGHT.*

1. What assurance from the bank is given by a certified check? That

    A. this particular check will be paid by the bank
    B. the credit rating of the depositor is good
    C. the depositor's checks are always good
    D. the depositor exists and has an account at the bank only

2. An instrument would NOT be negotiable if it is made payable to

    A. cash
    B. John Salisbury
    C. the order of John Salisbury
    D. bearer

3. What is the legal obligation of the payee who endorses his name on the back of a check?

    A. No obligation at all since he is not the drawer
    B. Only the legal obligation to cash the check before 7 days
    C. Only the legal obligation to cash the check before 30 days
    D. The obligation to pay the amount of the check if it is dishonored by the drawer

4. A bank is ALWAYS the drawee of a(n)

    A. personal check
    B. order bill of lading
    C. Series E United States Government Bond
    D. promissory note

5. Which act requires all persons who extend consumer credit in the regular course of business to inform the debtor of the amount of the financing charges in dollars and as an annual percentage rate? _____ Act.

    A. Interstate Commerce        B. Truth-in-Lending
    C. Sherman Anti-Trust         D. Clayton

6. Bicknell accepted a promissory note from Scott and negotiated it to Seamans. As the holder of this instrument, Seamans should NOT

    A. transfer or negotiate it
    B. attempt to enforce payment of it
    C. discharge it upon receiving payment
    D. surrender the instrument to the maker if it is dishonored

7. Through a bank teller's error, a bank refused to pay a check under the belief that there were not sufficient funds in the account to cover the check.
As a result of this error, the bank became liable to the

A. payee
B. drawer
C. endorsers
D. holder in due course

8. Brubaker was in need of $300 in cash. He borrowed that amount and signed a contract whereby he pledged his car as security. Title to the car passed to the lender until the debt was repaid, but possession remained with Brubaker.
Brubaker's contract was an example of a(n)

   A. installment sale
   B. conditional sale
   C. chattel mortgage
   D. seller's lien

9. Ella Simpkins died without leaving a will and without heirs.
Her property would pass to the state government by

   A. adverse possession
   B. eminent domain
   C. mandamus
   D. escheat

10. Medical provisions of hospital insurance and voluntary medical insurance for those people 65 years of age and over are contained in the Social Security Amendments Act of 1965.
These provisions are COMMONLY referred to as

    A. disability insurance
    B. Medicaid
    C. workmen's compensation
    D. Medicare

11. Upon the death of the insured, the life insurance company GENERALLY pays the

    A. cash surrender value of the policy to the beneficiary
    B. face value of the policy to the beneficiary
    C. cash surrender value of the policy to the insurer
    D. face value of the policy to the heir as stated by statute

12. In New York State, the MINIMUM age at which one may purchase insurance on his own life is _____ years.

    A. 21     B. 18     C. 15     D. 12

13. Which level of government establishes the laws governing intestacy?

    A. Federal     B. State     C. City     D. County

14. A formal written document by which one person gives another the authority to enter into contracts for him is known as a(n)

    A. independent contractor
    B. novation
    C. power of attorney
    D. writ of execution

15. Which date on a promissory note would make it payable at a definite time?

    A. One week after graduation
    B. Thirty days after the sale of my house
    C. Ten days after my twenty-first birthday
    D. Ten days after sight

16. What type of insurance protects an employee from financial loss resulting from personal injuries suffered on the job? _____ insurance.

    A. Workmen's Compensation
    B. State Disability
    C. fidelity
    D. fiduciary

17. An agent's authority may NOT ordinarily be revoked under which of the following types of agency agreements?
    An agency

    A. coupled with an interest
    B. for compensation
    C. by performance
    D. by implication

18. Unless it is otherwise designated, all stock issued by a corporation is called _____ stock.

    A. treasury
    B. preferred
    C. no-par
    D. common

19. Which is the MAIN disadvantage of a partnership?

    A. It requires special permission from the state to operate as a business.
    B. It is required to pay an organizational tax to the state.
    C. Each partner is personally liable for all debts incurred by the firm.
    D. It is legally separated from the owners of the business.

20. Which would USUALLY be found in the Articles of Copartnership?
    The

    A. type of invoices to be used by the firm
    B. credit and collection policies of the firm
    C. maximum amount of money the firm may borrow
    D. method of sharing profits

21. Shirley Baker's uncle promised to give her $100 on her 18th birthday.
    Is this a binding contract?

    A. Yes; a promise to pay money to another is legal and valid.
    B. Yes; an agreement is always enforceable at law.
    C. No; a promise may be revoked if there is not valid consideration for it.
    D. No; an agreement is void unless there are two competent parties.

22. Kelsey offered to sell to Langdon, a close friend, a rare antique vase for $450. Langdon did not have the money to buy it but told his brother about the offer. When Langdon's brother offered Kelsey $450, Kelsey refused to sell the antique vase to him.
    Can Langdon's brother enforce the offer made by Kelsey?

    A. Yes; the Statute of Frauds does not require contracts for the sale of goods under $500 to be in writing.
    B. Yes; this is a legally binding agreement in which all the terms are definite and certain.
    C. No; a person may change his mind and withdraw an offer at any time prior to its acceptance.
    D. No; an offer may only be accepted by the person to whom the offer is made.

23. Charlene Victor, a noted writer, was engaged to speak before a civic club. Her plane was unable to maintain its scheduled run because of intense fog. Upon learning that she would be unable to arrive at the meeting on time, Victor called another noted writer, Ashton, and asked him to appear in her place. When Ashton arrived, the club refused to let him speak.
Did the club have a legal reason for refusing to let Ashton speak in Victor's place?

    A. Yes; when the obligation under a contract requires special talent, it may not be assigned to a third party without approval of all parties.
    B. Yes; rights under a contract may be assigned to a competent third party only after notice is given to the party in the original agreement.
    C. No; where it is impossible to perform a contract, the contract may be assigned to a third party.
    D. No; one's obligations under a contract may be assigned to a competent third party.

24. Chalmers owned very little personal property and rented the house in which he lived. He felt there was no need to make out a will.
Is Chalmers CORRECT?

    A. Yes; a will is not really necessary unless a person has at least $10,000 in property.
    B. Yes; the cost of making a will is so great that it would probably take all his money.
    C. No; even though his property holdings are limited, he could be sure that they would go to whom he wished.
    D. No; if a person does not make a will, all his property passes to the state.

25. At the age of 17, Becking purchased a radio from Ramos and Company on the installment plan. After reaching majority, Becking made a payment when it became due. Becking later decided to return the radio and to demand the return of the money that he had paid.
Could Becking legally do so?

    A. Yes; a minor may disaffirm all agreements with the exception of those for necessities.
    B. Yes; a minor may disaffirm all agreements made with an adult on the grounds that the other party to the agreement is an adult.
    C. No; a minor who ratifies an agreement after reaching majority may not later disaffirm the agreement.
    D. No; a minor may not disaffirm any agreement after reaching majority.

26. Thompson rented a floor sander from Dugan's Hardware for one week and paid a fee of $35. Three days before the rental period expired, Dugan's Hardware had an opportunity to sell the floor sander at a good profit and demanded its return at once.
Must Thompson return the floor sander immediately?

    A. Yes; in a mutual benefit bailment for hire, the bailor has the right to exclusive possession of the property.
    B. Yes; the bailor always has the right to possession of bailed property if it can be sold at a profit.
    C. No; in a mutual benefit bailment for hire, the bailor must give the bailee the option of buying the goods.
    D. No; in a mutual benefit bailment for hire, the bailee has exclusive right over the goods during the period of the contract.

27. Myron answered a newspaper advertisement offering 19-inch color television sets for sale at $329. The store informed Myron that all sale models had been sold. Myron insisted they must sell him one at the advertised price because he was accepting their offer.
Is Myron CORRECT?

27.____

    A. Yes; it is illegal for stores to advertise sales if they do not have a sufficient quantity of the goods offered for sale.
    B. Yes; customers accepting offers made by advertisements create a legal and enforceable contract.
    C. No; stores have no obligation to fill customers' orders once their supply of goods runs out.
    D. No; advertisements are not offers but are merely invitations to offer and stores do not have to accept all offers.

28. Music Mart sold and delivered an expensive tapeplayer to Robideau, a minor, on credit. Later, discovering that Robideau had falsified his age on the agreement, Music Mart sought to void the contract and recover possession of the goods.
Will Music Mart succeed?

28.____

    A. Yes; contracts made by minors for luxuries are voidable at the option of either party.
    B. Yes; when a minor falsifies his age, the adult may avoid the contract and recover the goods.
    C. No; ordinarily, a contract between a minor and an adult is voidable only at the option of the minor.
    D. No; adults may only avoid agreements made with minors if the contract is for necessaries.

29. Marta Salomi received a letter from the Sweeta Corporation stating that the company would send her a year's supply of low-calorie sweetener in individually wrapped packets at an introductory price of $10.00. In the letter, the company stated that if it did not hear from Marta within 7 days, it would ship the merchandise to her. Marta made no reply. The year's supply of sweetener arrived in the mail C.O.D., and Marta refused to sign for and accept the merchandise. The company filed suit.
Is Marta obligated to pay?

29.____

    A. Yes; there is an implied contract with the Sweeta Corporation for the year's supply of sweetener.
    B. Yes; the offer was properly communicated to Marta and her silence constituted the acceptance.
    C. No; Marta's acceptance did not follow the terms of the offer.
    D. No; Marta's silence and failure to act cannot be regarded as an acceptance of the company's offer.

30. A tenant paid his monthly rent to Burke's agent, Pulcari, who failed to report it to Burke. Later, Burke sued the tenant for nonpayment.
Is the tenant obliged to pay this rent again?

    A. Yes; the rent should have been paid to the owner.
    B. Yes; as far as the owner knew, the rent had not been paid.
    C. No; payment to Pulcari was the same as payment to Burke.
    D. No; the only recourse open to Burke is to have the tenant evicted.

## KEY (CORRECT ANSWERS)

| | | | |
|---|---|---|---|
| 1. | A | 16. | A |
| 2. | B | 17. | A |
| 3. | D | 18. | D |
| 4. | A | 19. | C |
| 5. | B | 20. | D |
| 6. | D | 21. | C |
| 7. | B | 22. | D |
| 8. | C | 23. | A |
| 9. | D | 24. | C |
| 10. | D | 25. | C |
| 11. | B | 26. | D |
| 12. | C | 27. | D |
| 13. | B | 28. | C |
| 14. | C | 29. | D |
| 15. | D | 30. | C |

# TEST 3

DIRECTIONS: Each question or incomplete statement is followed by several suggested answers or completions. Select the one that BEST answers the question or completes the statement. *PRINT THE LETTER OF THE CORRECT ANSWER IN THE SPACE AT THE RIGHT.*

Questions 1-5.

DIRECTIONS: Questions 1 through 5 are to be answered on the basis of the information below.

1. This business paper is legally known as a  1._____
   - A. chattel mortgage
   - B. bill of lading
   - C. bill of sale
   - D. warehouse receipt

2. This business transaction is an example of a bailment for  2._____
   - A. storage
   - B. service
   - C. security
   - D. hire

3. In this business transaction, Ace Furniture Mart is known as the  3._____
   - A. consignor
   - B. consignee
   - C. bailor
   - D. bailee

4. How may this business paper be negotiated?  4._____
   - A. By delivery *only*
   - B. By endorsement *only*
   - C. By endorsement and delivery *only*
   - D. It may not be negotiated.

75

5. If Ace Furniture Mart should fail to pay the charges, Mayfair Storage, Inc. could exercise a _____ lien.

   A. mechanic's
   B. judgment
   C. bailee's
   D. mortgagee's

Questions 6-10.

DIRECTIONS: Questions 6 through 10 are to be answered on the basis of the information below.

Rovito purchased a used automobile for $4,500. He immediately purchased the following insurance coverage:

Minimal no-fault coverage
Bodily injury: 50,000/100,000
Medical payments: $5,000 per person
Property damage: $10,000
Collision: $100 deductible
Comprehensive: $200 deductible

6. Rovito hit a parked car while backing out of his driveway. The damage to his car was $450.
   His insurance company will pay him

   A. $350   B. $450   C. $4,500   D. nothing

7. Rovito was welding a trailer hitch onto the car when he carelessly set fire to the car, which was totally destroyed.
   How much will the insurance company pay Rovito?

   A. The purchase price of $4,500
   B. The present market value of the car less $200
   C. The present market value of the car less $100
   D. Nothing

8. If Rovito's car caused an accident seriously injuring six persons in another automobile, the MAXIMUM amount Rovito's insurer will pay would be

   A. $5,000   B. $30,000   C. $50,000   D. $100,000

9. During a severe thunderstorm, a tree fell on Rovito's parked car.
   Which insurance, if any, would cover this damage?

   A. Property damage
   B. Comprehensive
   C. Collision
   D. Bodily injury

10. Rovito was at fault in an accident that injured three persons, all of whom sued him.
    What action should Rovito take upon being served with the legal papers of suit?

    A. Hire the best lawyer he can afford.
    B. Offer to pay the $50,000 each called for in the policy himself.
    C. Notify the insurance company to offer the injured the $50,000 each called for in the policy.
    D. Notify the insurance company at once since they must defend him.

Questions 11-15.

DIRECTIONS: Questions 11 through 15 are to be answered on the basis of the instrument below.

> I, J.A. Mahoney, do hereby lease the residence at 4080 East Main Road, Easton, New York, to P.F. Moore for a period of two years for the sum of two hundred fifty dollars ($250.00) a month, payable monthly in advance.
>
> Date: April 2, 2008                                   *J.A. Mahoney*
>                                                       *P.F. Moore*

11. When Moore leased the house from Mahoney, Moore became the . 11._____

    A. assignor    B. assignee    C. lessee    D. lessor

12. When the lease was signed, Mahoney required Moore to pay $250 in advance to insure the faithful performance of the lease. 12._____
    This payment of $250 is called a(n)

    A. escrow              B. option
    C. surety              D. security deposit

13. The terms of this lease created a relationship known as a 13._____

    A. tenancy for years
    B. tenancy from year to year
    C. periodic tenancy
    D. tenancy at will

14. While Moore occupies the house, when may Mahoney, as owner of the property, enter the premises for inspection? 14._____

    A. At any time
    B. At no time
    C. On weekends only
    D. By permission of the tenant

15. If a fire totally destroys the house after 12 months of the lease, Moore's further liability for rent would be 15._____

    A. nothing
    B. $3,000
    C. $3,000, less the $250 paid in advance
    D. $3,000, less the cost of living quarters until the house is rebuilt

Questions 16-20.

DIRECTIONS: Questions 16 through 20 are to be answered on the basis of the information below.

Three weeks after Shaw was married, he purchased a life insurance policy for $20,000 and named his wife as beneficiary. He also went to a lawyer and had a will drawn up, leaving his entire estate to his wife, and named her as executrix of the will.

16. The insurance policy that Shaw purchased would ordinarily become effective when

    A. the application was made
    B. the application was received by the insurer
    C. the first premium was paid and the policy was issued
    D. Shaw passed a physical examination

17. When the life insurance policy has been in force over two years, it cannot be avoided by the insurer in the state because of the _____ clause.

    A. cash surrender value
    B. incontestability
    C. insurable interest
    D. waiver of premium

18. Shaw may change or modify his original will by preparing a(n)

    A. rider
    B. attachment
    C. codicil
    D. endorsement

19. When Shaw dies, his will must be submitted for probate in which local court? _____ court.

    A. District
    B. Family
    C. Supreme
    D. Surrogate

20. If Shaw's wife should predecease him by one day, the terms of the will would NORMALLY be carried out by a court-appointed

    A. administrator
    B. beneficiary
    C. executor
    D. testator

Questions 21-25.

DIRECTIONS: Questions 21 through 25 are to be answered on the basis of the information below.

Landry owned and operated a service station in a small village. He sold the station to Haroldson, agreeing not to open another service station for two years within an area of ten miles. Nine months later, Landry opened a used-car business with a service department, just five blocks from his former location. Haroldson immediately commenced court action to enforce their agreement.

21. Landry would receive official notification of Haroldson's action when he is served with a(n)

    A. indictment
    B. injunction
    C. summons
    D. subpoena

22. Landry's action in opening the used-car business with a service department in just nine months would be an example of a(n)

    A. felony
    B. infraction
    C. misdemeanor
    D. tort

23. The court of original jurisdiction to decide this controversy would be the _____ court.　　23.____

    A. appellate　　B. civil　　C. criminal　　D. surrogate

24. This court action against Landry would be scheduled for trial by the　　24.____

    A. attorney for the plaintiff
    B. court bailiff
    C. clerk of the court
    D. judge

25. The remedy that Haroldson's attorney would seek in the above court action would be a(n)　　25.____

    A. foreclosure　　　　　　B. injunction
    C. recision　　　　　　　　D. replevin

Questions 26-30.

DIRECTIONS: Questions 26 through 30 are to be answered on the basis of the information below.

Morris, an automobile dealer, employed Williams to sell new cars for him.

26. Williams would be known as a _____ agent.　　26.____

    A. special　　　　　　B. general
    C. public　　　　　　　D. del credere

27. While Williams was giving a prospective customer a demonstration ride, he caused an accident in which the customer was injured.　　27.____
    Which statement BEST describes the liability of Morris?
    A(n)

    A. principal is personally liable for his own negligence
    B. principal is liable for the negligence of his agent while the agent is carrying out his principal's business
    C. agent is personally liable only for acts performed within the scope of his employment
    D. principal is liable for an agent's acts only when the principal receives a direct benefit from such acts

28. Williams was also hospitalized in the same accident. He required hospitalization and was out of work for six weeks. Williams' hospital bill, as well as a weekly income, would be paid under provisions of the　　28.____

    A. Unemployment Insurance Act
    B. State Disability Benefits Law
    C. Federal Fair Labor Standards Act
    D. Workmen's Compensation Act

29. Before his accident, Williams had purchased some gasoline for the automobile he was demonstrating.
Williams' right to collect from Morris for this expense is called his right of

    A. subrogation
    B. compensation
    C. reimbursement
    D. indemnification

30. Williams' obligation to give Morris the cash taken in from customers is called the duty of

    A. accounting
    B. obedience
    C. diligence
    D. loyalty

# KEY (CORRECT ANSWERS)

| | | | |
|---|---|---|---|
| 1. | D | 16. | C |
| 2. | A | 17. | B |
| 3. | C | 18. | C |
| 4. | D | 19. | D |
| 5. | C | 20. | A |
| 6. | A | 21. | C |
| 7. | B | 22. | D |
| 8. | D | 23. | B |
| 9. | B | 24. | C |
| 10. | D | 25. | B |
| 11. | C | 26. | A |
| 12. | D | 27. | B |
| 13. | A | 28. | D |
| 14. | D | 29. | C |
| 15. | A | 30. | A |

# TEST 4

DIRECTIONS: Each question or incomplete statement is followed by several suggested answers or completions. Select the one that BEST answers the question or completes the statement. *PRINT THE LETTER OF THE CORRECT ANSWER IN THE SPACE AT THE RIGHT.*

1. The HIGHEST court in the State of New York is the

    A. Supreme Court  
    B. Probate Court  
    C. Court of Appeals  
    D. District Court

2. Walters struck a properly parked car while backing carelessly out of his driveway. Walters is guilty of the tort of

    A. negligence  
    B. nuisance  
    C. assault and battery  
    D. conversion

3. A new law enacted by a city council would be known as a(n)

    A. decree  
    B. injunction  
    C. ordinance  
    D. warrant

4. By orally repeating a rumor which he knew to be false, Maresco caused injury to Hanson's reputation. Maresco was guilty of

    A. trespass   B. libel   C. assault   D. slander

5. Lisa Brown, a merchant, offered to sell Wilson an air conditioner for $248.75. When Wilson said he needed time to think about the offer, Brown made a written promise to keep the offer open for 5 days.
Which statement concerning Brown's written promise is TRUE?

    A. Brown may not withdraw the offer until the end of the fifth day.  
    B. The written promise is called a pledge.  
    C. Brown may withdraw the offer at any time before an acceptance is made.  
    D. The written promise created a binding contract for the purchase of the air conditioner.

6. The written agreement of a minor to purchase a stereo system for personal use is

    A. valid   B. void   C. voidable   D. implied

7. Rider sold an old clock to Weeks for $10 cash. Later, Rider learned that the clock was worth $100.
If Rider should sue, she is legally entitled to recover

    A. $10   B. nothing   C. the clock   D. $90

8. Benton owed Harrington $250. Before the debt became due, Harrington gave his collection rights to the Easy Collection Agency.
In this situation, Harrington would be classified as the

    A. assignor   B. assignee   C. debtor   D. obligor

9. Actions for bankruptcy are brought before the _____ courts.

   A. Federal   B. state   C. county   D. local

10. Garland, age 17, purchased an automobile.
    If this contract is considered legally voidable, at which time may he avoid this contract? Only

    A. during his minority
    B. within one year from date of purchase
    C. after attaining his majority
    D. during his minority and within a reasonable time after attaining 18

11. Marcia Gray purchased an oil painting at a public auction.
    Title passed to Gray when

    A. the bid was made
    B. the auctioneer brought down his hammer and said *Sold*
    C. Gray paid the cashier in the auction gallery
    D. the painting was delivered to Gray

12. When Turney was unable to pay the $500 he owed Heston, Heston agreed to let Turney paint Heston's house in payment.
    When Turney finished painting the house, his original obligation was discharged by

    A. breach
    B. impossibility of performance
    C. accord and satisfaction
    D. disability

13. Mason was to do some carpentry work for Armand for $350.
    The terms of the contract called for one-half of the contract price to be paid when the work started. When Mason began work and requested $175, Armand offered only $150, which Mason refused.
    The contract was terminated by

    A. breach                B. substantial performance
    C. tender                D. alteration

14. A debt has been outlawed by the Statute of Limitations.
    The debtor promises, in writing, to repay this debt.
    What effect, if any, does this written promise have on the debt?
    It

    A. always revives the debt for 4 years
    B. revives the debt for different times, depending upon the type of agreement involved
    C. always revives the debt for 6 years
    D. has no effect on the debt

15. If he so chooses, a minor may legally avoid a contract for

    A. purchase of tools needed to earn a living
    B. a business in which a 17-year-old minor is engaged

C. purchase of winter clothing which the minor needs and which is actually supplied to him
D. purchase of an expensive pleasure automobile

16. If an offer is made by mail, a contract results when the offeree('s)

   A. writes his acceptance
   B. mails his written acceptance
   C. letter of acceptance reaches the post office in the offerer's city
   D. letter of acceptance is received by the offeror

17. A person who becomes hopelessly in debt may have his debts discharged through bankruptcy proceedings or by

   A. delaying payment of his debts for a period of three years
   B. notifying creditors in writing that they will receive only a percentage of the amount due
   C. arranging a composition of creditors who all agree to accept a percentage of the total amount due them
   D. paying those debts that can be paid and notifying the other creditors in writing of his inability to make any further payments

18. Watson, an automobile dealer, offered in writing to sell an automobile to Keller for $800 cash. Keller wanted to think further about the offer, so Watson agreed, in writing, to accept $50 in return for keeping the offer open for one week.
Which statement concerning this agreement is CORRECT?
Watson

   A. may sell the automobile to anyone else at any time
   B. must sell the automobile to Keller if Keller accepts within the week
   C. need not sell the automobile to Keller if Keller accepts within the week
   D. must sell the automobile to Keller if Keller accepts the offer two weeks after the agreement was made

19. If the finder of a briefcase returns it to the owner and receives a reward, the contract is terminated by

   A. mutual agreement        B. breach
   C. alteration              D. performance

20. After having contracted with Thompson to buy 500 boxes of oranges at $6 a box, Harvey refused to accept delivery of the oranges and Thompson was forced to sell them to Jackson for $4 a box.
What is Thompson entitled to do?
Thompson is

   A. entitled to sue Harvey for $2 a box, plus any necessary expenses incurred in selling the oranges to Jackson
   B. entitled to sue Harvey for $6 a box
   C. not entitled to any damages because he sold the oranges to Jackson
   D. not entitled to any damages because there was no warranty as to quality

21. If one person gives another a signed offer which does not state how much time he will have to act on it, the offer may

    A. be revoked by the offeror at any time
    B. be revoked by the offeror at any time before acceptance if the offeree is notified
    C. not be revoked, even though there is no consideration paid to keep the offer open
    D. not be revoked for a period of 4 months

22. Wilks, a plumber, supplied labor and material amounting to $1,500 in repairing the heating system in Abel's home.
    If Abel should fail to pay him, what action may Wilks take?
    He may

    A. send Abel a notice of assessment
    B. obtain a judgment by default
    C. file a mechanic's lien on Abel's home
    D. file a tax lien on Abel's home

23. Black stole a car from Matthews and had his friend, Barton, sell it to Calvin, an innocent purchaser.
    Who is the TRUE owner of the car?

    A. Barton    B. Black    C. Calvin    D. Matthews

24. Jones sold 5,000 bushels of apples to Benton. At the time of this sale, these apples were being stored at the Frosty Cold Storage Company.
    If Benton is to remove the apples from the premises of the cold storage company, which of the following original copies must he present to the storage company?
    A(n)

    A. straight bill of lading
    B. negotiable warehouse receipt
    C. order bill of lading
    D. non-negotiable warehouse receipt

25. Which bailee is obligated to exercise only slight care over the subject matter of the bailment?
    A

    A. warehouseman
    B. person who rents an outboard motor
    C. person who finds a diamond ring
    D. person who borrows his neighbor's garden shovel

26. Kraft purchased from Autrey a watch that had been stolen. Kraft was later forced to return the watch to its rightful owner.
    Kraft has rights against Autrey because of an

    A. express warranty of title
    B. express warranty of quality
    C. implied warranty of title
    D. implied warranty of fitness of purpose

27. An example of a bailee in a mutual benefit bailment is a    27.____

    A. cleaning establishment that renders the service of drycleaning clothes for a fee
    B. person who finds a watch
    C. person who trades a pen for a book
    D. person who holds or keeps a dog for one week as a special favor to a friend

28. Placing goods in a commercial warehouse for storage or safekeeping is an example of a    28.____

    A. gratuitous bailment
    B. bailment for the sole benefit of the bailor
    C. bailment for the sole benefit of the bailee
    D. mutual benefit bailment

29. When a tenant fails to pay his rent as called for in the lease, the landlord's FIRST remedy is to    29.____

    A. seize the tenant's furniture until the rent is paid
    B. sue for the back rent
    C. lock the premises to keep tenant from further occupancy
    D. have a mover take the tenant's furniture to storage until the rent is paid

30. Marge Anderson rented a house from Biddle for five years at a monthly rental. The lease made no statement as to subletting and no agreement as to when the monthly rental was due.    30.____
    Under these conditions, which statement concerning the monthly rental and subletting would take effect?
    The monthly rental was due _____ and Anderson _____ sublet.

    A. at the end of the month; could
    B. at the end of the month; could not
    C. in advance; could not
    D. in advance; could

## KEY (CORRECT ANSWERS)

| | | | |
|---|---|---|---|
| 1. | C | 16. | B |
| 2. | A | 17. | C |
| 3. | C | 18. | B |
| 4. | D | 19. | D |
| 5. | A | 20. | A |
| 6. | C | 21. | B |
| 7. | B | 22. | C |
| 8. | A | 23. | D |
| 9. | A | 24. | B |
| 10. | D | 25. | C |
| 11. | B | 26. | C |
| 12. | C | 27. | A |
| 13. | A | 28. | D |
| 14. | B | 29. | B |
| 15. | D | 30. | A |

# TEST 5

DIRECTIONS: Each question or incomplete statement is followed by several suggested answers or completions. Select the one that BEST answers the question or completes the statement. *PRINT THE LETTER OF THE CORRECT ANSWER IN THE SPACE AT THE RIGHT.*

1. Which type of fire is regarded as a *friendly fire*? A(n)

    A. fire started by a lighted cigarette tossed into a waste paper container
    B. fire started by soot in a chimney
    C. unusually hot fire in a fireplace, which scorches a nearby table
    D. fire started by lightning striking a building

2. Unless otherwise stated in a lease, those fixtures permanently attached to real property when a lease expires become the property of the

    A. landlord   B. tenant   C. sublessor   D. sublessee

3. A fire insurance contract becomes binding when the

    A. first premium is paid
    B. policy has been written
    C. application is made
    D. application is accepted by an authorized agent of the insurance company

4. Ferris borrowed money from the Community Building and Loan Association to purchase a home. The Community Building and Loan Association required a lien upon the realty as security for the loan.
    This lien is called a

    A. mechanic's lien            B. license
    C. mortgage                   D. lease

5. The duties of a tenant GENERALLY include

    A. paying the taxes and assessments due on the property
    B. using the apartment in accordance with the terms of the lease
    C. paying all upkeep expenses
    D. meeting all insurance premiums on the property

6. One who is hired to transport goods or persons by anyone desiring such services is called a

    A. gratuitous bailor          B. consignor
    C. common carrier             D. private carrier

7. When purchasing a new car, Albert was given the choice of delivery f.o.b. shipping point or f.o.b. destination.
    Of these terms, delivery f.o.b. destination would be to Albert's legal advantage because

    A. title will pass when the car is placed in the hands of the carrier
    B. shipping expenses on the car will be paid by the buyer upon delivery

C. Albert will not sustain the loss if the car is damaged in transit
D. all losses caused by damage to the car will fall upon the carrier

8. The holder of a promissory note fails to present the note to the maker for payment on the date on which it is due.
What effect does this have on the liability for payment?
It

   A. requires court action in order to make the holder liable for payment
   B. requires court action in order to hold previous endorsers liable for payment
   C. releases the maker from liability for payment
   D. releases previous endorsers from liability for payment

9. A _____ is an example of a promissory note.

   A. bond
   B. bank draft
   C. money order
   D. traveler's check

10. Johnson requested a bank in Buffalo to write him a check on its own funds in the bank so that he would be able to pay a bill.
This check is legally known as a

   A. cashier's check
   B. bank draft
   C. traveler's check
   D. certified check

11. A promissory note falls due on a legal holiday.
Under the Uniform Commercial Code, the holder must present the instrument on the

   A. legal holiday
   B. day before the legal holiday
   C. day after the legal holiday
   D. next business day for both parties

12. The legal relationship between a depositor and his bank is BEST described as that of

   A. employer and employee
   B. debtor and creditor
   C. landlord and tenant
   D. principal and agent

13. When a creditor fails to bring suit against a debtor for an unpaid amount within a fixed time, the law says that the debt is

   A. outlawed
   B. automatically extended
   C. canceled except for the interest
   D. paid

14. When a promissory note reads *with interest* but does not state the rate to be charged, the maker pays

   A. no interest at all
   B. the minimum contract rate of interest
   C. the maximum contract rate of interest
   D. the legal rate of interest

15. To be negotiable, a promissory note MUST

    A. be payable to order or bearer
    B. be dated
    C. contain the words *value received*
    D. indicate the place where it is payable

16. The written contract of life insurance is called the

    A. binder  B. policy  C. rider  D. floater

17. Roberts applied for a $5,000 whole life (straight life) policy and wanted his mother to collect upon his death.
    His mother would be known as the

    A. benefactor
    C. contingent
    B. beneficiary
    D. fiduciary

18. Brown, a driver for a trucking company, had to have the truck repaired in a distant city and charged the cost to the company.
    An agency was created by

    A. necessity
    C. ratification
    B. estoppel
    D. appearance

19. Rowe, Harrison, and Zoeller are general partners in an automobile sales agency. The partnership agreement made no mention of division of profits or losses. The auto firm sustained a loss of $60,000 in its first year of operation.
    What would be Harrison's share of the loss?

    A. Nothing  B. $20,000  C. $30,000  D. $60,000

20. Officers in a corporation are chosen by a

    A. unanimous vote of common stockholders
    B. two-thirds vote of all stockholders
    C. board of directors
    D. majority vote of preferred stockholders

21. Murphy borrowed $400 from Grace Swenk, agreeing to repay with interest in excess of the legal rate.
    Must Murphy repay the loan and interest when it becomes due?

    A. Yes; agreements involving usury are valid.
    B. Yes; agreements involving usury are voidable only on the part of the lender.
    C. No; agreements involving usury are voidable on the part of the borrower.
    D. No; agreements involving usury are void.

22. Janet Wynn, a minor, had heard that anything she purchased could be returned to the seller and her money would have to be refunded.
    Is Wynn's information CORRECT?

    A. Yes; a minor's contracts are voidable at the minor's choice.
    B. Yes; a minor's purchase must be taken back by the seller if the minor is less than 18 years of age.

C. No; a minor may not disaffirm contracts she has made if they are for necessities.
D. No; a minor is responsible for the contracts she makes just as an adult is.

23. Fuller wanted to purchase a used car from Jarvis Auto Company on the installment plan. The Jarvis Auto Company would not sell Fuller the car unless he could get someone else to guarantee payment. Fuller's father telephoned the Jarvis Auto Company and said that he would make payment if his son did not pay.
If the son fails to make payment, will his father be legally liable under his oral promise?

   A. Yes; the sale of personal property need not be in writing to be enforceable.
   B. Yes; the promise to pay for the debts of another need not be in writing if it is a promise by a parent.
   C. No; the promise to pay the debts of another must be in writing to be enforceable.
   D. No; the sale of personal property must be in writing to be enforceable.

24. Johnson borrowed his neighbor's lawnmower. After mowing his lawn, Johnson left the lawnmower in his front yard, intending to return it the next day. That night, the lawnmower was stolen.
Is Johnson liable for the loss?

   A. Yes; in a bailment for the sole benefit of the bailee, the bailee must take great care of the property.
   B. Yes; in a bailment for the sole benefit of the bailee, the bailee must take slight care of the property.
   C. No; in a bailment for the sole benefit of the bailee, the bailee must take ordinary care of the property.
   D. No; in a bailment for the sole benefit of the bailor, the bailee must take slight care of the property.

25. Caldwell did not tell the common carrier of the perishable nature of goods he was shipping.
Would the carrier be liable if the goods spoiled?

   A. Yes; a common carrier is liable as the insurer of goods.
   B. Yes; a common carrier is liable for losses due to the spoilage.
   C. No; a common carrier is not liable for losses due to an act of God.
   D. No; a common carrier is not liable for losses due to the inherent nature of the goods.

26. The landlord of an apartment building refused to repair the plumbing. As a result, all the apartments had an unpleasant odor. The landlord insisted that normal repairs were the responsibility of the tenant and that this was a normal repair.
Was the landlord CORRECT?

   A. Yes; unless agreed upon in the lease, the tenant is liable for any and all repairs.
   B. Yes; the landlord never has any responsibility to make repairs.
   C. No; the landlord is responsible for repairs to those areas jointly used and for proper sanitary conditions.
   D. No; the landlord is liable for any and all repairs.

27. A man completed his will and left all his property to his wife. She was subsequently killed in an automobile accident.
 Can he now change his will?

    A. Yes; but only if he first destroys the old one.
    B. Yes; a person may make a new will any time.
    C. No; a will is a very formal document and once written, it is registered and may not be changed.
    D. No; only a judge from the court that has jurisdiction over wills may permit a change in a will.

27.____

28. Robinson was hired as a clerk-typist in an office of a trucking firm. He and all other workers were covered by a union agreement, with specific duties outlined for each job classification. One day, Robinson was ordered to help unload some heavy crates from a truck. He refused because this work was not in his job classification. Robinson's employer attempted to discharge him.
 Should the employer be successful?

    A. Yes; an employee may not avoid tasks simply because they are unpleasant.
    B. Yes; an employer has the right to assign any lawful task to any worker.
    C. No; an employee need not do tasks assigned to him that are beyond the usual job or not covered by his contractual agreement.
    D. No; an employee is guaranteed freedom of choice of work by the Constitution.

28.____

29. Bond was employed by Nelson Appliance Repair Co. to pick up and deliver appliances in need of repair. While making a delivery of a repaired color television to Gordon, Bond dropped the set, completely destroying it.
 Could Gordon hold Nelson Appliance Repair Co. liable for the loss of this set?

    A. Yes; an employer is always liable for any acts of employees.
    B. Yes; an employer is liable for the acts of employees within the scope and course of their employment.
    C. No; an employer is not liable for acts of employees unless the employer approved of such acts.
    D. No; an employer is never liable for the negligent acts of his employees.

29.____

30. Drexler and Knox are partners in a retail shoe store. Without the permission of Knox, Drexler purchased a new cash register.
 Is the partnership bound by this purchase?

    A. Yes; a partnership is liable for all acts of the partners within the scope of the business.
    B. Yes; a partnership is liable for any agreement that a partner makes.
    C. No; a partnership is not liable for any individual acts of its partners.
    D. No; partners may not make contracts in the name of the firm without the consent of the other partners.

30.____

# KEY (CORRECT ANSWERS)

| | | | |
|---|---|---|---|
| 1. | C | 16. | B |
| 2. | A | 17. | B |
| 3. | D | 18. | A |
| 4. | C | 19. | B |
| 5. | B | 20. | C |
| 6. | C | 21. | D |
| 7. | C | 22. | C |
| 8. | D | 23. | C |
| 9. | A | 24. | A |
| 10. | A | 25. | D |
| 11. | D | 26. | C |
| 12. | B | 27. | B |
| 13. | A | 28. | C |
| 14. | D | 29. | B |
| 15. | A | 30. | A |

# EXAMINATION SECTION
# TEST 1

DIRECTIONS: Each question or incomplete statement is followed by several suggested answers or completions. Select the one that BEST answers the question or completes the statement. *PRINT THE LETTER OF THE CORRECT ANSWER IN THE SPACE AT THE RIGHT.*

Questions 1-5.

DIRECTIONS: Questions 1 through 5 are to be answered on the basis of the information below.

Alex was present when Martin entered into an oral agreement with Cott for the purchase of miscellaneous household furniture for $900.

1. Martin changed his mind, and Cott sued for breach of contract.
   The order for Alex to appear in court to give testimony is known as a(n)

   A. order bill          B. summons
   C. subpoena            D. writ of execution

2. If Alex failed to appear in court, he would be guilty of

   A. contempt of court   B. breach of contract
   C. deceit              D. trespass

3. If Alex lied on the witness stand, he would be guilty of

   A. battery             B. conversion
   C. fraud               D. perjury

4. Alex was called as a witness by the attorney for the plaintiff.
   The questions put to Alex by the plaintiff's attorney constituted the

   A. complaint           B. affidavit
   C. direct examination  D. cross examination

5. An agreement in which Cott agreed to pay Alex $500 to testify falsely in favor of Cott during the trial would be

   A. valid
   B. void
   C. voidable at the option of Cott
   D. voidable at the option of Alex

Questions 6-10.

DIRECTIONS: Questions 6 through 10 are to be answered on the basis of the information below.

Dorothy Nolan leased an apartment from Reynolds for a period of two years at a monthly rental of $750.

6. Reynolds required Nolan to place with him one month's additional rent to insure the faithful performance of the lease.
   This sum of money is referred to as a(n)

   A. easement
   B. option
   C. security deposit
   D. lien

7. Which fixture placed in the apartment by Nolan must be left there when the lease expires?
   A(n)

   A. portable dishwasher
   B. garbage disposal unit attached to the plumbing
   C. free-standing refrigerator
   D. microwave oven

8. Nolan would be required to pay the rent and the

   A. real estate taxes
   B. cost of replacing the electric wiring in the apartment
   C. fire insurance premiums on the building
   D. cost of telephone installation

9. Thirty days before the end of the second year, Nolan received notice reminding her that there was an automatic renewal clause in the lease.
   Such a clause means that the lease

   A. would be renewed automatically for another year regardless of Nolan's wish
   B. would be renewed only if both Nolan and Reynolds agreed in writing
   C. would be renewed automatically unless Nolan notified Reynolds within the appropriate time that she did not wish to renew it
   D. could not be renewed for more than 30 days

10. After six months, Reynolds wanted Nolan to move out of the apartment. Nolan did not want to move, so Reynolds cut off the water supply to Nolan's apartment for days at a time. Nolan finally moved.
    However, Nolan claimed that Reynolds was liable to her for damages caused by Reynolds'

    A. foreclosure proceedings
    B. escrow proceedings
    C. constructive eviction
    D. dispossession proceedings

Questions 11-15.

DIRECTIONS: Questions 11 through 15 are to be answered on the basis of the instrument on the next page.

On June 24, 2006, Morrison entered into the agreement that is written below.

## RETAIL INSTALLMENT CONTRACT

SAFEWAY CORPORATION
245 W. 40th STREET
NEW YORK, N.Y. 10017

### NOTICE TO BUYER

1. Do not sign this contract before you read it.
2. You have the right to pay in advance the full amount due.
3. Keep this contract to protect your legal rights.
4. Safeway retains a security interest until full payment is made.
5. The buyer shall be liable for losses or damages to property.
6. I acknowledge receipt of a copy of this contract.

*Steven Morrison*      6/24/06
Signature of buyer and date

STEVEN MORRISON
(Print) Name of buyer

R.D. #2
(Print) Street Address

GASPORT      N.Y.      14201
City      State      Zip Code

*George W. Fox*
Signature of Sales Representative

### SAFEWAY PRODUCTS SOLD

| Part No. | Qty. | Part Name | Price |
|---|---|---|---|
| X57619T | 1 | Vacuum Cleaner | $190.00 |

| | |
|---|---|
| Total | $190.00 |
| Tax | 13.30 |
| Cash Price | 203.30 |
| Trade-in Allowance | 40.00 |
| Finance Charge | 10.00 |
| Unpaid Balance | 173.30 |

Total of unpaid balance is payable in _17_ monthly installments of _$10.00_ each and a final installment of the remaining unpaid balance on or before the _1st_ day of each month beginning _8/1/06_ until fully paid.

11. The relationship between Fox and the Safeway Corporation is that of      11.____

     A. lessor and lessee      B. mortgagor and mortgagee
     C. agent and principal      D. vendor and vendee

12. In this sales agreement, Morrison is legally known as the      12.____

     A. vendor      B. vendee      C. consignor      D. consignee

13. If a fire in Morrison's home destroys the vacuum cleaner before it is completely paid for, the loss will fall upon

    A. the financing company
    B. Fox
    C. the Safeway Corporation
    D. Morrison

14. Title to the vacuum cleaner will pass to Morrison when the

    A. agreement is made
    B. downpayment is made
    C. final installment is paid
    D. first installment is paid

15. Proper filing of this retail installment contract will protect

    A. the seller's interest against third parties
    B. the buyer's interest against third parties
    C. third parties against the seller
    D. third parties against the buyer

Questions 16-20.

DIRECTIONS: Questions 16 through 20 are to be answered on the basis of the information below

Lawson planned a trip and had written for hotel reservations. He received a confirmation of his reservation at the DeLuxe Motor Hotel before he left home on July 1. He and his wife arrived at the hotel on July 2 and registered immediately. They were given a room on the third floor.

16. Lawson notified the hotel manager that his watch was missing.
    The hotel would NOT be liable to Lawson for his loss if

    A. the watch had been stolen from Lawson's room by a hotel employee
    B. the watch had been taken by a thief who had broken into Lawson's room
    C. Lawson had left his watch with a bellboy to take to a jewelry shop to make repairs
    D. Lawson had left the watch in the hotel restroom

17. Lawson and his wife cease to be guests of the hotel when

    A. they tell the room clerk they are leaving
    B. the bellhop picks up their luggage
    C. they check out and leave the hotel
    D. they pay their bill

18. When the Lawsons arrived, they were met at the airport by a limousine from the DeLuxe Motor Hotel. Lawson turned his luggage over to the driver, entered the limousine, and traveled to the hotel.
    Lawson became a guest of the hotel when he

    A. turned his luggage over to the driver of the limousine
    B. sent a letter to the hotel asking for a reservation
    C. signed the hotel register
    D. entered the door of his hotel room

19. The hotel owner is prohibited by law from 19._____

 A. lowering rates for available rooms
 B. providing lavish accommodations to customers
 C. refusing accommodations because of race, religion, or economic status of persons who apply
 D. joining a cooperative hotel-owners association

20. If Lawson could not pay his bill when he was ready to leave, which of the following steps should the hotel take to insure payment of the bill? 20._____

 A. Keep his luggage as security
 B. Refuse to let him check out
 C. Call the police and have Lawson arrested
 D. Report Lawson to the Better Business Bureau

Questions 21-25.

DIRECTIONS: Questions 21 through 25 are to be answered on the basis of the will below.

Henry Petersen, who prepared the following will, died January 8, 2002.

I, HENRY PETERSEN, now residing at 151 Hudson Avenue, Rochester, Monroe County, New York, being of sound mind and memory, do hereby make, publish, and declare this to be my Last Will and Testament.

### ARTICLE ONE
I hereby revoke all wills and codicils made by me at any time heretofore.

### ARTICLE TWO
I direct that all my just debts and funeral expenses be paid as soon as practicable after my death.

### ARTICLE THREE
I give and bequeath to my eldest son, Michael, my library consisting of 150 volumes including the works of Shakespeare, or if he shall predecease me, the library is to be turned over to his wife, Mildred.

### ARTICLE FOUR
I give and bequeath to my son, Robert, the sum of $1,000.

### ARTICLE FIVE
I give, devise, and bequeath to my wife, Rhoda Petersen, the house, located at 151 Hudson Avenue, Rochester, Monroe County, New York, and all the personal property, including my own personal effects, and household articles contained therein, but excepting the library heretofore bequeathed to my son Michael.

### ARTICLE SIX
All the rest of my property, both real and personal, and wherever located, not herein before disposed of, I give, devise, and bequeath to my wife, Rhoda, if she survives me, and if she does not, to my two children in equal shares.

### ARTICLE SEVEN
I nominate, constitute, and appoint my wife, RHODA PETERSEN, to act as executrix under this my will, and to serve without bond.

IN WITNESS WHEREOF, I hereunto subscribe my name this _25th_ day of _March_, in the year One Thousand Nine Hundred and Ninety-nine.

                                           _Henry Petersen_
                                           HENRY PETERSEN

The foregoing Instrument, consisting of one page, was signed, published, and declared by HENRY PETERSEN, the Testator, to be his Last Will and Testament, in our presence, and we at his request, and in his presence, and in the presence of each other, hereunto subscribe our names as witnesses this _25th_ day of _March_, 1999.

_Carl Martens_              residing at _39 Rand St., Rochester, N.Y._
_Roberta Brenner_       residing at _119 Embury St., Rochester, N.Y._

21. It is NOT absolutely necessary to include in a will a clause such as the one contained in ARTICLE ONE of the will because

    A. at death the will with the most recent date is evidence of the intention of the testator to revoke prior wills
    B. a beneficiary in a prior will by law has priority over a beneficiary in a later will regardless of the testator's expressed intention
    C. a statement in a will revoking prior wills is not conclusive proof of an intention to revoke prior wills
    D. a later will which revokes prior wills may not be admitted to probate without consent of the beneficiary or beneficiaries of the prior wills

22. Assume that ARTICLE TWO had not been included when the above will was prepared. Upon the death of Henry Petersen, his debts would then be

    A. discharged
    B. paid up
    C. still payable by his estate
    D. revoked

23. According to the terms of the will, Henry Petersen devised certain property to a designated beneficiary.
The devise consisted of

    A. the just debts and funeral expenses
    B. all the real and personal property making up the estate wherever located
    C. the personal property, including personal effects and household articles contained therein
    D. the house located at 151 Hudson Avenue, Rochester, Monroe County, New York

24. The person designated in the will to carry out the wishes of the testator is

    A. Michael Petersen
    B. Robert Petersen
    C. Rhoda Petersen
    D. Carl Martens or Roberta Brenner

25. Assume that Henry Petersen disinherited his wife Rhoda by leaving her the sum of $1.00 in his will, when the actual value of the entire estate after taxes, just debts, and funeral expenses was $90,000 in real property and $62,000 in personal property.
    Rhoda could then contest the will and receive at least

    A. $90,000  B. $62,000  C. $152,000  D. $52,000

Questions 26-30.

DIRECTIONS: Questions 26 through 30 are to be answered on the basis of the information below.

On March 6, 2006, Brown Paper, Inc. signed a written contract with Wilcox to manage their paper store in Utica, New York, for a period of two years at an annual salary of $45,000 plus a bonus of 2% of the net profit.

26. This contract was required to be in writing under the Statute of Frauds because it

    A. involved over $500 in money
    B. could not be completed within one year
    C. was for personal services
    D. involved paying the debts of another

27. The relationship between Brown Paper, Inc. and Wilcox is known as

    A. bailor and bailee
    B. vendor and vendee
    C. general partnership
    D. principal and agent

28. If Wilcox, acting within the apparent scope of his authority as manager, makes a fraudulent statement that causes a third party to suffer a financial loss, the third party may bring suit against

    A. Brown Paper, Inc. *only*
    B. Wilcox *only*
    C. both Brown Paper, Inc. and Wilcox
    D. neither Brown Paper, Inc. nor Wilcox

29. In the relationship of manager for Brown Paper, Inc., Wilcox is expected to

    A. exercise skill, care, and prudence
    B. receive specific approval for all major decisions
    C. act only within the express authority given him by Brown Paper, Inc.
    D. obtain power of attorney from Brown Paper, Inc.

30. If Wilcox should decide to purchase and sell paper products for his personal profit during the hours when the store is closed, this would be violating Wilcox's duty of

    A. accounting
    B. care and skill
    C. loyalty
    D. obedience

## KEY (CORRECT ANSWERS)

| | | | |
|---|---|---|---|
| 1. | C | 16. | D |
| 2. | A | 17. | C |
| 3. | D | 18. | A |
| 4. | C | 19. | C |
| 5. | B | 20. | A |
| 6. | C | 21. | A |
| 7. | B | 22. | C |
| 8. | D | 23. | D |
| 9. | C | 24. | C |
| 10. | C | 25. | D |
| 11. | C | 26. | B |
| 12. | B | 27. | D |
| 13. | D | 28. | C |
| 14. | C | 29. | A |
| 15. | A | 30. | C |

# TEST 2

DIRECTIONS: Each question or incomplete statement is followed by several suggested answers or completions. Select the one that BEST answers the question or completes the statement. *PRINT THE LETTER OF THE CORRECT ANSWER IN THE SPACE AT THE RIGHT.*

1. The law permitting the Federal government to lay and collect taxes on incomes is an example of _____ law.

    A. common
    B. commercial
    C. constitutional
    D. moral

    1.____

2. A court order prohibiting the performance of a certain act is a(n)

    A. injunction
    B. mandamus
    C. specific performance order
    D. execution

    2.____

3. In the event of breach of contract, the injured party may be awarded the estimated amount lost as a definite result of the breach.
   This form of settlement is known as

    A. garnishment
    B. specific performance
    C. replevin
    D. damages

    3.____

4. Which contract must be in writing to comply with the Statute of Frauds?
   A

    A. contract to repair a radio
    B. contract for the sale of personal property with the value of $135
    C. contract for the sale of real property
    D. quasicontract

    4.____

5. Becker offered a $500 reward through the newspaper for the return of a watch he had lost. The next day, Becker published a cancellation of the offer in the same newspaper. Lester read about the reward, but he did not see the cancellation. Lester later found the watch and sought to collect the reward.
   Lester was NOT entitled to collect the reward because the general offer

    A. was revoked
    B. lapsed
    C. was not communicated
    D. was not accepted

    5.____

6. Serious illness would terminate a contract for painting a(n)

    A. house
    B. portrait
    C. picket fence
    D. automobile

    6.____

7. The party who transfers his rights under a contract to a third party is called the

    A. consignor   B. assignor   C. debtor   D. bailor

    7.____

8. Arnett made a written contract with Best to build a house for $300,000. When the house was completed, Best had not yet paid all of the agreed sum.
   The contract was considered to be

    8.____

A. implied and executory  B. implied and executed
C. express and executory  D. express and executed

9. Levin owes Walters $750. When the debt is due, Walters accepts a claim which Levin has against Johnson for the same amount.
Into which classification would this contract fall?

A. Agency  B. Assignment
C. Bailment  D. Barter

10. Arlene Robinson owned a corner lot which Taylor wanted to buy. In a telephone conversation, Robinson agreed to sell the lot to Taylor for $90,000. At the date set for the closing of title, Robinson refused to sell the lot to Taylor unless Taylor would pay her an additional $30,000. What rights, if any, does Taylor have?

A. To sue for specific performance
B. To sue for money damages
C. To sue for action re replevin
D. None

11. To be valid, an offer need NOT be

A. definite and certain  B. communicated
C. seriously intended  D. in writing

12. Bloom had contracted with Dr. James, a licensed dentist, to take an impression of his mouth and to fit him with a set of false teeth. Dr. James became ill and told Bloom that an arrangement had been made with another dentist in town to complete the work. Bloom refused to permit the second dentist to do the work.
Legally, which would be the BEST reason for Bloom's refusal?

A. The second dentist was recently graduated from dental college and had just received his license.
B. The office of the second dentist was on the opposite side of the town and would require a long trip for Bloom.
C. Contracts calling for personal skill may not be assigned without consent of all parties.
D. Dr. James had violated the medical society's code of ethics by discussing Bloom's case with another dentist.

13. Walker offered to sell Bowers a tent he had used for camping trips. Bowers replied that he was not interested in buying the tent because he had no place to store it. Walker's offer was terminated by

A. rejection  B. revocation
C. disability  D. a counteroffer

14. Halpin made an agreement to repaint Myson's automobile for $750. Halpin later refused to paint the car as agreed. Halpin's action constituted

A. a breach of contract  B. a misdemeanor
C. a waiver  D. fraud

15. Which statement meets the requirements of a valid offer? I will sell you my

    A. car for a reasonable price
    B. computer today for $300
    C. book after I finish reading it
    D. watch for several bushels of tomatoes

16. The acceptance of an offer must ALWAYS

    A. be in writing
    B. be given orally
    C. follow a definite form
    D. be indicated by some word or act

17. A written acceptance of a mail offer becomes binding when

    A. the acceptance is properly written
    B. the acceptance is properly mailed
    C. a reasonable time has passed
    D. the acceptance is received by the offeror

18. Philips placed his furniture in the Saf-T-Fine storehouse for temporary storage. The storehouse should have been expected to provide Philips with a

    A. bill of lading         B. bill of sale
    C. chattel mortgage       D. warehouse receipt

19. What does a bailment transfer?

    A. Personal property without a change of ownership
    B. Personal property with a change of ownership
    C. Ownership without a transfer of property
    D. Real property without a change of ownership

20. In a security agreement (conditional sale), title USUALLY passes to the buyer at the time of the

    A. sale                   B. downpayment
    C. final payment          D. delivery of the goods

21. A person who buys a store's equipment receives title to it by a

    A. bill of sale           B. deed
    C. chattel mortgage       D. replevin

22. Arthur took his CB radio into a repair shop for repairs. During the night, the shop was entered by vandals, and the radio was stolen.
    The value of the radio could be recovered from the repair shop if it could be shown that

    A. Arthur had title to the goods while they were in the repair shop
    B. Arthur had paid for the repairs in advance
    C. the repair shop had failed to carry insurance to cover this type of situation
    D. the repair shop had not exercised ordinary skill and care in safeguarding the radio

23. Under the provisions of the Uniform Commercial Code, a _____ would NOT be considered as *goods*.

    A. watch
    B. coat
    C. bookcase
    D. summer cottage

24. The rule of caveat emptor applies when

    A. goods are sold by description
    B. the buyer has an opportunity to inspect the goods
    C. the seller gives an express warranty
    D. the goods are purchased by mail

25. Which step should be taken by a buyer of real property to determine whether or not the seller has good title to the property being sold?

    A. An encumbrance
    B. A title search
    C. A satisfaction piece
    D. Condemnation proceedings

26. Assume that the Federal government passes a bill to establish a military base in a section of a state.
    On what legal basis will Henderson, an owner of a farm in this section, lose title to his property?

    A. Adverse possession
    B. Dedication
    C. Eminent domain
    D. Public grant

27. A(n) _____ signifies ownership of real property.

    A. deed
    B. easement
    C. lease
    D. mortgage

28. Innkeepers or hotelkeepers are liable for the loss of a guest's baggage when the loss is caused by

    A. flood
    B. lightning
    C. public enemies
    D. negligence of an employee

29. Common carriers contract with shippers to deliver goods to a specified place and person. The written evidence of this agreement between the carrier and the shipper is referred to as a(n)

    A. bill of lading
    B. bill of sale
    C. abstract of title
    D. accommodation paper

30. A common carrier is liable for losses to shipments caused by

    A. a hurricane
    B. lightning
    C. an act of a public enemy
    D. rioting strikers

## KEY (CORRECT ANSWERS)

| | | | |
|---|---|---|---|
| 1. | C | 16. | D |
| 2. | A | 17. | B |
| 3. | D | 18. | D |
| 4. | C | 19. | A |
| 5. | A | 20. | C |
| 6. | B | 21. | A |
| 7. | B | 22. | D |
| 8. | C | 23. | D |
| 9. | B | 24. | B |
| 10. | D | 25. | B |
| 11. | D | 26. | C |
| 12. | C | 27. | A |
| 13. | A | 28. | D |
| 14. | A | 29. | A |
| 15. | B | 30. | D |

# TEST 3

DIRECTIONS: Each question or incomplete statement is followed by several suggested answers or completions. Select the one that BEST answers the question or completes the statement. *PRINT THE LETTER OF THE CORRECT ANSWER IN THE SPACE AT THE RIGHT.*

1. A formal supplement or addition to a will is known as a(n)

    A. codicil     B. easement     C. abstract     D. devise

2. Morgan planned to take an airplane trip. He purchased a life insurance policy which would cover his life only during the trip.
   Such a life insurance policy would be a(n) _____ policy.

    A. endowment     B. straight life
    C. term     D. annuity

3. Life insurance companies may avoid paying the face amount of the policy if the insured commits suicide

    A. within the first two policy years
    B. within three policy years
    C. before age 18
    D. before age 21

4. Mr. Benton, a debtor who executed a promissory note, is known as the

    A. payee     B. maker     C. drawer     D. drawee

5. A personal check on which the bank has guaranteed payment is known as a

    A. cashier's check     B. bank draft
    C. certified check     D. traveler's check

6. Which expression, used to designate the time of payment of a note, would make the note non-negotiable?

    A. On June 1, 2006
    B. One year after my death
    C. On demand
    D. Within one year from April 1, 2006

7. The Fair Labor Standards Law requires employers to

    A. pay their employees time and a half for overtime work
    B. withhold Federal taxes from the employees' pay
    C. carry unemployment insurance on covered employees
    D. carry disability insurance on covered employees

8. When an employer closes his place of work in an effort to resist union demands, he is engaging in a practice called

    A. a boycott     B. a lockout
    C. featherbedding     D. a strike

9. When a contract of employment is made between an employer and a group of workers represented by a union negotiator, the agreement is known as a(n)

   A. apprenticeship agreement
   B. laissez-faire agreement
   C. collective bargaining agreement
   D. Fair Labor Practices action

10. The manager of a department store is an example of a _____ agent.

    A. general            B. special
    C. gratuitous         D. del credere

11. One who is engaged to perform for another, but is not under the other person's direct control or direction, is called a(n)

    A. employee               B. employer
    C. independent contractor D. principal

12. Abramson, an agent, sells a car at a higher price than expected. The additional profit belongs to the

    A. agent           B. principal
    C. tax department  D. buyer

13. The life of a corporation will NOT be affected by

    A. court decree  B. consolidation
    C. expiration    D. death of a stockholder

14. In the absence of any special agreement by the partners, which would NOT be a right possessed by each general partner?
    To

    A. inspect partnership books
    B. change the nature of the partnership
    C. share in the management
    D. share in the profits

15. Which document is evidence of ownership in a corporation?

    A. Stock certificate   B. Registered bond
    C. Stock subscription  D. Promissory note

16. Upon dissolution of a partnership, which parties would have FIRST claim against the firm's assets?

    A. Partners
    B. Debtors of the partnership
    C. Creditors of the partnership
    D. Creditors of the individual partners

17. What is the liability of a minority stockholder for Zender Corporation?

    A. Unlimited liability for all the debts of the corporation
    B. Unlimited liability for debts of the corporation while he is a stockholder

C. Limited liability for 50% of his investment in the corporation
D. Liability limited to the value of his total investment in the corporation

18. If the agreement does not specify how the profits are to be shared, how will they be divided?

   A. According to each partner's total investment
   B. Equally among the partners
   C. According to the amount of time each partner spends in conducting the partnership business
   D. According to each partner's cash investment

19. If a retiring partner fails to notify creditors and the public of his retirement, he will remain liable for

   A. debts contracted before his retirement
   B. debts contracted after his retirement, but not before
   C. debts up to the amount of his original investment only
   D. all debts, current and future

20. Thomas owes James $2,500. When the debt is due, Thomas offers $1,500 in cash and a camera worth about $500 in full settlement of the debt. James accepts.
Is the entire debt cancelled?

   A. Yes; payment of a smaller sum before a debt is due constitutes adequate consideration.
   B. Yes; a debt is discharged when a creditor accepts a part payment of money, plus some other valuable consideration, in settlement of a claim.
   C. No; paying less than the full amount of a debt already due does not bar action to recover the balance.
   D. No; payment of a smaller sum in satisfaction of a larger debt will fail unless a release in writing is given by the creditor.

21. The president, treasurer, and other officers of a corporation are USUALLY chosen by the

   A. employees        B. state
   C. directors        D. stockholders

22. Wilkes agrees to drill a well for Forman for $2,500. After drilling several feet, Wilkes ran into rock. He then informed Forman that he had underestimated the cost of drilling. Forman orally promised to pay Wilkes an additional $1,000 if he would complete the job.
Was this promise to pay an additional $1,000 binding upon Forman?

   A. Yes; a promise to pay extra compensation for an existing obligation is binding.
   B. Yes; according to common law, a person is entitled to a fair profit on his contracts.
   C. No; a mistake on the part of one of the parties to a contract voids that contract.
   D. No; an oral promise to pay additional consideration to perform an existing obligation is not binding.

23. Judson, in selling a used automobile to Bush, told her that it was *the best buy in the city.* After purchasing the automobile, Bush found that Judson's statement was false.
Did Bush have a claim for damages?

A. Yes; a statement made by the seller to induce the buyer to purchase constitutes a warranty.
B. Yes; a seller is liable for fraudulent statements made in selling goods.
C. No; an expression of opinion by the seller is not a warranty.
D. No; a seller is not liable for breach of warranty if no consideration was given for the warranty.

24. When Bartle began painting his house, he found that his own ladder was too short for the job. He asked a neighbor, Cullen, if he might borrow his ladder which was longer. Cullen's ladder had been cracked, although the crack was not noticeable. Cullen, who knew of the crack, did not mention this crack to Bartle. The ladder broke when Bartle was on it, and he was injured.
Does Bartle have any right of legal action against Cullen?

   A. Yes; even in a gratuitous bailment, the bailee has the right to a safe article, or he must be warned if it is not.
   B. Yes; anyone who is injured using another's property always has a right of legal action against the owner.
   C. No; when one borrows another's property, he does so at his own risk.
   D. No; in a sole benefit bailment, the bailee is required to exercise reasonable care in the use of the borrowed article.

25. While Adams was away from home on a business trip, his wife purchased some necessary medical supplies in his name. When Adams returned, he refused to pay the bill, claiming that his wife had no legal authority to make such a purchase.
Is Adams liable for the purchase?

   A. Yes; a husband is liable for all contracts made in his name by his wife.
   B. Yes; when necessary, a wife may become her husband's agent.
   C. No; a husband is never liable for contracts made in his name by his wife.
   D. No; a husband is liable for contracts made in his name by his wife only when she has expressly been appointed his agent.

26. Zorn finds a valuable pen and pencil set on the street and claims that the set now belongs to him.
Is he CORRECT?

   A. Yes; *finders keepers, losers weepers*.
   B. Yes; the finder of lost property takes immediate title through possession.
   C. No; a finder of lost property is the owner against everyone except the true owner.
   D. No; all local ordinances require that all found property, regardless of value or the location where property is found, be immediately reported to the local authorities.

27. A used television set on display in a store was marked *As is, $39*. The seller let the buyer try the set in the store. At that time, it worked perfectly, but it failed to operate at all in the buyer's home. It was later found to need a new picture tube. The buyer insisted that the store was legally responsible for the replacement of this tube.
Was he CORRECT?

   A. Yes; there was an implied warranty that the goods were usable for the purpose intended.
   B. Yes; the Uniform Commercial Code imposes upon all sellers a 90-day warranty of their product.

C. No; by trying out the set in the store, the buyer waived all warranties.
D. No; when goods are sold *as is,* there are no warranties as to their quality.

28. On July 1, Markson purchased a power lawnmower on approval, with a 10-day time limit specified. On July 9, Markson went to Canada for a two-week vacation. Upon his return on July 23, he called the store and told them he did not want to keep the mower.
Is the store legally obligated to accept the return of the mower?

   A. Yes; Markson never gave his approval of the purchase.
   B. Yes; a sale on approval means that goods may be returned any time they do not meet with the approval of the buyer.
   C. No; Markson's approval was implied by his keeping the mower beyond the 10-day limit.
   D. No; Markson left the state before the end of the 10-day limit.

29. The following statement was on a note dated June 1, 2008 and signed by Roger Cole: *I hope to pay the $2000 I owe to Lillian Riley on or before the 30th day of June of this year.*
Is it a negotiable instrument?

   A. Yes; all the essential elements are present in the correct form.
   B. Yes; even though the form is unusual, all necessary elements are present.
   C. No; the intent to pay is not strong enough to be considered as an unconditional promise.
   D. No; the time of payment is not definite.

30. Scott Allen issued his promissory note due in sixty days to Marge Simson in the amount of $4000. Simson was on vacation when the note fell due and did not present it for payment until more than one week later. Allen refused payment, claiming that the late presentation was improper; therefore, he was no longer liable.
Is he CORRECT?

   A. Yes; a promissory note must be presented no more than one week after the due date.
   B. Yes; a promissory note must be presented on the due date in order to bind the maker.
   C. No; there is no time limit for the presentation of a promissory note.
   D. No; presentation on the due date is not necessary to bind the maker.

# KEY (CORRECT ANSWERS)

| | | | | |
|---|---|---|---|---|
| 1. | A | | 16. | C |
| 2. | C | | 17. | D |
| 3. | A | | 18. | B |
| 4. | B | | 19. | D |
| 5. | C | | 20. | B |
| 6. | B | | 21. | C |
| 7. | A | | 22. | D |
| 8. | B | | 23. | C |
| 9. | C | | 24. | A |
| 10. | A | | 25. | B |
| 11. | C | | 26. | C |
| 12. | B | | 27. | D |
| 13. | D | | 28. | C |
| 14. | B | | 29. | C |
| 15. | A | | 30. | C |

# TEST 4

DIRECTIONS: Each question or incomplete statement is followed by several suggested answers or completions. Select the one that BEST answers the question or completes the statement. *PRINT THE LETTER OF THE CORRECT ANSWER IN THE SPACE AT THE RIGHT.*

Questions 1-5.

DIRECTIONS: Questions 1 through 5 are to be answered on the basis of the information below.

Reed owned a chair which formerly belonged to George Washington. In a telephone conversation on March 2, Reed offered to sell the chair to Benson for $315 and agreed to hold the offer open until March 12. On March 11, Reed received a letter from Benson accepting the offer. Reed refused to deliver the chair to Benson, who then threatened to take legal action to get the chair.

1. Since his case dealt with the sale of goods, Benson would have to begin suit against Reed within a period of NOT MORE THAN _____ year(s).

   A. 1   B. 2   C. 6   D. 4

2. Benson's threat to take legal action is considered

   A. an injunction  
   B. duress  
   C. undue influence  
   D. a legal right

3. If Benson takes the case to court, he will be known as the

   A. summoned party  
   B. subpoenaed party  
   C. plaintiff  
   D. defendant

4. The legal remedy Benson threatened to seek in court is known as

   A. specific performance  
   B. accord and satisfaction  
   C. injunction  
   D. recision

5. Benson's case would involve a field of law known as _____ law.

   A. common  
   B. civil  
   C. criminal  
   D. administrative

Questions 6-10.

DIRECTIONS: Questions 6 through 10 are to be answered on the basis of the notice below.

To: Ann McLoughlin                                      March 26, 2006
    532 Chestnut Street
    Lockport, N.Y. 14201

You are hereby notified that on *March 26, 2006*, *William Boles* has assigned to this company his right to receive payment due of *$250.00* under a contract with you dated *February 12, 2006* for the sale of a *General Electric television set*.

BENDIX COLLECTION AGENCY
*William Bendix*
WILLIAM BENDIX, PRESIDENT

2 (#4)

6. This document is a notification of a(n)  6.____

   A. assignment  B. bailment
   C. conveyance  D. sale

7. The Bendix Collection Agency is legally known as the  7.____

   A. consignor  B. consignee  C. assignor  D. assignee

8. Ann McLoughlin is legally known as the  8.____

   A. bailor  B. bailee  C. debtor  D. creditor

9. William Boles is legally known as the  9.____

   A. bailee  B. bailor  C. assignee  D. assignor

10. If Ann McLoughlin had paid $100 on account to Boles before she received this notification, her liability to the Bendix Collection Agency would be  10.____

    A. $100.00  B. $150.00  C. $250.00  D. nothing

Questions 11-15.

DIRECTIONS: Questions 11 through 15 are to be answered on the basis of the following information.

Miller contracted to purchase a motorcycle for $3500 from Hill, a local used-car and motorcycle dealer. The agreement provided for a deposit payment of $500, with the balance to be paid upon the delivery of the motorcycle at Miller's home the next day.

11. Which statement, if made by Hill to induce Miller to purchase the motorcycle, constitutes an express warranty?  11.____

    A. This is the finest motorcycle you can buy for the money.
    B. You won't have to spend a cent for repairs for the next 30,000 miles.
    C. This motorcycle was formerly owned by Allen Jackson.
    D. You will win any motorcycle races with this machine.

12. Under the terms of this agreement, Miller would legally be known as a(n)  12.____

    A. bailee  B. assignee  C. drawee  D. vendee

13. If the motorcycle was badly damaged while it was being delivered to Miller, the risk of loss would have to be borne by  13.____

    A. Hill, entirely
    B. Miller, entirely
    C. both Hill and Miller, equally
    D. Miller for the first $500, and Hill for the rest

14. Upon delivery of the motorcycle, Miller refused to accept it or to pay the balance of the purchase price.  14.____
    Under the Uniform Commercial Code, which legal action may NOT be taken by Hill?

    A. Cancel the contract and sue for damages.
    B. Resell the motorcycle elsewhere and recover damages, if any.

113

C. Hold the motorcycle for the buyer and if a resale is not possible, sue for the purchase price.
D. Sue for the purchase price and resell the motorcycle as soon as possible.

15. After the motorcycle was delivered to Miller, he discovered that Hill had not been the true owner. In fact, the machine had been stolen from Rall.
Would Miller have to return the motorcycle to the true owner?

    A. Yes; it is the duty of the purchaser to determine the true ownership of the goods.
    B. Yes; a thief cannot pass title even to an innocent purchaser for value.
    C. No; one who has a voidable title may pass a good title to an innocent purchaser for value.
    D. No; the true owner who made the theft possible should stand the loss.

Questions 16-20.

DIRECTIONS: Questions 16 through 20 are to be answered on the basis of the information below.

Robinson owned a one-family house in a small village. He agreed to let the Taylor family occupy the house for two years, for a monthly rental payment of $600. He also required them to pay an additional $600 to him at the beginning of the two years, to be returned at the end of the two years if all rent payments had been made on time and if no damage had been done to the property.

16. This agreement between Robinson and the Taylor family is known as a(n)

    A. lease                B. policy
    C. land contract        D. installment contract

17. The extra $600 paid to Robinson at the beginning of the two years is known as a

    A. downpayment          B. performance bond
    C. security deposit     D. special assessment

18. If nothing is mentioned in the agreement about minor repairs, who is responsible for them?

    A. Robinson *only*
    B. Taylor *only*
    C. Robinson and Taylor, equally
    D. Taylor for the first $600, and then Robinson for any additional costs

19. Would this agreement between Robinson and Taylor have to be in writing to be enforceable?

    A. Yes; any contract pertaining to real estate has to be in writing.
    B. Yes; any contract which cannot be completed within one year from the beginning of its term has to be in writing.
    C. No; it is not necessary for any rental agreement to be in writing.
    D. No; this agreement does not have to be in writing because it covers only a one-family house.

20. If nothing is mentioned in the agreement, who would be responsible for the installation of a new heating system for the house?    20.____

    A. Robinson *only*
    B. Taylor *only*
    C. Robinson and Taylor, equally
    D. Taylor, up to a maximum of $600, and Robinson for any additional amount

Questions 21-25.

DIRECTIONS:   Questions 21 through 25 are to be answered on the basis of the information below.

Cullen has a homeowner's policy on his house. His neighbor, Sally Lufkin, has a standard state fire insurance policy on her house. Each policy has a face value of $200,000. Cullen's premium is $750 per year, and Lufkin's is $500 per year.

21. Is it true that Cullen is paying more than Lufkin for the same protection?    21.____

    A. Yes; except for the name, the policies are the same.
    B. Yes; the face amount is the same for both.
    C. No; a homeowner's policy actually pays double the face amount.
    D. No; a homeowner's policy provides additional types of protection.

22. A tree on the boundary line fell over, causing damage to both houses.    22.____
    The loss for this damage will be paid by the insurance company to

    A. Lufkin *only*
    B. Cullen *only*
    C. both Cullen and Lufkin
    D. neither Cullen nor Lufkin

23. Lightning strikes both houses, but does not start a fire. The loss for this damage will be paid by the insurance company to    23.____

    A. Lufkin *only*
    B. Cullen *only*
    C. both Cullen and Lufkin
    D. neither Cullen nor Lufkin

24. A severe windstorm tore off parts of the roofs from both houses.    24.____
    The loss for this damage will be paid by the insurance company to

    A. Lufkin *only*
    B. Cullen *only*
    C. both Cullen and Lufkin
    D. neither Cullen nor Lufkin

25. A grass fire damaged both houses.    25.____
    The loss for this type of damage will be paid by the insurance company to

    A. Lufkin *only*            B. Cullen *only*
    C. both Cullen and Lufkin   D. neither Cullen nor Lufkin

Questions 26-30.

DIRECTIONS: Questions 26 through 30 are to be answered on the basis of the information below.

Henry A. Smith, who is married and has three children, lives in Syracuse, New York. On June 15, Mr. Smith made a will specifying how his estate was to be distributed upon his death. The estate at that time consisted of both personal and real property. The will named Robert Jones, a friend, as one of the beneficiaries, and John T. Brooks, a neighbor, to carry out the provisions of the will.

26. Mr. Brooks is called the

    A. administrator          B. testator
    C. devisor                D. executor

27. Mr. Smith is known as the

    A. beneficiary            B. legatee
    C. testator               D. devisee

28. In order to be valid, this will must be signed by AT LEAST how many witnesses? _____ person(s).

    A. 1        B. 2        C. 3        D. 4

29. Which court will supervise the proper distribution of Mr. Smith's estate after his death?

    A. Surrogate's Court      B. County Court
    C. Court of Claims        D. Supreme Court

30. The will may be declared INVALID if

    A. Mrs. Smith's financial status is such that she personally requires all of her husband's remaining assets
    B. some of the persons named in the will are under 18 years of age
    C. Mr. Smith has debts that were not mentioned in the will
    D. Mr. Smith made another will after the one made

# KEY (CORRECT ANSWERS)

| | | | |
|---|---|---|---|
| 1. | D | 16. | A |
| 2. | D | 17. | C |
| 3. | C | 18. | B |
| 4. | A | 19. | B |
| 5. | B | 20. | A |
| 6. | A | 21. | D |
| 7. | D | 22. | B |
| 8. | C | 23. | C |
| 9. | D | 24. | B |
| 10. | B | 25. | C |
| 11. | C | 26. | D |
| 12. | D | 27. | C |
| 13. | A | 28. | B |
| 14. | D | 29. | A |
| 15. | B | 30. | D |

# TEST 5

DIRECTIONS: Each question or incomplete statement is followed by several suggested answers or completions. Select the one that BEST answers the question or completes the statement. *PRINT THE LETTER OF THE CORRECT ANSWER IN THE SPACE AT THE RIGHT.*

1. Which government official represents a person who requests legal counsel in a criminal proceeding?
   The

   A. public defender
   B. district attorney
   C. justice of the peace
   D. probate judge

2. A body of law that states the rights and limitations of both the Federal and State governments would be classified as _____ law.

   A. administrative
   B. constitutional
   C. common
   D. statutory

3. A Federal Communications Commission restriction on the amount of cigarette advertising permitted on television would be an example of _____ law.

   A. administrative
   B. constitutional
   C. international
   D. statutory

4. A legal notice commanding a witness to a crime to appear in court is known as a

   A. complaint
   B. judgment
   C. summons
   D. subpoena

5. The jurisdiction of the Surrogate Court would include hearing the case of a person involved in

   A. an arson charge
   B. a breach of contract proceeding
   C. contesting the validity of a will
   D. suing the Federal government for negligence

6. Under state law, a successful plaintiff may obtain a court order requiring the defendant's employer to pay a certain part of the defendant's salary to the plaintiff until the judgment is satisfied.
   This court is known as a(n)

   A. injunction
   B. writ of mandamus
   C. garnishment
   D. affidavit

7. In a lawsuit, which procedure comes FIRST?
   The _____ the jury.

   A. impaneling of
   B. verdict of
   C. attorney's opening address to
   D. judge's charging

8. In a legal action for breach of contract, the court awarded the plaintiff money damages. The purpose of this particular judgment was to

   A. punish the defendant
   B. compensate the plaintiff for his loss
   C. allow the injured party to gain from the wrongful acts of the defendant
   D. permit the plaintiff to avoid carrying out his part of the contract

9. Wolters placed a notice of reward for her lost dog in the local newspaper. Such notices are considered as

   A. general offers
   B. contracts
   C. invitations to buy
   D. acceptances

10. Giving up the right to do what one is legally entitled to do is a definition of

    A. duress
    B. forbearance
    C. protest
    D. undue influence

11. The Statute of Limitations specifies the

    A. contracts that are unenforceable by custom and tradition
    B. number of witnesses needed for a legal will
    C. contracts that must be in writing to be enforceable
    D. time limit for starting a lawsuit

12. Morton owed Dowd $6,000. The debt was due on May 1. Under which set of circumstances would the debt NOT be charged?

    A. On the due date, Dowd agreed to accept $500 and a watch valued at $40 in full settlement of the debt.
    B. Dowd insisted the debt was $600, but Morton claimed it was $400. They compromised on $500 in full settlement.
    C. On April 15, Dowd agreed to accept $500 in full settlement.
    D. On July 1, Dowd orally agreed to accept $500 in full settlement of the $600 debt.

13. Howard, a businessman, died.
    Which contract entered into prior to his death would be discharged as a result of Howard's death?
    A

    A. contract involving the sale of real estate
    B. contract involving the purchase of merchandise
    C. contract to speak before a convention of business leaders
    D. loan to the business from a local bank

14. Which agreement would be illegal and therefore void? A contract

    A. in reasonable restraint of trade
    B. to buy a stereo set
    C. to pay a usurious rate of interest
    D. to build a house

15. Hurst entered into a written agreement with Burrows to buy a horse. In the meantime, without the knowledge of either party, the horse died.
This contract was discharged by

    A. performance
    B. breach
    C. mutual agreement
    D. impossibility

16. On April 1, Heights Market owed Abel Meat Provision Company $10,000 for meat it had purchased. On April 2, Heights paid $2,000 to Abel. On April 15, Abel transferred its customers' accounts to Triangle Finance Company. On April 30, Heights paid Abel an additional $2,000 on account. On May 9, Heights received notice of the assignment. After receiving this notice, how much money was Heights Market legally obligated to pay Triangle Financing Company?

    A. Nothing   B. $6,000   C. $8,000   D. $10,000

17. Payne, who owned and operated a small retail grocery store, sold her store to Hutton. In the written contract, Payne promised that she would not engage in a similar business anywhere in the state for a period of 10 years.
Payne was NOT legally bound to this promise because a

    A. contract that unreasonably restrains trade is unenforceable
    B. contract that covers business agreements between merchants comes under the Uniform Commercial Code
    C. contract that is not completed within 6 years is outlawed by the Statute of Limitations
    D. promise to refrain from doing what one is entitled to do is not valid consideration

18. If a minor purchases an expensive camera for his hobby, the contract may be avoided by

    A. the minor *only*
    B. the merchant *only*
    C. either the minor or the merchant
    D. neither the minor nor the merchant

19. One dollar given in return for a promise to keep a certain offer open for fifteen days is known as a(n)

    A. warranty
    B. option
    C. offer
    D. acceptance

20. A contract for the sale of goods is terminated by

    A. either party's moving from the state in which he lives
    B. a change of mind on the part of either party
    C. death of the seller
    D. mutual agreement

21. Which statement concerning the refusal of tender of payment is CORRECT?
It will

    A. force a settlement by arbitration
    B. force payment with legal tender
    C. not discharge future interest payments
    D. not discharge the obligation

22. Margaret Downs, 17 years of age, was enrolled in the Shorthand 2 class of her high school. She signed a contract with the Speed-O-Shorthand Correspondence School for a course in the same shorthand method offered at her high school and paid a $250 deposit. Immediately upon receipt of her first lesson from the correspondence school, Downs returned the lessons unused and demanded the return of her money.
Which would PROBABLY result from Downs' action to recover her deposit?
She would

    A. be held liable for full payment of this course because a minor's contract for any educational services is legally considered as dealing with a necessity of life
    B. be held liable for the initial deposit only because a minor is liable only for actual necessities supplied
    C. not be held liable on this contract and would be legally entitled to receive a refund of her deposit because a minor is not liable for education already available and furnished
    D. not be held liable on her entire contract and would be legally entitled to a partial refund of her deposit, but she would be guilty of committing a tort

23. Which statement concerning rights acquired under a contract is CORRECT?
Rights are

    A. never negotiable
    B. always negotiable
    C. sometimes assignable
    D. always assignable

24. The usual manner of discharging a contract is by

    A. subsequent impossibility
    B. death of one of the parties
    C. assignment
    D. performance

25. A warehouseman is legally classified as a(n)

    A. mutual benefit bailee
    B. extraordinary bailee
    C. vendee of goods
    D. gratuitous bailee

26. Jones was a guest at the Lightstone Inn for a period of three weeks. When Jones left the Inn, he was unable to pay his bill.
If the innkeeper attempted to retain some of Jones' property because of his failure to pay the bill, the innkeeper would be exercising his right of

    A. pledge    B. tariff    C. lien    D. demurrage

27. A bailment in which one party does NOT receive any consideration or benefit is a(n) _____ bailment.

    A. gratuitous
    B. mutual-benefit
    C. tortious
    D. extraordinary

28. A bailment is BEST described by the statement that the owner parts with

   A. title to the real property but not with possession of the real property
   B. title to the personal property but not with possession of the property
   C. possession of the personal property but not with title to the property
   D. possession of the real property but not with title to the property

29. What type of bailment is created by someone who uses a book free of charge with the owner's permission?
   A(n)

   A. extraordinary bailment
   B. mutual benefit bailment
   C. bailment for the sole benefit of the bailor
   D. bailment for the sole benefit of the bailee

30. Slight care is required to be exercised by the bailee in which bailment agreement?

   A. James takes care of Henry's car without receiving any pay.
   B. Smith borrows White's watch for personal use.
   C. Hunter rents a bicycle from Walsh.
   D. Watts checks her baggage for $2.50 at a local bus terminal.

---

## KEY (CORRECT ANSWERS)

| | | | |
|---|---|---|---|
| 1. | A | 16. | B |
| 2. | B | 17. | A |
| 3. | A | 18. | A |
| 4. | D | 19. | B |
| 5. | C | 20. | D |
| 6. | C | 21. | D |
| 7. | A | 22. | C |
| 8. | B | 23. | C |
| 9. | A | 24. | D |
| 10. | B | 25. | A |
| 11. | D | 26. | C |
| 12. | D | 27. | A |
| 13. | C | 28. | C |
| 14. | C | 29. | D |
| 15. | D | 30. | A |

# EXAMINATION SECTION
## TEST 1

DIRECTIONS: Each question or incomplete statement is followed by several suggested answers or completions. Select the one that BEST answers the question or completes the statement. *PRINT THE LETTER OF THE CORRECT ANSWER IN THE SPACE AT THE RIGHT.*

1. A salesperson says, *This stereo is the best you can buy for the money.* The salesperson's statement is an example of an

    A. offer to sell
    B. opinion
    C. express warranty
    D. implied warranty

    1._____

2. In a cash sale, title to the goods passes when the

    A. contract is made
    B. goods are delivered to the buyer
    C. goods are paid for
    D. goods are put into a deliverable state

    2._____

3. A consumer complaining about the quality of his local telephone service may seek further action through the _____ Commission.

    A. Interstate Commerce
    B. Public Service
    C. Federal Trade
    D. Federal Communications

    3._____

4. Which statement concerning an installment sale is CORRECT?

    A. Title and possession pass immediately.
    B. Title passes immediately, but possession does not pass until final payment is made.
    C. Possession passes immediately, but title does not pass until final payment is made.
    D. Title and possession pass after the first payment is made.

    4._____

5. Johnson signed a lease in which she agreed to pay $800 a month for the rental of an apartment for three years. This tenancy is legally known as a

    A. periodic tenancy
    B. month-to-month tenancy
    C. year-to-year tenancy
    D. tenancy for years

    5._____

6. The _____ lien on real property takes priority over all of the other liens listed.

    A. tax
    B. mechanic's
    C. mortgagee's
    D. judgment

    6._____

7. Placing the title of real property into the hands of a third party, such as a bank, to be delivered to the buyer after payment of purchase price is an example of

    A. adverse possession
    B. eminent domain
    C. delivery in escrow
    D. redemption

    7._____

8. Which of the following companies is NOT a common carrier?

    A. Greyhound Bus
    B. Western Union Telegraph
    C. New York Central Railway
    D. Yellow Taxicab

    8._____

9. Which business paper can NOT be used as evidence of ownership?

   A. deed
   B. lease
   C. certificate of title
   D. bill of lading

10. A minor may legally obtain a senior driver's license upon the successful completion of a New York State high school driver training course at the age of

   A. 21   B. 18   C. 17   D. 16

11. An insurance contract in which the amount to be paid is determined by the amount of the loss is referred to as a(n)

   A. valued policy
   B. open policy
   C. binder
   D. endorsement

12. Martell, age 30, wishes to insure his own life.
    In order to receive the face value of the policy when he reaches age 50, which type of life insurance policy should he buy?
    A(n)

   A. 20-payment life policy
   B. term policy
   C. 20-year endowment policy
   D. annuity policy with payments beginning at age 50

13. An order drawn by a bank on funds which it has on deposit in another bank is called a

   A. cashier's check
   B. certified check
   C. sight draft
   D. bank draft

14. Ward signed an unconditional promise to pay a certified sum of money on a definite day to the order of Toback.
    Toback is known as the

   A. payee   B. maker   C. drawer   D. drawee

15. A special form of draft which is drawn by the seller of goods upon the purchaser of those goods is a

   A. bank draft
   B. sight draft
   C. time draft
   D. trade acceptance

16. A personal check written on July 17, but dated July 16, is an example of a(n) _____ check.

   A. antedated
   B. canceled
   C. forged
   D. postdated

17. Hogan wished to make a bank deposit by mail.
    The SAFEST kind of endorsement for her to use on checks in this deposit would be a(n) _____ endorsement.

   A. special
   B. blank
   C. restrictive
   D. accommodation

18. A promissory note is NOT negotiable if it is  18.____

    A. not dated
    B. payable 30 days after the death of the maker
    C. signed by two persons
    D. payable 30 days after the date of the note

19. Eckleson negotiated a check that she received from Farmington by making the following  19.____
    endorsement:
    
    *Pay to the order of Toby Gardner*
    *Roberta Eckleson*
    
    Gardner may now legally negotiate this check by

    A. endorsement *only*
    B. delivery *only*
    C. either endorsement or delivery
    D. both endorsement and delivery

20. Phillips hired Wertman, a licensed plumber, to repair some plumbing in his home.  20.____
    In this relationship, Wertman would be legally known as an

    A. agent                    B. independent contractor
    C. employee                 D. employer

21. Frank Wallace had debts of $40,000, while his assets were only $26,000. He petitioned  21.____
    the court to be declared a bankrupt. Sheryl Porter, one of Wallace's creditors, had a
    claim of $1,200, but received $780 in the settlement. After the discharge in bankruptcy,
    Porter telephoned Wallace and told him that she would expect payment of the balance of
    the debt.
    Is Wallace legally liable to Porter for the balance of the debt?

    A. Yes; payment of a sum less than the amount due will not cancel the debt unless
       both parties agree.
    B. Yes; a discharge in bankruptcy does not discharge a debt but only bars court
       action until the debtor is able to fulfill his obligation.
    C. No; a discharge in bankruptcy bars legal action against the bankrupt for the balance of the debts due to his creditors.
    D. No; a discharge in bankruptcy terminates all outstanding claims.

22. Allen, a paint dealer, offered a well-known brand of paint at $4 per gallon through an  22.____
    advertisement in a local newspaper. Powers, a painter, order 100 gallons and enclosed
    his check for $400 in payment. Allen refused to sell him the paint and returned his check.
    Did a contract exist?

    A. Yes; there was an offer and an acceptance, and an enforceable contract was
       thereby created.
    B. Yes; Allen obviously was prejudiced against Powers and, therefore, Allen had no
       legal defense.
    C. No; according to the Statute of Frauds, the contract should have been in writing to
       be enforceable.
    D. No; an advertisement is merely an invitation to trade and, therefore, does not constitute a legally enforceable offer.

23. Fisher orally agreed to make a fur coat for Mrs. Calder to her individual measurements for $1,950. When the coat was finished, Mrs. Calder refused to accept it, pleading the Statute of Frauds as a defense.
Was this a good defense?

    A. Yes; contracts for labor and materials for more than $500 must be in writing.
    B. Yes; contracts for the sale of goods, wares, or merchandise for a price of $2,000 or less need not be in writing.
    C. No; a sales contract does not need a written note or memorandum.
    D. No; contracts for labor and materials need not be in writing.

24. Feldman purchased a 50-foot length of garden hose at the local hardware store and mentioned to the salesclerk that he was going to use the hose to water some shrubs around his house. When he tried to use the hose, he found that it was so old that it pulled apart in several places. Would there be any breach of warranty on the part of the store?

    A. Yes; there was an implied warranty that the goods were of the finest quality.
    B. Yes; there was an implied warranty that the goods were fit for the purpose intended.
    C. No; no warranties were expressed by the salesclerk.
    D. No; unless the store states a definite warranty, there are none in a sale.

25. Baker, an agent for Fuller, negligently operated her automobile while engaged in calling on customers and injured Collins, a pedestrian. Collins sought to hold Fuller liable for damages.
Could she do so?

    A. Yes; principals are liable for their agents' torts while the agents are carrying out the principals' business.
    B. Yes; principals are always liable for any act committed by their agents.
    C. No; principals are not liable for negligent acts of their agents.
    D. No; principals are not liable for their agents' actions in their dealings with third parties.

26. A landlord frequently used his passkey to enter the apartment of a tenant, claiming that he was checking on the condition of the apartment to see if any repairs were needed. Actually, he only wanted to see what his tenants were doing.
Was this action by the landlord legal?

    A. Yes; he was only looking for repairs and protecting his property.
    B. Yes; a landlord may enter an apartment unannounced.
    C. No; the tenant is supposed to have exclusive use of the apartment.
    D. No; once rented, the apartment may never again be entered by the landlord.

27. West entered a bus depot to buy a ticket. Before she was able to buy her ticket, she tripped and fell over a mop and pail left in the way by a cleaning man. West claims the bus company is liable for her injury.
Is she CORRECT?

    A. Yes; a carrier is liable for the injuries to anyone who enters its premises.
    B. Yes; a common carrier is liable for injuries sustained by its passengers as a result of the negligence of the carrier or its employees.

C. No; a common carrier has no liability for those who are not its passengers.
D. No; a common carrier does not become responsible for a passenger's injuries until the passenger enters the conveyance.

28. Moody purchased an insurance policy on her life. Five years later, she committed suicide.
Would the insurance company be able to avoid paying Moody's beneficiary the face amount of the policy?

   A. Yes; suicide is a felony and makes the insurance void.
   B. Yes; the company has to pay back just the premiums paid by Moody.
   C. No; the length of time Moody held the policy was long enough to void the suicide clause.
   D. No; once the policy is issued, the insurance company may not avoid payment for any reason.

28._____

29. What type of action is indicated by the case title *Harvey Lund v. Dorothy King*?

   A. Civil
   B. Criminal
   C. Punitive
   D. Bankruptcy

29._____

30. When a tenant vacated his apartment at the end of his lease, the landlord insisted that it was the obligation of the tenant to repaint the entire apartment.
In the absence of any provision in the lease, was the landlord CORRECT?

   A. Yes; a tenant must always leave the premises ready for the next tenant by painting before leaving.
   B. Yes; all decorating is the responsibility of the tenant and not the landlord.
   C. No; a tenant must leave the premises as he found them.
   D. No; a tenant is never responsible for any decorating.

30._____

## KEY (CORRECT ANSWERS)

| | | | |
|---|---|---|---|
| 1. | B | 16. | A |
| 2. | C | 17. | C |
| 3. | B | 18. | B |
| 4. | C | 19. | D |
| 5. | D | 20. | B |
| 6. | A | 21. | C |
| 7. | C | 22. | D |
| 8. | B | 23. | D |
| 9. | B | 24. | B |
| 10. | C | 25. | A |
| 11. | B | 26. | C |
| 12. | C | 27. | B |
| 13. | D | 28. | C |
| 14. | A | 29. | A |
| 15. | D | 30. | C |

# TEST 2

DIRECTIONS: Each question or incomplete statement is followed by several suggested answers or completions. Select the one that BEST answers the question or completes the statement. *PRINT THE LETTER OF THE CORRECT ANSWER IN THE SPACE AT THE RIGHT.*

Questions 1-5.

DIRECTIONS: Questions 1 through 5 are to be answered on the basis of the following will.

---

LAST WILL AND TESTAMENT

I, John Wayman, of the city of Albany, State of New York, being of sound mind, do hereby make and declare this my last will and testament.

    First.    I direct that all my just debts, funeral, and other expenses, be paid as soon as may be practicable after my death.

    Second. To my nephew, Peter Roberts, I bequeath the sum of two thousand dollars ($2,000).

    Third.    All the residue of my estate, whether real or personal, I devise and bequeath to my wife, Mary W. Wayman, for her own use and benefit.

    Fourth.    I hereby nominate and appoint as Executor of this my last will and testament, my nephew, Peter Roberts, who is to act without bond and without being required to give security.

    Fifth.    I hereby revoke any and all other former wills made by me.

In witness whereof, I have hereunto subscribed my name and set my seal to this will, on this third day of February, in the year Two Thousand and Eighteen.

*John Wayman*
---

*Lawrence Smith, 29 Arch Street, Albany, New York Ronald Schelle, 3720 Columbia Street, East Greenbush, N.Y. Mary Williams, 427 Shirley Street, Albany, New York*

June 2, 2018

P.S. In the event of my wife's death, I wish my nephew, Peter Roberts, to have all of my property, both personal and real.

*John Wayman*
---

*Lawrence Smith, 29 Arch Street, Albany, New York Ronald Schelle, 3720 Columbia Street, East Greenbush, N.Y. Mary Williams, 427 Shirley Street, Albany, New York*

---

1. The testator of this will is

    A.  John Wayman                          B.  Peter Roberts
    C.  Mary W. Wayman              D.  Lawrence Smith

1.\_\_\_\_

2. After John Wayman's death, to which court should this will be presented?

   A. Federal District
   B. Equity
   C. Surrogate
   D. Appellate

3. The legal name given to the P.S. is

   A. attestation
   B. codicil
   C. release
   D. allonge

4. To make this will valid under state law, John Wayman would have to be

   A. at least 30 years of age
   B. in good health
   C. a resident of the state
   D. of sound mind and judgment

5. The MOST important reason for making out a will is to

   A. distribute the property according to the wishes of the deceased
   B. dispose of property in a legal manner
   C. keep creditors from collecting debts
   D. eliminate inheritance taxes

Questions 6-10.

DIRECTIONS: Questions 6 through 10 are to be answered on the basis of the information below.

The RST Corporation was incorporated to operate within the state to manufacture electronic data processing equipment.

6. If only one class of stock is authorized, which must it be?

   A. Common    B. Preferred    C. Treasury    D. Registered

7. Berman, an investor, wanted to acquire stock in the RST Corporation. Which method would NOT be available to her?

   A. Through a stockbroker
   B. Through the Secretary of State's office
   C. Directly from a stockholder
   D. By original subscription

8. Generally, the liability for the debts of the corporation would fall upon the

   A. stockholders
   B. board of directors
   C. officers
   D. corporation itself

9. Which Federal agency is PRIMARILY responsible for protecting investors against fraudulent securities sales?

   A. Interstate Commerce Commission
   B. Federal Trade Commission
   C. Securities and Exchange Commission
   D. Federal Bureau of Investigation

10. The right of employees of the RST Corporation to organize for the purpose of negotiating wages and working conditions is called

    A. featherbedding
    B. unionizing
    C. boycotting
    D. collective bargaining

Questions 11-15.

DIRECTIONS: Questions 11 through 15 are to be answered on the basis of the following information.

Farr leased an apartment from Owens for one year. There were three other apartments in the same building.

11. Unless there was an agreement otherwise, Farr could automatically

    A. renew the lease
    B. use the property for commercial purposes
    C. sublet the property
    D. remove the fixtures

12. Farr would like a picture window installed in his living room.
    What must he do if he is willing to pay the cost of installation himself?

    A. Arrange for the work to be done and notify the landlord before the work is completed.
    B. Arrange for the work to be done and inform the landlord when the work is finished.
    C. Arrange with a carpenter to do the work and pay him.
    D. Get the landlord's permission before arranging for the work to be done.

13. During the winter months, the furnace broke down. Several weeks passed before Owens completed the repairs. This delay in making repairs caused Farr to move out.
    Such a delay is known as

    A. dispossession
    B. constructive eviction
    C. foreclosure
    D. repossession

14. After the year had expired, Farr, without notice, remained in possession of the apartment.
    As a result, Farr became a

    A. sublessor
    B. sublessee
    C. squatter
    D. holdover

15. Farr purchased a garbage disposal unit and had it installed in the kitchen plumbing.
    This unit would be referred to as a(n)

    A. fixture
    B. attachment
    C. retainer
    D. leasehold

Questions 16-20.

DIRECTIONS: Questions 16 through 20 are to be answered on the basis of the information below.

On September 20, 2018, Paul R. Dean submitted an application for life insurance to the Mutual Life Insurance Company, Inc.

16. Mr. Dean was actually born in 1955. On the application, he made a mistake by writing 1958 rather than 1955.
    Upon discovery, this error would cause the policy to be

    A. declared void by the insurer
    B. adjusted to the correct age
    C. payable at the face value excluding any declared dividends
    D. unaffected after the insurer had accepted the application

17. Mr. Dean is applying for life insurance in which the premiums are payable for a stated number of years, after which the insurance will cover him until his death.
    This is known as _____ insurance.

    A. term
    B. ordinary life
    C. limited payment
    D. endowment

18. The term *premium* as used in insurance is BEST defined as the

    A. written insurance contract
    B. periodic payment made by the insured to the insurer
    C. subject matter of the insurance contract
    D. party who is to receive the compensation under the insurance contract

19. On November 15, 2018, the Mutual Life Insurance Company, Inc. discovered that Mr. Dean had applied for life and disability insurance with another insurance company in 2015 and had been refused coverage.
    This fact would

    A. cancel the policy
    B. cause a reduction in the amount payable at death
    C. cause a lapse in the policy until a corrected statement was made, signed, and submitted by the insured
    D. have no effect on the policy

20. If the life insurance policy should lapse, the insured is entitled to the

    A. cash surrender value
    B. proceeds
    C. premiums paid
    D. amount as stipulated in the settlement option

Questions 21-25.

DIRECTIONS: Questions 21 through 25 are to be answered on the basis of the information below.

Felix, a potato farmer, shipped 300 sacks of potatoes from Mattituck, Long Island, to the American Produce Co., Chicago, Illinois. The potatoes were shipped via railroad, terms F.O.B. Mattituck, Long Island.

21. The Long Island Railroad, which accepted the potatoes from Felix, undertakes to transport goods for any person who may request its services.
This railroad would be classified under these circumstances as a

    A. consignee
    B. consignor
    C. common carrier
    D. private carrier

22. The rates charged by the Long Island Railroad for shipping goods from Mattituck, Long Island, to Chicago, Illinois, would be subject to the regulations of the _____ Commission

    A. Federal Trade
    B. Public Service
    C. Interstate Commerce
    D. Intrastate Commerce

23. Risk of loss to the 300 sacks of potatoes passed to the American Produce Company when the potatoes

    A. were placed in the hands of the railroad at Mattituck
    B. reached their destination at Chicago
    C. were paid for by the American Produce Company
    D. were taken from the grower's storage bin and prepared for shipment

24. The potatoes were shipped according to the railroad's regular shipping conditions and without any unusual delay. When they reached their destination, however, potatoes in several of the bags had spoiled. The railroad would be liable for

    A. the value of the spoiled potatoes
    B. negligence in not speeding up the delivery so as to prevent spoilage
    C. negligence in having accepted goods that were subject to delay
    D. no part of the loss because of the inherent nature of the goods

25. When the potatoes arrived in Chicago, Illinois, the American Produce Company was unable to unload them for several days. The carrier levied a charge for this delay. Such a charge is referred to as

    A. demurrage
    B. fee simple
    C. a tariff
    D. a lien

Questions 26-30.

DIRECTIONS: Questions 26 through 30 are to be answered on the basis of the information below.

Robinson wanted a garage built on her property. On May 1, she wrote a letter to Slater, giving all necessary specifications, and asked him if he would be interested in doing the job. Slater mailed a letter on May 12, stating that he would furnish the materials and the labor for $1,800. On May 16, Robinson sent a letter to Slater telling him that the price was acceptable and asking him to go ahead with the job. Slater received the letter on May 18 and began construction on May 21.

26. The above contract did not need to be in writing because the

    A. price involved was under $3,000
    B. contract concerns the sale of personal property

C. contract is for labor and materials
D. contract is for personal service

27. The offer in the above agreement was made by

A. Slater on May 12
B. Slater on May 21
C. Robinson on May 1
D. Robinson on May 16

28. The acceptance of the above order took place on May

A. 12
B. 16
C. 18
D. 21

29. On June 2, a strike of cement workers made it impossible for Slater to obtain premixed concrete for the garage floor.
What would be the effect of Slater's inability to obtain premixed concrete for this contract?
The

A. contract would be discharged by impossibility of performance
B. contract would be discharged if it cost Mr. Slater more money to obtain the concrete elsewhere
C. contract would be discharged if Mr. Slater were to be required to mix the concrete himself
D. impossibility would not affect this contract

30. Robinson agreed to pay Slater an extra $200 if he would complete the garage by the agreed time.
This promise to pay an additional $200 would be binding upon him if Robinson

A. agreed to pay the sum in cash at the time the garage was completed
B. agreed to pay the entire $200 at the time the garage was completed
C. put her promise to pay an additional $200 in writing
D. was able to get Slater to promise in writing that the garage would be completed on schedule

## KEY (CORRECT ANSWERS)

| | | | |
|---|---|---|---|
| 1. | A | 16. | B |
| 2. | C | 17. | C |
| 3. | B | 18. | B |
| 4. | D | 19. | D |
| 5. | A | 20. | A |
| 6. | A | 21. | C |
| 7. | B | 22. | C |
| 8. | D | 23. | A |
| 9. | C | 24. | D |
| 10. | D | 25. | A |
| 11. | C | 26. | C |
| 12. | D | 27. | A |
| 13. | B | 28. | B |
| 14. | D | 29. | D |
| 15. | A | 30. | C |

# TEST 3

DIRECTIONS: Each question or incomplete statement is followed by several suggested answers or completions. Select the one that BEST answers the question or completes the statement. *PRINT THE LETTER OF THE CORRECT ANSWER IN THE SPACE AT THE RIGHT.*

1. An ordinance passed by a city council would become part of _____ law.

    A. constitutional
    B. common
    C. statutory
    D. international

2. The rule of precedent refers to

    A. statutory law
    B. common law
    C. constitutional law
    D. ordinances

3. A decree of a court of proper jurisdiction determining that one party is indebted to another and fixing the amount of such indebtedness is known as a(n)

    A. judgment
    B. summons
    C. lawsuit
    D. injunction

4. In which court would the trial of a person accused of transporting stolen stocks and bonds from New York City to Chicago, Illinois be held?

    A. New York State Court of Appeals
    B. New York State Supreme Court
    C. United States District Court
    D. United States Supreme Court

5. Which BEST describes an income execution (garnishee proceedings)?

    A. A written agreement between debtor and creditor in which the debtor agrees to pay a certain amount each pay period to the creditor
    B. A proposal by the debtor that he will pay a certain proportion of the debt each pay period to the creditor
    C. The acceptance by the creditor of the debtor's offer to pay a certain proportion of the debt each pay period
    D. A court order directing the employer to withhold a certain amount of money each pay period from the employee's earnings

6. A petit or trial jury has the responsibility of determining the facts of a case and stating its decision in the form of a(n)

    A. verdict
    B. judgment
    C. indictment
    D. deposition

7. Smith had one child when he made his will. Later, a second child was born. What action should Smith take to assure that this second child will share equally with the first child in any estate Smith might leave upon his death?

    A. Do nothing, since all children automatically by law are given the same amount
    B. Leave a note to this effect in his safe deposit box
    C. Tell Mrs. Smith and a witness about his wishes regarding his estate settlement
    D. Add a codicil to the original will

8. When Frieda Wilbur sold her neighborhood grocery store, she promised not to open or operate another grocery store for one year in the same neighborhood.
This agreement in restraint of trade is

   A. reasonable
   B. unreasonable
   C. void
   D. voidable

9. Wing said to Foster, *I will sell you my automobile for $800 cash*. Foster replied, *I'll take it at that price if you will take $500 in cash and my 30-day note for the balance*. Foster's reply legally constituted a

   A. counteroffer
   B. revocation
   C. binding acceptance
   D. novation

10. The Statute of Frauds specifies

    A. what acts constitute fraud
    B. who may make binding contracts
    C. the length of time during which legal action must be started
    D. what agreements must be in writing to be enforceable

11. Johnson lost his wallet and placed a reward notice in the local newspaper, stating that anyone who returned the wallet could collect a ten-dollar reward. Ellis, who did not know of the reward, found and returned the wallet. After returning the wallet, Ellis read the reward notice in the newspaper.
Which statement BEST describes Ellis' rights in this situation?
Ellis may

    A. legally collect the reward within a reasonable period of time
    B. not legally collect the reward
    C. demand return of the wallet until the reward is paid
    D. successfully sue for breach of contract

12. The carrying out of the original terms by both parties to a contract is referred to as

    A. accord and satisfaction
    B. agreement
    C. lapse of time
    D. performance

13. Miller, an opera star, contracts to sing over a television network at $5,000 per performance.
If Miller dies before the date of her first performance, the contract is

    A. assigned by operation of law to her executor
    B. terminated by operation of law
    C. breached and her estate is liable for damages
    D. enforceable by Miller's heirs

14. A quotation of prices in a newspaper advertisement is USUALLY regarded as a(n)

    A. general offer which may be accepted by any party who reads it
    B. invitation to others to make offers
    C. valid offer communicated indirectly to the offeree
    D. valid offer which, upon acceptance, will be enforced as a quasi-contract

15. In a letter to David Hall, Elizabeth Walsh offered to sell her paintings. A contract was created when _____ letter of acceptance.

    A. Hall wrote the
    B. Hall mailed the
    C. Walsh received Hall's
    D. Walsh notified Hall that she had received his

16. Becker offers to hire Lucey as a sales representative for a salary of $500 a week plus *a fair share of the profits of the business.*
    Lucey will NOT be able to hold Becker to this agreement because it is a(n)

    A. general offer          B. invitation
    C. indefinite offer       D. oral offer

17. The term *caveat emptor,* where the buyer has an opportunity to inspect the goods which he or she is buying, means that the sale is legally regarded to be

    A. at the seller's risk
    B. at the buyer's risk
    C. with the privilege of return
    D. on an approval basis

18. Which bailee is obligated to exercise only slight care over the subject matter of the bailment?
    A

    A. warehouseman
    B. person who rents an outboard motor
    C. person who finds a diamond ring
    D. person who borrows his neighbor's garden shovel

19. Which statement is an express warranty?

    A. This car is a bargain.
    B. This car has a lot of miles in it yet.
    C. This car has an eight-cylinder motor.
    D. I feel that this car has been given excellent care by its former owner.

20. Smith sold his car to Butler for $500. Smith made the following statement for the purpose of inducing Butler to buy the car: *You should not have to spend a cent for repairs for the next 5,000 miles.* Before he had driven 3,000 miles, Butler spent $100 for repairs to keep the car in running order.
    Smith's statement to Butler was

    A. *binding,* because it constituted an express warranty
    B. *binding,* because it constituted an implied warranty
    C. *not binding,* because it expressed a mere opinion
    D. *not binding,* because repairs are essential to keep a car in running order

21. Dunn purchased a new rug under a conditional sales agreement. The terms of the agreement called for a downpayment of $60 and 10 regular monthly installments of $20 each.
    Title to the rug passed to Dunn when

A. the agreement was made
B. a copy of the sale was filed in the proper public office
C. the rug was delivered to Dunn
D. the final installment was paid

22. Esther Martin saw a detailed listing and a picture of a home dehumidifier in a mail-order catalog and ordered one. Which phrase BEST describes this contract?

    A. Sale by sample
    B. Sale by description
    C. Bulk sale
    D. No sale, because there was no personal contract

23. After careful examination, Emerson bought Dietz's motorcycle for $350, paying cash. At the time of the sale, Dietz assured Emerson that this motorcycle was *a tremendous buy at that price*. Soon thereafter, Emerson discovered he could buy the identical model at another dealer's for $250.
    If Emerson brought suit against Dietz, how much money could Emerson legally recover as damages?

    A. $100
    B. $100 and court costs
    C. $350
    D. Nothing

24. An oil well owned by Anderson constitutes part of his

    A. real property
    B. personal property
    C. encumbrances
    D. fungible goods

25. Which does the Interstate Commerce Commission have the authority to regulate?

    A. The business of a common carrier operating within a state
    B. Freight rates for goods being transported from one state to another state
    C. Speed limits for trucks and buses on state highways
    D. The hiring and firing of employees working for a common carrier

26. The party to whom goods are to be shipped by the carrier is known as the

    A. consignee    B. consignor    C. assignee    D. assignor

27. Morris was injured on Nolan's property due to a defective railing on Nolan's front porch. If Morris should sue Nolan for the damages caused as a result of this injury, Nolan would have some financial protection if she carried which type of insurance?

    A. Title
    B. Health and accident
    C. Hospitalization
    D. Public liability

28. A car was totally destroyed by fire.
    To have this car replaced by the insurance company, which type of automobile insurance would be needed?

    A. Collision
    B. Comprehensive
    C. No-fault
    D. Property damage

29. Which expression, when used to designate the promise of the maker to pay the note, would result in a negotiable note?
I promise to pay to

    A. the order of Harry Smith if I inherit my father's property
    B. the order of Harry Smith if I graduate from high school
    C. bearer thirty days after presentation out of the rentals I collect
    D. bearer thirty days after presentation and request you to deduct the amount from my account

30. When the drawer of a check tells his bank not to pay the check, he is said to be _____ the check.

    A. dishonoring
    B. forging
    C. negotiating
    D. stopping payment on

---

# KEY (CORRECT ANSWERS)

| | | | | |
|---|---|---|---|---|
| 1. | C | | 16. | C |
| 2. | B | | 17. | B |
| 3. | A | | 18. | C |
| 4. | C | | 19. | C |
| 5. | D | | 20. | C |
| 6. | A | | 21. | D |
| 7. | D | | 22. | B |
| 8. | A | | 23. | D |
| 9. | A | | 24. | A |
| 10. | D | | 25. | B |
| 11. | B | | 26. | A |
| 12. | D | | 27. | D |
| 13. | B | | 28. | B |
| 14. | B | | 29. | D |
| 15. | B | | 30. | D |

# TEST 4

DIRECTIONS: Each question or incomplete statement is followed by several suggested answers or completions. Select the one that BEST answers the question or completes the statement. *PRINT THE LETTER OF THE CORRECT ANSWER IN THE SPACE AT THE RIGHT.*

1. Nancy Smith endorses her paycheck, *For deposit only - Nancy Smith.* This endorsement is

    A. blank
    B. special
    C. restrictive
    D. qualified

2. Lillian Jones of Albany wishes to buy merchandise from a manufacturer in Chicago. Jones asks her bank to give her a check drawn on a Chicago bank. This type of check is called a

    A. cashier's check
    B. bank draft
    C. sight draft
    D. trade acceptance

3. Which endorsement made by Edward Thompson, the payee of a check, has the effect of making the check payable to the bearer?

    A. Edward Thompson

    B. Pay to the order of Frank Williams
       Edward Thompson

    C. Pay to Frank Williams only
       Edward Thompson

    D. Pay to Frank Williams or order
       Edward Thompson

4. For a debtor to prove that a bill submitted by a creditor has already been paid, the MOST conclusive evidence would be the debtor's

    A. checkbook stub
    B. canceled voucher check
    C. bank reconciliation statement
    D. personal bookkeeping records

5. The words of negotiability are contained in which phrase? _____ Roberta Ochs.

    A. Pay to
    B. Please pay
    C. Pay to holder,
    D. Pay to the order of

6. Unemployment Insurance, Disability Insurance, Old Age Insurance, Medicare, and Survivors' Insurance are all various types of insurance brought into being as a result of which act and its amendments?
   The _____ Act.

A. National Labor Relations
B. Federal Fair Labor Standards
C. Social Security
D. National Labor Management Relations

7. Ordinarily, any profit that an agent makes in connection with the discharge of his or her duties

   A. belongs to the principal
   B. must be equally shared with the principal
   C. should be deposited in the agent's personal bank account
   D. becomes the property of the agent upon the principal's death

8. The charges made by the local government against real property owners for local improvements, such as the paving of a street, are called

   A. liens
   B. mortgages
   C. attachments
   D. assessments

9. A contract which creates an *estate or tenancy for years* is known as a

   A. mortgage   B. deed   C. lease   D. bailment

10. Dorothy Beyer promised to sell a building lot to Kenyon. Kenyon agreed to buy the lot. This contract would be binding if

    A. the amount of money concerned was less than $500
    B. both parties had witnesses to the agreement
    C. Kenyon gave $100 as a downpayment
    D. the agreement was in writing, regardless of the amount of money involved

11. A condominium is a

    A. type of ownership in which the tenant owns an apartment within an apartment house
    B. type of deed in which the owner receives only a lifetime use of the property purchased
    C. type of loan made to purchase real property
    D. right that the mortgagor has in property in which he or she holds a mortgage

12. One who makes a will is legally known as a(n)

    A. testator
    B. executor
    C. legatee
    D. administrator

13. Which term is applicable to the partnership type of business?

    A. Limited liability
    B. Preemptive right
    C. Ultra vires
    D. Unlimited liability

14. Which one of the following statements distinguishes a corporation from a partnership?

    A. The corporation is not organized for profit, whereas the partnership is.
    B. The management of a corporation is usually less efficient than that of a partnership.

C. A corporation does not cease to exist on the death or withdrawal of one of its members.
D. A partnership is a legal entity.

15. Ellis transferred ten shares of stock in the River Realty Company, Inc. to Joan Sweeney. As proof that she is a stockholder, Sweeney should receive a

    A. transcript
    B. stock certificate
    C. bond certificate
    D. charter

16. The report by a grand jury that a crime has been committed and that a certain person should be tried for that crime is a(n)

    A. indictment
    B. injunction
    C. judgment
    D. summons

17. Which is a MAJOR function of a grand jury?

    A. Replacing the district attorney in certain criminal cases
    B. Determining the facts at issue during a trial in open court
    C. Hearing evidence in order to determine if a crime has been committed
    D. Trying cases against public officials

18. Threatening to harm a person physically, without actually doing it, is known as the tort of

    A. battery *only*
    B. assault *only*
    C. assault and battery
    D. deceit

19. Where a tort has been committed, the type of action GENERALLY taken is a

    A. civil action brought by the injured party for money damages
    B. civil action brought by the injured party for specific performance
    C. criminal action brought by the district attorney's office
    D. criminal action brought by the attorney general of the state

20. Perjury is classified legally as a(n)

    A. offense
    B. misdemeanor
    C. felony
    D. violation

21. Johnson promised his nephew Arthur $5,000 if Arthur would go back to college and complete his engineering course. Arthur did so, but his uncle, claiming that there was no consideration for his promise, refused to pay Arthur the $5,000 after he had finished college. Was Johnson's promise legally binding?

    A. Yes; consideration may consist of doing something one is not legally obligated to do.
    B. Yes; consideration may consist of a promise for a promise.
    C. No; a promise not based upon a valuable consideration is not binding.
    D. No; a social agreement is not enforceable at law.

22. Jackson made an agreement with a cabinetmaker to build a desk to Jackson's own specifications.
    Would this contract come under the provisions of the *sales of goods* section of the Uniform Commercial Code?

A. Yes; anything that passes from one person to another for consideration is a sale.
B. Yes; any personal property that changes hands is a sale.
C. No; only those items sold between merchants are considered as sales.
D. No; this would be a contract for labor and materials, not a sale of goods.

23. Early in the morning, the Truck Transport Company received at its terminal platform several baskets of peaches for shipment that day. The receiving clerk who checked in the baskets and filled out the bill of lading left the peaches on the platform exposed to the elements. Late that afternoon, a hailstorm, which was unusual for the area and time of year, ruined the entire shipment of peaches.
Would the common carrier be excused for the damage to the peaches because of its argument that loss was due to an Act of God?

   A. Yes; an unusual storm is considered an Act of God and the common carrier is released from its extreme liability.
   B. Yes; any damage caused by the elements releases a common carrier from its extreme liability.
   C. No; a common carrier is liable for any damage to goods while in its custody.
   D. No; a common carrier must take all reasonable precautions to protect goods while in its custody.

24. Taylor purchased a house by making a downpayment and borrowing the remainder from the local savings and loan association. A friend suggested that Taylor purchase a homeowner's policy instead of a standard fire insurance policy.
Is this good advice?

   A. Yes; the homeowner's policy gives much broader coverage than the standard fire insurance policy.
   B. Yes; the homeowner's policy has a lower premium than the standard fire insurance policy.
   C. No; Taylor is ineligible because he does not completely own his house.
   D. No; homeowner's insurance is very expensive compared to standard fire insurance policies.

25. Adams promised his daughter $5,000 if she would never marry. Would this agreement be enforceable by law?

   A. Yes; agreements containing a forebearance is enforceable.
   B. Yes; agreements where the consideration is marriage are always enforceable.
   C. No; agreements never to marry are unenforceable.
   D. No; agreements containing a forebearance are unenforceable.

26. Lois McKee, the manager of a small chain store, was directed by the owner to sell for cash only. She found that she could increase sales for the company by giving credit to certain individuals until Saturday of each week. Sessler, a credit customer, could not pay as agreed.
Is McKee responsible to the owner of the store for Sessler's debt?

   A. Yes; an agent owes her principal obedience and is liable to him for any loss resulting from any failure to obey.
   B. Yes; a principal is not bound to third parties for acts committed by his agent outside the scope of her authority.

C. No; the scope of authority of a manager is very broad.
D. No; the agent, if she acts in good faith, is not liable to her principal.

27. Walker worked in a plant in which all of the employees belonged to a particular labor union. The union negotiated a contract for all the employees of the plant. A majority of the union membership voted to accept the negotiated contract.
If Walker did not vote for the contract, would he be bound by it?

   A. Yes; in collective bargaining agreements, the contract accepted by a majority of the union members is binding upon all members.
   B. Yes; once the union representative has come to agreement with the employer, all the employees are bound to this agreement whether a vote is taken or not.
   C. No; in order to be bound by any union agreement, all members of the union must vote in favor of the agreement.
   D. No; if some union members are not in favor of a contract negotiated by their representative and accepted by majority vote, these members have the right to negotiate their own contract.

27.____

28. When a tenant vacated his apartment at the end of his lease, the landlord insisted that it was the obligation of the tenant to repaint the entire apartment.
In the absence of any provision in the lease, was the landlord CORRECT?

   A. Yes; a tenant must always leave the premises ready for the next tenant by painting before leaving.
   B. Yes; all decorating is the responsibility of the tenant and not of the landlord.
   C. No; a tenant must leave the premises as he found them, with normal wear and tear excepted.
   D. No; a tenant is never responsible for any decorating.

28.____

29. Atkinson, Garland, and Jones orally agreed to organize a partnership to operate a drugstore for 3 years. After 2 years, Garland wished to end the partnership.
Is he legally bound to stay in the partnership until the end of the third year?

   A. Yes; a contract to form a partnership may be oral.
   B. Yes; as this partnership had been in operation for two years, the oral contract had been ratified and, consequently, it is too late to be broken.
   C. No; if the partnership is to continue for more than 1 year, it must be in writing in order to satisfy the requirements of the Statute of Frauds.
   D. No; a partner has the right to withdraw from the firm at any time without any liability.

29.____

30. Stephanie Bacon, a stockholder in the Comstock Corporation, cannot attend the annual meeting of the stockholders, but desires to vote on a very important issue that will be taken up at this meeting.
Is it possible for her to have a vote on this matter at the meeting?

   A. Yes; she may arrange to call in her vote by telephone while the voting is taking place.
   B. Yes; she may give her right to vote to someone else by signing a paper called a proxy.
   C. No; a stockholder may only vote in person at the annual meeting of a corporation.
   D. No; one who cannot attend a stockholders' meeting forfeits the right to vote.

30.____

# KEY (CORRECT ANSWERS)

| | | | |
|---|---|---|---|
| 1. | C | 16. | A |
| 2. | B | 17. | C |
| 3. | A | 18. | B |
| 4. | B | 19. | A |
| 5. | D | 20. | C |
| 6. | C | 21. | A |
| 7. | A | 22. | D |
| 8. | D | 23. | D |
| 9. | C | 24. | A |
| 10. | D | 25. | C |
| 11. | A | 26. | A |
| 12. | A | 27. | A |
| 13. | D | 28. | C |
| 14. | C | 29. | C |
| 15. | B | 30. | B |

# TEST 5

DIRECTIONS: Each question or incomplete statement is followed by several suggested answers or completions. Select the one that BEST answers the question or completes the statement. *PRINT THE LETTER OF THE CORRECT ANSWER IN THE SPACE AT THE RIGHT.*

Questions 1-5.

DIRECTIONS: Questions 1 through 5 are to be answered on the basis of the business paper below.

---

ROGERS & JONES, INC.
1150 Main St.
Buffalo, N.Y.

Date: *May 3, 2009*
Terms: *1/10, n/60*

Sold To: C.N. Helbert Co.
266 Broad Street
Syracuse, New York
Shipped by: Supersonic Freight Line

| 1 | X55 Motor for M-3 water pump | $375.00 |

---

1. C.N. Helbert Co. is known as the

   A. vendor    B. buyer    C. consignor    D. bailor

2. Title to the motor passed to the C.N. Helbert Co. when

   A. Rogers & Jones, Inc. delivered it to the freight depot at Buffalo
   B. the motor arrived at the freight station in Syracuse
   C. the motor was picked up by the truck of the C.N. Helbert Co. at the freight depot in Syracuse
   D. C.N. Helbert Co. made payment for the motor

3. Rogers & Jones, Inc. gave the C.N. Helbert Co.

   A. what is known as *caveat emptor*
   B. an implied warranty that the motor would satisfactorily operate the M-3 pump
   C. an implied warranty that the motor could be used satisfactorily in pumping oil
   D. no warranty of any kind

4. If the C.N. Helbert Co. made a payment of $50 on the motor on August 7, 2009, the balance of the debt would be *outlawed* on

   A. May 3, 2013         B. July 2, 2013
   C. August 7, 2013      D. May 3, 2016

5. The Supersonic Freight Line would be responsible for the loss if

   A. an officer of the law took the motor from the carrier
   B. the motor was damaged by lightning which struck the freight truck

146

C. the motor was damaged while being transported by the carrier because it had not been properly crated by Rogers & Jones, Inc.
D. the motor was stolen from a locked freight truck

Questions 6-10.

DIRECTIONS: Questions 6 through 10 are to be answered on the basis of the information below.

Rogers, an antique dealer, contracted to sell to Martha Niles a certain piece of antique furniture for $5,000. The piece was the only one of its type known to antique dealers. The agreement between Rogers and Niles provided for delivery by Rogers within five days.

6. The agreement between Rogers and Niles is legally considered a contract for

   A. labor and materials
   B. bailment of goods
   C. the sale of goods
   D. the sale of realty

7. The furniture is an example of

   A. real property
   B. personal property
   C. a choses in action
   D. an accessory

8. Shortly after the contract was made, and before delivery, Rogers changed his mind and refused to deliver the furniture to Niles.
   Under these circumstances, Niles' MOST effective legal remedy would be to

   A. obtain an injunction
   B. obtain a decree of specific performance
   C. sue Rogers for money damages
   D. cancel the contract with Rogers

9. Risk of loss, destruction, or damage to the furniture passed to Niles when

   A. she selected the antique furniture
   B. the furniture was delivered to a common carrier
   C. the furniture was delivered to Niles
   D. she paid for the furniture

10. Legally, if the antique furniture were sold on an *as is* basis, the seller may only be held liable for breach of an

    A. express warranty
    B. implied warranty of merchantability
    C. implied warranty of fitness for a particular purpose
    D. implied warranty of title

Questions 11-15.

DIRECTIONS: Questions 11 through 15 are to be answered on the basis of the information below.

Martin took out a fire insurance policy for $20,000 on his home and extended coverage on his personal property for $5,000 with the XYZ Insurance Company. The house had cost Martin $25,000 when he bought it.

11. A short time later, Martin carelessly dropped a cigarette on a couch and set it afire. It cost $150 to have this couch repaired.
How much will Martin recover from the XYZ Insurance Company?

    A. Nothing    B. $100    C. $120    D. $150

12. The couch fire also caused smoke damage to the draperies and walls amounting to $80. This loss will be borne by

    A. Martin *only*
    B. the bank holding Martin's mortgage
    C. the insurance company *only*
    D. Martin and the insurance company on an equal basis

13. If Martin wished to combine several different policies related to his home (fire, liability, casualty, theft) into one comprehensive policy, which type of policy would be of special interest to him?

    A. Special endorsements
    B. Homeowner's
    C. Standard fire
    D. Standard fire, with extended coverage

14. If fire partially destroyed his home, what amount of money would Martin collect from the insurance company?
The

    A. face value of the policy carried regardless of the value of the property
    B. cost of the property
    C. assessed valuation of the property
    D. value of the property at the time of the loss

15. One year later, while he still held the policy with the XYZ Insurance Company, Martin purchased a $10,000 policy from the Friendly Insurance Company and a $5,000 policy from the Reliable Insurance Company.
If the property is completely destroyed by fire, how would the cost be shared by the three insurance companies?

    A. The XYZ Company would pay the entire loss.
    B. The loss would be shared equally.
    C. Each company would pay the full face value of its policy.
    D. The loss would be shared in proportion to the share of the total insurance each insurance company had.

Questions 16-20.

DIRECTIONS: Questions 16 through 20 are to be answered on the basis of the information below.

Brown, a serviceman, rented a store building from Elton for a period of 10 years at a rental of $1,800 a year.

16. To be enforceable, the contract between Brown and Elton was required to be in writing because   16.____

    A. it could not be completed within a period of one year
    B. it concerned a business enterprise
    C. it concerned a rental of over $500 per year
    D. Brown was not a competent party

17. Brown was required to place money with Elton to insure Brown's faithful performance of the lease.   17.____
    This is known as a(n)

    A. option                    B. security deposit
    C. royalty                   D. assessment

18. Brown may recover damages from Elton if Elton does not give Brown   18.____

    A. a warranty of title       B. an option to buy
    C. a security deposit        D. undisturbed possession

19. At the termination of the lease, Brown continues in possession of the property and continues paying the rent.   19.____
    Such an act is known as

    A. holding over              B. adverse possession
    C. repossessing              D. dispossessing

20. If Brown was unable to pay the rent on the leased property, Elton could begin an action to take back possession of the property.   20.____
    Such an action is called a(n)

    A. lien                      B. foreclosure
    C. eviction                  D. attachment

Questions 21-25.

DIRECTIONS: Questions 21 through 25 are to be answered on the basis of the information below.

Crawford died without a will. He was survived by his wife and four children.

21. Which term is used to indicate that Crawford died without a will?   21.____

    A. Testate                   B. Legatee
    C. Intestate                 D. Devised

22. Handling the estate of a deceased person is the responsibility of the _____ Court.   22.____

    A. Justice of the Peace      B. City
    C. County                    D. Surrogate's

23. If Mrs. Crawford is appointed by the court to take charge of the property, she will be known as the

    A. administrator
    B. executor
    C. administratix
    D. executrix

24. Mrs. Crawford would be entitled after setoffs to _____ the remaining _____ personal property.

    A. 1/3; real and
    B. 2/3; real and
    C. 1/3; 'real property and all of the
    D. 2/3; real property and all of the

25. Crawford owed a balance of $700 on an automobile registered in his name only. What happens to this obligation as a result of Crawford's death?
    The obligation

    A. is discharged
    B. becomes an obligation of his estate
    C. becomes an obligation of the family
    D. becomes an obligation of the state

Questions 26-30.

DIRECTIONS: Questions 26 through 30 are to be answered on the basis of the information below.

George Snyder, Cheryl Brooks, and Neil Perkins are partners in a retail drugstore. Snyder and Brooks are registered pharmacists, and Perkins is a salesman. Snyder invested $3,000; Brooks, $8,000; and Perkins, $9,000. The partnership agreement said nothing about the division of profits or the sharing of losses.

26. If a profit of $40,000 was made, how would the profits have to be divided?
    Each would

    A. get an amount in proportion to his or her investment
    B. get one-third
    C. get an amount equal to his or her investment and then the remainder of the profit would be divided equally
    D. be entitled only to a 6% return on his or her investment with the rest of the profit kept in reserve

27. A characteristic of this general partnership is

    A. its continuous existence
    B. the limited liability of its members
    C. the distribution of profits in the form of dividends
    D. the fact that each owner is an agent

28. If Snyder compounded a prescription incorrectly and a person became ill as a result of this, against whom could legal action be taken by the injured party?  28.____

    A. Snyder only since it was his mistake
    B. either Snyder or Brooks since both are registered pharmacists
    C. Perkins only because he is not licensed
    D. any one or all of the partners

29. Johnson made an investment in the partnership but agreed not to take an active part in the management of the business.  29.____
    He is known as a

    A. limited partner
    B. silent partner
    C. debtor of the partnership
    D. creditor of the partnership

30. Any partner who withdraws from the partnership will be liable for subsequent contracts made by the reorganized partnership with former creditors unless  30.____

    A. he gives creditors actual notice of his withdrawal
    B. he publishes notice of his withdrawal in the newspaper
    C. his former partners agree to release him from such obligations
    D. he is insolvent

## KEY (CORRECT ANSWERS)

| | | | |
|---|---|---|---|
| 1. | B | 16. | A |
| 2. | A | 17. | B |
| 3. | B | 18. | D |
| 4. | C | 19. | A |
| 5. | D | 20. | C |
| 6. | C | 21. | C |
| 7. | B | 22. | D |
| 8. | B | 23. | C |
| 9. | C | 24. | A |
| 10. | D | 25. | B |
| 11. | D | 26. | B |
| 12. | C | 27. | D |
| 13. | B | 28. | D |
| 14. | D | 29. | B |
| 15. | D | 30. | A |

# GLOSSARY OF BUSINESS LAW

## CONTENT

| | Page |
|---|---|
| abandon ---- act of god | 1 |
| administrative agency ---- antitrust acts | 2 |
| appeal ---- bill of exchange (draft) | 3 |
| bill of lading ---- circumstantial evidence | 4 |
| civil action ---- confidential relationship | 5 |
| conflict of laws ---- cy-pres doctrine | 6 |
| damages ---- disparagement of goods | 7 |
| distress for rent ---- escrow | 8 |
| estate ---- federal trade commission act | 9 |
| fellow-servant rule ---- grand jury | 10 |
| grant ---- indictment | 11 |
| inheritance ---- judgment note | 12 |
| judgment n.o.v ---- lex loci fori | 13 |
| lex loci sitae rei ---- merger of corporations | 14 |
| mesne ---- nuncupative will | 15 |
| obiter dictum ---- person | 16 |
| personal defenses ---- presumption of innocence | 17 |
| presumption of payment ---- protest | 18 |
| proximate cause ---- ratio legis | 19 |
| real defenses ---- reasale price maintenance agreement | 20 |
| rescission upon agreement ---- run with the land | 21 |
| sale of return ---- special agent | 22 |
| special damages ---- summons | 23 |
| superior servant rule ---- theory of the case | 24 |
| third-party beneficiary ---- unfair competition | 25 |
| unfair labor practice acts ---- warranties of insured | 26 |
| warranties of seller of goods ---- zoning restrictions | 27 |

# GLOSSARY OF BUSINESS LAW

## A

**abandon**: give up or leave employment; relinquish possession of personal property with intent to disclaim title.

**abate**: put a stop to a nuisance; reduce or cancel a legacy because the estate of the testator is insufficient to make payment in full.

**ab initio**: from the beginning.

**abrogate**: recall or repeal; make void or inoperative.

**absolute liability**: liability for an act that causes harm even though the actor was not at fault.

**absolute privilege**: protection from liability for slander or libel given under certain circumstances to statements regardless of the fact that they are false or maliciously made.

**abstract of title**: history oj the transfers of title to a given piece of land, briefly stating the parties to and the effect of all deeds, wills, and judicial proceedings relating to the land.

**acceleration clause**: provision in a contract or any legal instrument that upon a certain event the time for the performance of specified obligations shall be advanced; for example, a provision making the balance due upon debtor's default.

**acceptance**: unqualified assent to the act or proposal of another; as the acceptance of a draft or bill of exchange, of an offer to make a contract, of goods delivered by the seller, or of a gift or a deed.

**accession**: acquisition of title to property by a person by virtue of the fact that it has been attached to property that he already owned or was the offspring of an animal he owned.

**accessory after the fact**: one who after the commission of a felony knowingly assists the felon.

**accessory before the fact**: one who is absent at the commission of the crime but who aided and abetted its commission.

**accident**: an event that occurs even though a reasonable man would not have foreseen its occurrence, because of which the law holds no one legally responsible for the harm caused.

**accommocfa'tion party**: a person who signs a commercial paper to lend credit to another.

**accord and satisfaction**: an agreement to substitute a different performance for that called for in the contract and the performance of that substitute agreement.

**accretion**: the acquisition of title to additional land when the owner's land is built up by gradual deposits made by the natural action of water.

**acknowledgment**: an admissioriqr confirmation, generally of an instrument and usually made before a person authorized to administer oaths, as a notary public; the purpose being to declare that the instrument was executed by the person making the instrument, or that it was his free act, or that he desires that it be recorded.

**action**: a proceeding brought to enforce any right.

**action in personam**: an action brought to impose a personal liability upon a person, such as a money judgment.

**action in rem**: an action brought to declare the status of a thing, such as an action to declare the title to property to be forfeited because of its illegal use.

**action of assumpsit**: an action brought to recover damages for breach of a contract or a quasi-contract.

**action of ejectment**: an action brought to recover the possession of land.

**action of mandamus**: an action brought to compel the performance of a ministerial or clerical act by an officer.

**action of quo warranto**: an action brought to challenge the authority of an officer to act or to hold office.

**action of replevin**: an action brought to recover the possession of personal property.

**action of trespass**: an action brought to recover damages for a tort.

**act of bankruptcy**: any of the acts specified by the national bankruptcy law which, when committed by the debtor within the four months preceding fhe filing of the petition in bankruptcy, is proper ground for declaring the debtor a bankrupt if the other requirements are met.

**act of god**: a natural phenomenon or act of nature that is not reasonably foreseeable.

**administrative agency**: a governmental commission or board given authority by statute to regulate particular matters.

**administrator-administratrix**: the person (man—woman) appointed to wind up and settle the estate of a person who has died without a will.

**adverse possession**: the hostile possession of real estate, which when actual, visible, notorious, exclusive, and continued for the required number of years, will vest the title to the land in the person in such adverse possession.

**advisory opinion**: an opinion that may be rendered in a few states when there is no actual controversy before the court and the matter is submitted by private persons or in some instances by the governor of the state, to obtain the co.urt's opinion.

**affidavit**: a statement of facts set forth in written form and supported by the oath or affirmation of the person making the statement, setting forth that such facts are true to his knowledge or to his information ane! belief the affidavit is executed before a notary public or other person authorized to administer oaths.

**affinity**: the relationship that exists by virtue of marriage.

**affirmative covenant**: an express undertaking or promise in a deed to do an act.

**agency**: the relationship that exists between a person identified as a principal and another by virtue of which the latter may make contracts with third persons on behah of the principal. (Parties-principal, agent, third person)

**agency coupled with an interest in the authority**: an agency in which the agent has given a consideration or has paid for the right to exercise the authority granted to him.

**agency coupled with an interest in the subject matter**: an agency in which for a consideration the agent is given an interest in the property with which he is dealing.

**agency shop**: a union contract provision requiring that nonunion employees pay to the union the equivalent of union dues in order to retain their employment.

**agent**: one who is authorized by the principal or by operation of law to make contracts with third persons on behalf of the principal.

**allonge**: a paper securely fastened to a negotiable instrument in order to provide additional space for indorsements.

**alluvion**: the additions made to/and by accretion.

**alteration**: any material change of the terms of writing made bya party thereto.

**ambulatory**: not effective and therefore may be changed, as in the case of a will that is not final until the testator has died.

**amicable action**: an action that all parties agree should be brought and which is begun by the filing of such an agreement, rather than by serving the adverse parties with process. Although the parties agree to litigate, the dispute is real and the decision is not an advisory opinion.

**amicus curiae**: literally a friend of the court; one who is appointed by the court to take part in litigation and to assist the court by furnishing his opinion in the matter.

**annexation**: attachment of personal property to realty in such a way as to make it become real property and part of the realty.

**annuity**: a contract by which the insured pays a lump sum to the insurer and later receives fixed annual payments.

**anomalous indorser**: a person who signs a negotiable instrument but is not otherwise a party to the instrument.

**anticipatory breach**: the repudiation by a promisor of the contract prior to the time he is required to perform when such repudiation is accepted by the promisee as a breach of the contract.

**anti-injunction acts**: statutes prohibiting the use of injunctions in labor disputes except under exceptional circumstances; notably the federal norris-la guardia act of 1932.

**anti-petrillo act**: a federat statute that makes it a crime to compel a radio broadcasting station to hire musicians not needed. to pay for services not performed or to refrain from broadcasting music of school children or from foreign countries.

**antitrust acts**: statutes prohibiting combinations and contracts in restraint of trade, notably the federal sherman antitrust act of 1890, now generally inapplicable to labor union activity.

**appeal**: taking the case to a reviewing court to determine whether the judgmentof the lower court or administrative agency was correct. (Parties-appellant, appellee)
**appellate jurisdiction**: the power of a court to hear and decide a given class of cases on appeal from another court or administrative agency.
**arbitration**: the settlement of disputed questions whether of law or fact, by one or more arbitrators by whose decision the parties agree to be bound. Increasingly used as a procedure for labor dispute settlement.
**assignment**: transfer of a right, generally used in connection with personal property rights, as rights under a contract, a negotiable instrument, an insurance policy, a mortgage, or a chattel real or lease. (parties--assignor, assignee)
**assumption of risk**: the common-law rule that an employee could not sue the employer for injuries caused by the ordinary risks of employment on the theory that he had assumed such risks by undertaking the work. the rule has been abolished in those areas governed by workmen's compensation laws and most employers' liability statutes.
**attachment**: the seizure of property of or a debt owed to, the debtor by the service of process upon a third person who is in possession of the property or who owes a debt to the debtor.
**attractive nuisance doctrine**: a rule imposing liability on a landowner for injuries sustained by small children playing on his land when the landowner permits a condition to exist or maintains equipment that he should realize would attract small children who could not realize the danger. The rule does not apply if an unreasonable burden would be imposed on the landowner in taking steps to protect the children.
**authenticate**: make or establish as genuine, official, or final, as by signing, countersigning, sealing, or any other act indicating approval.

# B

**bad check laws**: laws making it a criminal offense to issue a bad check with intent to defraud.
**baggage**: such articles of necessity or personal convenience as are usually carried for personal use by passengers of common carriers.
**bail**: variously used in connection with the release of a person or property from the custody of the law, referring (a) to the act of releasing or bailing (b) to the persons who assume liability in the event that the released person does not appear or it is held that the property should not be released, and (c) to the bond or sum of money that such persons furnish the court or other official as indemnity for non-performance of the obligation.
**bailee' lien**: a specific, possessory lien of the bailee on the goods for work done to them. Commonly extended by statute to any bailee's claim for compensation and eliminating the necessity of retention of possession.
**bailment**: the relation that exists when personal property is delivered into the possession of another under an agreement, express or implied, that the identical property will be returned or will be delivered in accordance with the agreement. (parties-bailor, bailee)
**bankruptcy**: a procedure by which one unable to pay his debts may be declared a bankrupt, after which all his assets in excess of his exemption claim are surrendered to the court for administration and distribution to his creditors, and the debtor is given a discharge that releases him from the unpaid balance due on most debts.
**bearer**: the person in physical possession of a negotiable instrument payable to bearer.
**beneficiary**: the person to whom the proceeds of a life insurance policy are payable, a person for whose benefit property is held in trust, or a person given property by a will.
**bequest**: a gift of personal property by will.
**bill of exchange (draft):** an unconditional order in writing by one person upon another, signed by the person giving it, and ordering the person to whom it is directed to payor deliver on demand or ata definite time a sum certain in money to order or to bearer.

**bill of lading**: a document issued by a carrier reciting the receipt of goods and the terms of the contract of transportation. Regulated by the uniform bills of lading act, the federal bills of lading act, or the uniform commercial code.

**bill of sale**: a writing signed by the seller reciting that he has sold to the buyer the personal property therein described.

**binder**: a memorandum delivered to the insured stating the essential terms of a policy to be executed in the future when it is agreed that the contract of insurance is to be effective before the written policy is executed.

**blank indorsement**: an indorsement that does not state to whom the instrument is to be paid.

**blue-sky laws**: state statutes designed to protect the public from the sale of worthless stocks and bonds.

**boardinghouse keeper**: one regularly engaged in the business of offering living accommodations to permanent lodgers or boarders as distinguished from transient guests.

**bona fide**: in good faith: without any fraud or deceit.

**bond**: an obligation or promise in writing and sealed, generally of corporations, personal representatives, trustees; fidelity bonds.

**boycott**: a combination of two or more persons to cause harm to another by refraining from patronizing or dealing with such other person in any way or inducing others to so refrain; commonly an incident of labor disputes.

**bulk sales acts**: statutes to protect creditors of a bulk seller by preventing him from obtaining cash for his goods and then leaving the state. Notice must be given creditors, and the bulk sale buyer is liable to the seller's creditors if the statute is not satisfied. Expanded to "bulk transfers" under the Code.

**business trust**: a form of business organization in which the owners of the property to be devoted to the business transfer the title of the property to trustees with full power to operate the business.

# C

**cancellation**: a crossing out of a part of an instrument or a destruction of all legal effect of the instrument, whether by act of party, upon breach by the other party, or pursuant to agreement or decree of court.

**capital**: net assets of a corporation.

**capital stock**: the declared money value of the outstanding stock of the corporation.

**cash surrender value**: the sum that will be paid the insured if he surrenders his policy to the insurer.

**cause of action**: the right to damages or other judicial relief when a legally protected right of the plaintiff is violated by an unlawful act of the defendant.

**caveat emptor**: let the buyer beware. This maxim is subject to modification by warranties.

**certificate of protest**: a written statement by a notary public setting forth the fact that the holder had presented the negotiable instrument to the primary party on the due date and that the latter had failed to make payment.

**cestui que trust**: the beneficiary or person for whose benefit the property is held in trust.

**charter**: the grant of authority from a government to exist as a corporation. Generally replaced today by a certificate approving the articles of incorporation.

**chattel mortgage**: a security device by which the owner of personal property transfers the title to a creditor as security for the debt owed by the owner to the creditor. Replaced under the Uniform Commercial Code by a secured transaction. (Parties-chattel mortgagor, chattel mortgagee)

**chattels personal**: tangible personal property.

**chattels real**: leases of land and buildings.

**check**: an order by a depositor on his bank to pay a sum of money to a payee: also defined as a bill of exchange drawn on a bank and payable on demand.

**chose in action**: intangible personal property in the nature of claims against another, such as a claim for accounts receivable or wages.

**chose in possession**: tangible personal property.

**circumstantial evidence**: relates to circumstances surrounding the facts in dispute from which the trier of fact may deduce what had happened.

**civil action**: in many states a simplified form of action combining all or many of the former common-law actions.

**civil court**: a court with jurisdiction to hear and determine controversies relating to private rights and duties.

**closed shop**: a place of employment in which only union members may be employed. Now generally prohibited by unfair labor practice statutes.

**codicil**: a writing by one who has made a will which is executed with all the formality of a will and is treated as an addition to or modification of the will.

**coinsurance**: a clause requiring the insured to maintain insurance on his property up to a stated amount and providing that to the extent that he fails to do so the insured is to be deemed a coinsurer with the insurer so that the latter is liable only for its proportionate share of the amount of insurance required to be carried.

**collateral note**: a note accompanied by collateral security.

**collective bargaining**: the process by which the terms of employment are agreed upon through negotiations between the employer or employers within a given industry or industrial area and the union or the bargaining representative of the employees.

**collective bargaining unit**: the employment area within which employees are by statute authorized to select a bargaining representative, who is then to represent all the employees in bargaining collectively with the employer.

**collusion**: an agreement between two or more persons to defraud the government or the courts, as by obtaining a divorce by collusion when no grounds for a divorce exist, or to defraud third persons of their rights.

**color of title**: circumstances that make a person appear to be the owner when he in fact is not the owner, as the existence of a deed appearing to convey the property to a given person gives him color of title although the deed is worthless because it was executed by one who was not the owner of the property.

**commission merchant**: a bailee to whom goods are consigned for sale.

**common carrier**: a carrier that holds out its facilities to serve the general public for compensation without discrimination.

**common law**: the body of unwritten principles originally based on the usages and customs of the community which were recognized and enforced by the courts.

**common stock**: stock that has no right or priority over any other stock of the corporation as to dividends or distribution of assets upon dissolution.

**common trust fund**: a plan by which the assets of small trust estates are pooled into a common fund, each trust being given certificates representing its proportionate ownership of the fund, and the pooled fund is then invested in investments of large size.

**community property**: the cotenancy held by husband and wife in property acquired during their marriage under the law of some of the states, principally in the southwestern united states.

**complaint**: the initial pleading filed by the plaintiff in many actions which in many states may be served as original process to acquire jurisdiction over the defendant.

**composition of creditors**: an agreement among creditors that each shall accept a part payment as full payment in consideration of the other creditors doing the same.

**concealment**: the failure to volunteer information not requested.

**conditional estate**: an estate that will come into being upon the satisfaction of a condition precedent or that will be terminated upon the satisfaction of a condition subsequent provided in the latter case that the grantor or his heirs re-enter and retake possession of the land.

**conditional sale**: a credit transaction by which the buyer purchases on credit and promises to pay the purchase price in installments, while the seller retains the title to the goods, together with the right of repossession upon default, until the condition of payment in full has been satisfied. The conditional sale is replaced under the Uniform Commercial Code by a secured transaction.

**confidential relationship**: a relationship in which, because of the legal status of the parties or their respective physical or mental conditions or knowledge, one party places full confidence and trust in the other and relies upon him entirely for guidance.

**conflict of laws**: the body of law that determines the law of which state is to apply when two or more states are involved in the facts of a given case.

**confusion of goods**: the mixing of goods of different owners that under certain circumstances results in one of the owners becoming the owner of all the goods.

**consanguinity**: relationship by blood.

**consideration**: the promise or performance by the other party that the promisor demands as the price of his promise.

**consignment**: a bailment made for the purpose of sale by the bailee. (parties-consignor, consignee)

**consolidation of corporations**: a combining of two or more corporations in which the corporate existence of each one ceases and a new corporation is created.

**constructive**: an adjective employed to indicate that the noun which is modified by it does not exist but the law disposes of the matter as though it did; as a constructive bailment or a constructive trust.

**contingent beneficiary**: the person to whom the proceeds of a life insurance policy are payable in the event that the primary beneficiary dies before the insured.

**contract**: a binding agreement based upon the genuine assent of the parties, made for a lawful object, between competent parties, in the form required by law and generally supported by consideration.

**contract carrier**: a carrier who transports on the basis of individual contracts that it makes with each shipper, contract to sell: a contract to make a transfer of title in the future as contrasted with a present sale.

**contribution**: the right of a cosurety who has paid more than his proportionate share of the loss to demand that the other surety pays him the amount of the excess payment he has made.

**contributory negligence**: negligence of the plaintiff that contributes to his injury and at common law bars him from recovery from the defendant although the defendant may have been more negligent than the plaintiff.

**conveyance**: a transfer of an interest in land, ordinarily by the execution and delivery of a deed.

**cooling-off period**: a procedure designed to avoid strikes by requiring a specified period of delay before the strike may begin during which negotiations for a settlement must continue.

**cooperative**: a group of two or more persons or enterprises that act through a common agent with respect to a common objective, as buying or selling.

**copyright**: a grant to an author of an exclusive right to publish and sell his work for a period of 28 years, renewable for a second period of 28 years.

**corporation**: an artificial legal person or being created by government grant, which for many purposes is treated as a natural person.

**cost plus**: a method of determining the purchase price or contract price by providing for the payment of an amount equal to the costs of the seller or the contractor to which is added a stated percentage as his profit.

**costs**: the expenses of suing or being sued, recoveroble in some actions by the successful party, and in others, subject to allocation by the court. Ordinarily they do not include attorney's fees or compensation for loss of time.

**counterclaim**: a claim that the defendant in an action may make against the plaintiff.

**covenants of title**: covenants of the grantor contained in a deed that guarantee such matters as his right to make the conveyance, his ownership of the property, the freedom of the property from encumbrances, or that the grantee will not be disturbed in the quiet enjoyment of the land.

**crime**: a violation of the law that is punished as an offense against the state or government.

**cross complaint**: a claim that the defendant may make against the plaintiff.

**cross-examination**: the examination made of a witness by the attorney for the adverse party.

**cumulative voting**: a system of voting for directors in which each stockholder has as many votes as the number of voting shares he owns multiplied by the number of directors to be elected, which votes he can distribute for the various candidates as he desires.

**cy-pres doctrine**: the rule under which a charitable trust will be carried out as nearly as possible in the way the settlor desired, when for any reason it cannot be carried out exactly in the way or for the purposes he had expressed.

# D

**damages**: a sum of money recovered to redress or make amends for the legal wrong or injury done.

**damnum absque injuria**: loss or damage without the violation of a legal right, or the mere fact that a person sustains a loss does not mean that his legal rights have been violated or that he is entitled to sue someone.

**declaratory judgment**: a procedure for obtaining the decision of a court on a question before any action has been taken or loss sustained. It differs from an advisory opinion in that there must be an actual, imminent controversy.

**dedication**: acquisition by the public or a government of title to land when it is given over by its owner to use by the public and such gift is accepted.

**deed**: an instrument by which the grantor (owner of land) conveys or transfers the title to a grantee.

**de facto**: existing in fact as distinguished from as of right, as in the case of an officer or a corporation purporting to act as such without being elected to the office or having been properly incorporated.

**deficiency judgment**: a personal judgment for the amount still remaining due the mortgagee after foreclosure, which is entered against any person liable on the mortgage bond. Statutes generally require the mortgagee to credit the fair value of the property against the balance due when the mortgagee has purchased the property.

**del credere agent**: an agent who sells goods for the principal and who guarantees to the principal that the buyer will pay for the goods.

**delegation**: the transfer of the power to do an act for another.

**de minimis non curat lex**: a maxim that the law is not concerned with trifles. Not always applied, as in the case of the encroachment of a building over the property line in which case the law will protect the landowner regardless of the extent of the encroachment.

**demonstrative evidence**: evidence that consists of visible, physical objects, as a sample taken from the wheat in controversy or a photograph of the subject matter involved.

**demonstrative legacy**: a legacy to be paid or distributed from a specified fund or property.

**demurrage**: a charge made by the carrier for the unreasonable detention of cars by the consignor or consignee.

**demurrer**: a pleading that may be filed to attack the sufficiency of the adverse party's pleading as not stating a cause of action or a defense.

**dependent relative revocation**: the doctrine recognized in some states that if a testator revokes or cancels a will in order to replace it with a later will, the earlier will is to be deemed revived if for any reason the later will does not take effect or no later will is executed.

**deposition**: the testimony of a witness taken out of court before a person authorized to administer oaths.

**devise**: a gift of real estate made by will.

**directed verdict**: a direction by the trial judge to the jury to return a verdict in favor of a specified party to the action.

**directors**: the persons vested with control of the corporation, subject to the elective power of the shareholders.

**discharge in bankruptcy**: an order of the bankruptcy court discharging the bankrupt debtor from the unpaid balance of most of the claims against him.

**discharge of contract**: termination of a contract by performance, agreement, impossibility, acceptance of breach, or operation of law.

**discovery**: procedures for ascertaining facts prior to the time of trial in order to eliminate the element of surprise in litigation.

**dishonor by nonacceptance**: the refusal of the drawee to accept a bill of exchange.

**dishonor by nonpayment**: the refusal to pay a negotiable instrument when properly presented for payment.

**dismiss**: a procedure to terminate an action by moving to dismiss on the ground that the plaintiff has not pleaded a cause of action entitling him to relief.

**disparagement of goods**: the making of malicious, false statements as to the quality of the goods of another.

**distress for rent**: the common-law right of the lessor to enter the premises when he was not paid the rent and to seize all personal property found on the premises. Statutes have modified or abolished this right in many states.

**distributive share**: the proportionate part of the estate of the decedent that will be distributed to an heir or legatee, and also as devisee in those jurisdictions in which real estate is administered as part of the decedent's estate.

**domestic bill of exchange**: a draft drawn in one state and payable in the same or another state.

**domestic corporation**: a corporation that has been incorporated by the state as opposed to incorporation by another state.

**domicile**: the home of a person or the state of incorporation of a corporation, to be distinguished from a place where a person lives but which he does not regard as his home, or a state in which a corporation does business but in which it was not incorporated.

**dominant tenement**: the tract of land that is benefited by an easement to which another tract, or servient tenement, is subject.

**double indemnity**: a provision for payment of double the amount specified by the insurance contract if death is caused by an accident and occurs under specified circumstances.

**double jeopardy**: the principle that a person who has once been placed in jeopardy by being brought to trial at which the proceedings progressed at least as far as having the jury sworn cannot thereafter be tried a second time for the same offense.

**draft**: see bill of exchange.

**draft-varying acceptance**: one in which the acceptor's agreement to pay is not exactly in conformity with the order of the instrument.

**due care**: the degree of care that a reasonable man would exercise to prevent the realization of harm, which under all the circumstances was reasonably forseeable in the event that such care were not taken.

**due process of law**: the guarantee by the 5th and 14th amendments of the federal constitution and of many state constitutions that no person shall be deprived of life, liberty, or property without due process of law, as presently interpreted, this prohibits any law either state or federal that sets up an unfair procedure or the substance of which is arbitrary or capricious.

**duress**: conduct that deprives the victim of his own free will and which generally gives the victim the right to set aside any transaction entered into under such circumstances.

# E

**easement**: a permanent right that one has in the land of another, as the right to cross another's land or easement of way.

**eleemosynary corporation**: a corporation organized for a charitable or benevolent purpose.

**embezzlement**: a statutory offense consisting of the unlawful conversion of property entrusted to the wrongdoer with respect to which he owes the owner a fiduciary duty.

**eminent domain**: the power of a government and certain kinds of corporations to take private property against the objection of the owner provided the taking is for a public purpose and just compensation is made therefor.

**encumbrance**: a right held by a third person in or a lien or charge against property, as a mortgage or judgment lien on land.

**equity**: the body of principles that originally developed because of the inadequacy of the rules then applied by the common-law courts of England.

**erosion**: the loss of land through a gradual washing away by tides or currents, with the owner losing title to the lost land.

**escheat**: the transfer to the state of the title to a decedent's property when he dies intestate not survived by anyone capable of taking the property as his heir.

**escrow**: a conditional delivery of property or of a deed to a custodian or escrow holder, who in turn makes final delivery to the grantee or transferee when a specified condition has been satisfied.

**estate:** the extent and nature of one's interest in land. Also the assets constituting the decedent's property at the time of his death.

**estate in fee simple:** the largest estate possible in which the owner has the absolute and entire property in the land.

**estoppel:** the principle by which a person is barred from pursuing a certain course of action or of disputing the truth of certain matters when his conduct has been such that it would be unjust to permit him to do so.

**evidence:** that which is presented to the trier of fact as the basis on which the trier is to determine what had happened.

**exception:** an objection, as an exception to the admission of evidence on the ground that it was hearsy; the exclusion of particular property from the operation of a deed.

**ex contractu:** a claim or matter that is founded upon or arises out of a contract.

**ex delicto:** a claim or matter that is founded upon or arises out of a tort.

**execution:** the carrying out of a judgment of a court, generally directing that property owned by the defendant be sold and the proceeds first used to pay the execution or judgment creditor.

**exemplary damages:** damages in excess of the amount needed to compensate for the plaintiff's injury, which are awarded in order to punish the defendant for his malicious or wanton conduct so as to make an example of him.

**exoneration:** an agreement or provision in an agreement that one party shall not be held liable for loss; the right of the surety to demand that those primarily liable pay the claim for which the surety is secondarily liable.

**expert witness:** one who has acquired special knowledge in a particular field through practical experience, or study, or both, which gives him a superior knowledge so that his opinion is admissible as an aid to the trier of fact.

**ex post facto law:** a law making criminal an act that was lawful when done or that increases the penalty for an act which was subject to a lesser penalty when done. Such laws are generally prohibited by constitutional provisions.

**extraordinary bailment:** a bailment in which the bailee is subject to unusual duties and liabilities, as a hotelkeeper or common carrier

# F

**facility-of-payment clause:** a provision commonly found in an industrial policy permitting the insurer to make payment to any member of a designated class or to any person the insurer believes equitably entitled thereto.

**factor:** a bailee to whom goods are consigned for sale.

**factors' acts:** statutes protecting persons who buy in good faith for value from a factor although the goods had not been delivered to the factor with the consent or authorization of their owner.

**fair employment practice acts:** statutes designed to eliminate discrimination in employment in terms of race, religion, natural origin, or sex.

**fair labor standards acts:** statutes, particularly the federal statute designed to prevent excessive hours of employment and low pay, the employment of young children, and other unsound practices.

**fair trade acts:** statutes that authorize the making of resale price maintenance agreements as to trade-mark and brand name articles, and generally provide that all persons in the industry are bound by such an agreement whether they have signed it, or not.

**featherbedding:** the exaction of money for services not performed or not to be performed, which is made an unfair labor practice generally and a criminal offense in connection with radio broadcasting.

**federal securities act:** a statute designed to protect the public from fraudulent securities.

**federal securities exchange act:** a statute prohibiting improper practices at and regulating security exchanges.

**federal trade commission act:** a statute prohibiting unfair methods of competition in interstate commerce.

**fellow-servant rule**: a common-law defense of the employer that barred an employee from suing an employer for injuries caused by a fellow employee.
**felony**: a criminal offense that is punishable by confinement in prison or by death or that is expressly stated by statute to be a felony.
**financial responsibility laws**: statutes that require a driver involved in an automobile accident to prove his financial responsibility in order to retain his license, which responsibility may be shown by procuring public liability insurance in a specified minimum amount.
**financing factor**: one who lends money to manufacturers on the security of goods to be manufactured thereafter.
**firm offer**: an offer stated to be held open for a specified time, which must be so held in some states even in the absence of an option contract, or under the code, with respect to merchants.
**fixture**: personal property that has become so attached to or adapted to real estate that it has lost its character as personal property and is part of the real estate.
**food, drug, and cosmetic act**: a federal statute prohibiting the interstate shipment of misbranded or adulterated foods, drugs, cosmetics, and therapeutic devices.
**forbearance**: refraining from doing an act.
**foreclosure**: procedure for enforcing a mortgage resulting in the public sale of the mortgaged property and less commonly in merely barring the right of the mortgagor to redeem the property from the mortgage.
**foreign (international) bill of exchange**: a bill of exchange made in one nation and payable in another.
**foreign corporation**: a corporation incorporated under the laws of another state.
**forgery**: the fraudulent making or altering of an instrument that apparently creates or alters a legal liability of another.
**fraud**: the making of a false statement of a past or existing fact with knowledge of its falsity or with reckless indifference as to its truth with the intent to cause another to rely thereon, and he does rely thereon to his injury.
**freight forwarder**: one who contracts to have goods transported and, in turn, contracts with carriers for such transportation.
**fructus industriales**: crops that are annually planted and raised.
**fructus naturales**: fruits from trees, bushes, and grasses growing from perennial roots.
**fungible goods**: goods of a homogenous nature of which any unit is the equivalent of any other unit or is treated as such by mercantile usage.
**future advance mortgage**: a mortgage given to secure additional loans to be made in the future as well as an original loan.

## G

**garnishment**: the name given in some states to attachment proceedings.
**general creditor**: a creditor who has a claim against the debtor but does not have any lien on any of the debtor's property, whether as security for his debt or by way of a judgment or execution upon a judgment.
**general damages**: damages that in the ordinary course of events follow naturally and probably from the injury caused by the defendant.
**general legacy**: a legacy to be paid out of the assets generally of the testator without specifying any particular fund or source from which the payment is to be made.
**general partnenhip**: a partnership in which the partners conduct as co-owners a business for profit, and each partner has a right to take part in the management of the business and has unlimited liability.
**gift causa mortis**: a gift made by the donor because he believed he faced immediate and impending death, which gift is revoked or is revocable under certain circumstances.
**grace period**: a period generally of 30 or 31 days after the due date of a premium of life insurance in which the premium may be paid.
**grand jury**: a jury not exceeding 23 in number that considers evidence of the commission of crime and prepares indictments to bring offenders to trial before a petty jury.

**grant**: convey real property; an instrument by which such property has been conveyed, particularly in the case of a government.
**gratuitous bailment**: a bailment in which the bailee does not receive any compensation or advantage.
**grievance settlement**: the adjustment of disputes relating to the administration or application of existing contracts as compared with disputes over new terms of employment.
**guarantor**: one who undertakes the obligation of guaranty.
**guaranty**: an undertaking to pay the debt of another if the creditor first sues the debtor and is unable to recover the debt from the debtor or principal. (In some instances the liability is primary, in which case it is the same as suretyship.)

# H

**hearsay evidence**: statements made out of court which are offered in court as proof of the information contained in the statements, which, subject to many exceptions, are not admissible in evidence.
**hedging**: the making of simultaneous contracts to purchase and to sell a particular commodity at a future date with the intention that the loss on one transaction will be offset by the gain on the other.
**heirs**: those persons specified by statute to receive the estate of a decedent that he has not disposed by will.
**holder**: the person in possession of a negotiable instrument payable to him as payee or indorsee, or the person in possession of a negotiable instrument payable to bearer.
**holder in due course**: the holder of a negotiable instrument under such circumstances that he is treated as favored and is given immunity from certain defenses.
**holder through a holder in due course**: a person who is not himself a holder in due course but is a holder of the instrument after it was held by some prior party who was a holder in due course, and who is given the same rights as a holder in due course.
**holographic will**: a will written by the testator in his own hand.
**hotelkeeper**: one regularly engaged in the business of offering living accommodations to all transient persons.
**hung jury**: a petty jury that has been unable to agree upon a verdict.

# I

**ignorantia legis non excusat**: ignorance of the law is not an excuse.
**implied contract**: a contract expressed by conduct or implied or deduced from the facts. Also used to refer to a quasi-contract.
**imputed**: vicariously attributed to or charged to another, as the knowledge of an agent obtained while acting in the scope of his authority is imputed to his principal.
**incidental authority**: authority of an agent that is reasonably necessary to execute his express authority.
**incontestable dause**: a provision that after the lapse of a specified time the insurer cannot dispute the policy on the ground of misrepresentation or fraud of the insured or similar wrongful conduct.
**in custodia legis**: in the custody of the law.
**indemnity**: the right of a person secondarily liable to require that a person primarily liable pay him for his loss when the secondary party discharges the obligation which the primary party should have discharged; the right of an agent to be paid the amount of any loss or damage sustained by him without his fault because of his obedience to the principal's instructions; an undertaking by one person for a consideration to pay another person a sum of money to indemnify him when he incurs a specified loss.

**independent contractor**: a contractor who undertakes to perform a specified task according to the terms of a contract but over whom the other contracting party has no control except as provided for by the contract.
**indictment**: a formal accusation of crime made by a grand jury which accusation is then tried by a petty or trial jury.

**inheritance**: the estate which passes from the decedent to his heirs.
**injunction**: an order of a court of equity to refrain from doing (negative injunction) or to do (affirmative or mandatory injunction) a specified act. Its use in labor disputes has been greatly restricted by statute.
**in pari delicto**: equally guilty; used in reference to a transaction as to which relief will not be granted to either party because both are equally guilty of wrongdoing.
**insolvency**: an excess of debts and liabilities over assets.
**insurable interest**: an interest in the non occurrence of the risk insured against, generally because such occurrence would cause financial loss, although sometimes merely because of the close relationship between the insured and the beneficiary.
**insurance**: a plan of security against risks by charging the loss against a fund created by the payments made by policyholders.
**intangible personal property**: an interest in an enterprise, such as an interest in a partnership or stock of a corporation, and claims against other persons, whether based on contract or tort.
**interlineation**: a writing between the lines or adding to the provisions of a document, the effect thereof depending upon the nature of the document.
**interlocutory**: an intermediate step or preceding that does not make a final disposition of the action and from which ordinarily no appeal may be taken.
**international bill of exchange**: an instrument made in one nation and payable in another.
**interpleader**: a form of action or proceeding by which a person against whom conflicting claims are made may bring the claimants into court to litigate their claims between themselves, as in the case of a bailor when two persons each claim to be the owner of the bailed property, or an insurer when two persons each claim to be the beneficiary of the insurance policy.
**inter se**: among or between themselves, as the rights of partners inter se or as between themselves.
**inter vivos**: any transaction which takes place between living persons and creates rights prior to the death of any of them.
**intestate**: the condition of dying without a will as to any property.
**intestate succession**: the distribution made as directed by statute of property owned by the decedent of which he did not effectively dispose by will.
**ipso facto**: by the very act or fact in itself without any further action by anyone.
**irrebuttable presumption**: a presumption which cannot be rebutted by proving that the facts are to the contrary; not a true presumption but merely a rule of law described in terms of a presumption.
**irreparable injury to property**: an injury that would be of such a nature or inflicted upon such an interest that it would not be reasonably possible to compensate the injured party by the payment of money damages because the property in question could not be purchased in the open market with the money damages which the defendant could be required to pay.

# J

**joint and several contract**: a contract in which two or more persons are jointly and severally obligated or are jointly and severally entitled to recover.
**joint contract**: a contract in which two or more persons is jointly liable or jointly entitled to performance under the contract.
**joint stock company**: an association in which the shares of the members are transferable and control is delegated to a group or board.
**joint tenancy**: the estate held by two or more jointly with the right of survivorship as between them, unless modified by statute.
**joint venture**: a relationship in which two or more persons combine their labor or property for a single undertaking and share profits and losses equally unless otherwise agreed.
**judgment**: the final sentence, order, or decision entered into at the conclusion of the action.
**judgment note**: a promissory note containing a clause authorizing the holder of the note to enter judgment against the maker of the note if it is not paid when due. Also called cognovit note.

**judgment n.o.v.**: a judgment which may be entered after verdict upon the motion of the losing party on the ground that the verdict is so wrong that a judgment should be entered the opposite of the verdict, or nonobstante veredicto (notwithstanding the verdict).

**judgment on the pleadings**: a judgment which may be entered after all the pleadings are filed when it is clear from the pleadings that a particular party is entitled to win the action without proceeding any further.

**judicial sale**: a sale made under order of court by an officer appointed to make the sale or by an officer having such authority as incident to his office. The sale may have the effect of divesting liens on the property.

**jurisdiction**: the power of a court to hear and determine a given class of cases; the power to act over a particular defendant.

**jurisdictional dispute**: a dispute between rival labor unions which may take the form of each claiming that particular work should be assigned to it.

**justifiable abandonment by employee**: the right of an employee to abandon his employment because of nonpayment of wages, wrongful assault, and the demand for the performance of services not contemplated or injurious working-conditions.

**justifiable discharge of employee**: the right of an employer to discharge an employee for nonperformance of duties, fraud, disobedience, disloyalty, or incompetence.

# L

**laches**: the rule that the enforcement of equitable rights will be denied when the party has delayed so long that rights of third persons have intervened or the death or disappearance of witnesses would prejudice any party through the loss of evidence.

**land**: earth, including all things imbedded in or attached thereto, whether naturally or by act of man.

**last clear chance**: the rule that if the defendant had the last clear chance to have avoided injuring the plaintiff, he is liable even though the plaintiff had also been contributorily negligent. In some states also called the humanitarian doctrine.

**law of the case**: matters decided in the course of litigation which are binding on the parties in the subsequent phases of the litigation.

**leading questions**: questions which suggest the desired answer to the witness, or assume the existence of a fact which is in dispute.

**lease**: an agreement between the owner of property and a tenant by which the former agrees to give possession of the property to the latter in consideration of the payment of rent. (parties-landlord or lessor, tenant or lessee)

**leasehold**: the estate or interest which the tenant has in land rented to him.

**legacy**: a gift of personal property made by will.

**legal tender**: such form of money as the law recognizes as lawful and declares that a tender thereof in the proper amount is a proper tender which the creditor cannot refuse.

**letters of administration**: the written authorization given to an administrator as evidence of his appointment and authority.

**letters testamentary**: the written authorization given to an executor as evidence of his appointment and authority.

**levy**: a seizure of property by an officer of the court in execution of a judgment of the court, although in many states it is sufficient if the officer is physically in the presence of the property and announces the fact that he is "seizing" it, although he then allows the property to remain where he found it.

**lex loci**: the law of the place where the material facts occurred as governing the rights and liabilities of the parties.

**lex loci contractus**: the law of the place where the contract was made as governing the rights and liability of the parties to a contract with respect to certain matters.

**lex loci fori**: the law of the state in which the action is brought as determining the rules of procedure applicable to the action.

**lex loci sitae rei**: the law of the place where land is located as determining the validity of acts done relating thereto.
**libel**: the defamation of another without legal justification.
**license**: a personal privilege to do some act or series of acts upon the land of another not amounting to an easement or a right of possession, as the placing of a sign thereon.
**lien**: a claim or right against property existing by virtue of the entry of a judgment against its owner or by the entry of a judgment and a levy thereunder on the property, or because of the relationship of the claimant to the particular property, such as an unpaid seller.
**life estate**: an estate for the duration of a life.
**limited jurisdiction**: a court with power to hear and determine cases within certain restricted categories.
**limited liability**: loss of contributed capital as maximum liability.
**limited partnership**: a partnership in which at least one partner has a liability limited to the loss of the capital contribution that he has made to the partnership, and such a partner neither takes part in the management of the partnership nor appears to the public to be a partner.
**lineal consanguinity**: the relationship that exists when one person is a direct descendant from the other.
**liquidated damages**: a provision stipulating the amount of damages to be paid in event of default or breach of contract.
**liquidation**: the process of converting property into money whether of particular items of property or all the assets of a business.
**lis pendens**: the doctrine that certain types of pending actions are notice to everyone so that if any right is acquired from a party to that action, the transferee takes that right subject to the outcome of the pending action.
**lobbying contract (illegal):** a contract by which one party agrees to attempt to influence the action of a legislature or congress, or any members thereof, by improper means.
**lottery**: any plan by which a consideration is given for a chance to win a prize.
**lucri causa**: with the motive of obtaining gain or pecuniary advantage.

# M

**majority**: of age, as contrasted with being a minor; more than half of any group, as a majority of stockholders.
**malice in fact**: an intention to injure or cause harm.
**malice in law**: a presumed intention to injure or cause harm when there is no privilege or right to do the act in question, which presumption cannot be contradicted or rebutted.
**maliciously inducing breach of contract**: the wrong of inducing an employee to break his contract with his employer or inducing the breach of any other kind of contract with knowledge of its existence and without justification.
**malum in se**: an offense that is criminal because contrary to the fundamental sense of a civilized community, as murder.
**malum prohibitum**: an offense that is criminal not because inherently wrong but is prohibited for the convenience of society, as overtime parking.
**marshalling assets**: the distribution of a debtor's assets in such a way as to give the greatest benefit to all of his creditors.
**martial law**: government exercised by a military commander over property and persons not in the armed forces, as contrasted with military law which governs the military personnel.
**mechanics' lien**: protection afforded by statute to various types of laborers and persons supplying materials, by giving them a lien on the building and land that has been improved or added to by them.
**mens rea**: the mental state that must accompany an act to make the act a crime, sometimes described as the "guilty mind," although appreciation of guilt is not required.
**merger by judgment**: the discharge of a contract through being merged into a judgment which is entered in a suit on the contract.
**merger of corporations**: a combining of corporations by which one absorbs the other and continues to exist, preserving its original charter and identity while the other corporation ceases to exist.

**mesne**: intermediate, intervening, as mesne profits, which are the fruits or income from the land received in between the time that the true owner was wrongfully dispossessed and the time that he recovers the land.

**misdemeanor**: a criminal offense which is neither treason nor a felony.

**misrepresentation**: a false statement of fact although made innocently without any intent to deceive.

**mobilia sequuntur personam**: the maxim that personal property follows the owner and in the eyes of the law is located at the owner's domicile.

**moratorium**: a temporary suspension by statute of the enforcement of debts or the foreclosure of mortgages.

**mortgage**: an interest in land given by the owner to his creditor as security for the payment to the creditor of a debt, the nature of the interest depending upon the law of the state where the land is located. (Parties--mortgagor, mortgagee)

**multiple insurers**: insurers who agree to divide a risk so that each is only liable for a specified portion.

# N

**National Labor Management Relations Act**: the federal statute, also known as the taft-hartley act, designed to protect the organizational rights of labor and to prevent unfair labor practices by management or labor.

**natural and probable consequences**: those ordinary consequences of an act which a reasonable man would foresee.

**negative covenant**: an undertaking in a deed to refrain from doing an act.

**negligence**: the failure to exercise due care under the circumstances in consequence of which harm is proximately caused to one to whom the defendant owed a duty to exercise due care.

**negligence per se**: an action which is regarded as so improper that it is declared by law to be negligent in itself without regard to whether due care was otherwise exercised.

**negotiable instruments**: drafts or bills of exchange, promissory notes, checks, and certificates of deposit in such form that greater rights may be acquired thereunder than by taking an assignment of a contract right.

**negotiation**: the transfer of a negotiable instrument by indorsement and delivery by the person to whom then payable in the case of order paper, and by physical transfer in the case of bearer paper.

**nominal damages**: a nominal sum awarded the plaintiff in order to establish that his legal rights have been violated although he in fact has not sustanied any actual loss or damages.

**nominal partner**: a person who in fact is not a partner but who holds himself out as a partner or permits others to do so.

**Norris-Laguardia Anti-Injunction Act**: a federal statute prohibiting the use of the injunction in labor disputes, except in particular cases.

**notice of dishonor**: notice given to parties secondarily liable that the primary party to the instrument has refused to accept the instrument or to make payment when it was properly presented for that purpose.

**novation**: the discharge of a contract between two parties by their agreeing with a third person that such third person shall be substituted for one of the original parties to the contract, who shall thereupon be released.

**nudum pactum**: a mere promise for which there is no consideration given and which therefore is ordinarily not enforceable.

**nuisance**: any conduct that harms or prejudices another in the use of his land or which harms or prejudices the public.

**nuisance per se**: an activity which is in itself a nuisance regardless of the time and place involved.

**nuncupative will**: an oral will made and declared by the testator in the presence of witnesses to be his will and generally made during the testator's last illness.

## O

**obiter dictum**: that which is said in the opinion of a court in passing or by the way, but which is not necessary to the determination of the case and is therefore not regarded as authoritative as though it were actually involved in the decision.

**obliteration**: any erasing, writing upon or crossing out that makes all or part of a will impossible to read, and which has the effect of revoking such part when done by the testator with the intent of effecting a revocation.

**occupation**: taking and holding possession of property; a method of acquiring title to personal property which has been abandoned.

**open-end mortgage**: a mortgage given to secure additional loans to be made in the future as well as the original loan.

**operation of law**: the attaching of certain consequences to certain facts because of legal principles that operate automatically, as contrasted with consequences which arise because of the voluntary action of a party designed to create those consequences.

**opinion evidence**: evidence not of what the witness himself observed but the conclusion which he draws from what he observed, or in the case of an expert witness, also from what he is asked or what he has heard at the trial.

**option contract**: a contract to hold an offer to make a contract open for a fixed period of time.

## P

**paper title**: the title of a person evidenced only by deeds or matter appearing of record under the recording statutes.

**parol evidence rule**: the rule that prohibits the introduction in evidence of oral or written statements made prior to or contemporaneously with the execution of a complete written contract, deed, or instrument, in the absence of clear proof of fraud, accident, or mistake causing the omission of the statement in question.

**passive trust**: a trust that is created without imposing any duty to be performed by the trustee and is therefore treated as an absolute transfer of the title to the trust beneficiary.

**past consideration**: something that has been performed in the past and which therefore cannot be consideration for a promise made in the present.

**PATENT**: the grant to an inventor of an exclusive right to make and sell his invention for a nonrenewable period of 17 years: a deed to land given by a government to a private person.

**pawn**: a pledge of tangible personal property rather than of documents representing property rights.

**pecuniary legacy**: a general legacy of a specified amount of money without indicating the source from which payment is to be made.

**per autre vie**: limitation of an estate. An estate held by A during the lifetime of B, is an estate of A per autre vie.

**per curiam opinion**: an opinion written "by the court" rather than by a named judge when all the judges of the court are so agreed on the matter that it is not deemed to merit any discussion and may be simply disposed of.

**perpetual succession**: a phrase describing the continuing life of the corporation unaffected by the death of any stockholder or the transfer by stockholders of their stock.

**perpetuities, rule against**: a rule of law that prohibits the creation of an interest in property which will not become definite or vested until a date further away than 21 years after the death of persons alive at the time the owner of the property attempts to create the interest.

**per se**: in, through, or by itself

**person**: a term that includes both natural persons, or living people, and artificial persons, as corporations which are created by act of government.

**personal defenses**: limited defenses that cannot be asserted by the defendant against a holder in due course or a holder through a holder in due course. This term is not expressly used in the Uniform Commercial Code.
**per stirpes**: according to the root or by way of representation. Distribution among heirs related to the decedent in different degrees, the property being divided into lines of descent from the decedent and the share of each line then divided within the line by way of representation.
**petty jury**: the trial jury of twelve. Also petit jury.
**picketing**: the placing of persons outside of places of employment or distribution so that by words or banners they may inform the public of the existence of a labor dispute.
**pleadings**: the papers filed by the parties in an action in order to set forth the facts and frame the issues to be tried, although under some systems, the pleadings merely give notice or a general indication of the nature of the issues.
**pledge**: a bailment given as security for the payment of a debt or the performance of an obligation owed to the pledgee. (Parties-pledgor. pledgee)
**police power**: the power to govern; the power to adopt laws for the protection of the public health, welfare, safety, and morals.
**policy**: the paper evidencing the contract of insurance.
**polling the jury**: the process of inquiring of each juror individually in open court as to whether the verdict announced by the foreman of the jury was agreed to by him.
**possession**: exclusive domain and control of property.
**possessory lien**: a right to retain possession of property of another as security for some debt or obligation owed the lienor which right continues only as long as possession is retained.
**possibility of reverter**: the nature of the interest held by the grantor after conveying land outright but subject to a condition or provision that may cause the grantee's interest to become forfeited and the interest to revert to the grantor of his heirs.
**postdate**: to insert or place a later date on an instrument than the actual date on which it was executed.
**power of appointment**: a power given to another, commonly a beneficiary of a trust, to designate or appoint who shall be beneficiary or receive the fund upon his death.
**power of attorney**: a written authorization to an agent by the principal.
**precatory words**: words indicating merely a desire or a wish that another use property for a particular purpose but which in law will not be enforced in the absence of an express declaration that the property shall be used for the specified purpose.
**pre-emptive offer of shares**: the right, subject to many exceptions, that each shareholder has that whenever the capital stock of the corporation is increased he will be allowed to subscribe to such a percentage of the new shares as his old shares bore to the former total capital stock.
**preferred creditor**: a creditor who by some statute is given the right to be paid first or before other creditors.
**preferred stock**: stock that has a priority or preference as to payment of dividends or upon liquidation, or both.
**preponderance of evidence**: the degree or quantum of evidence in favor of the existence of a certain fact when from a review of all the evidence it appears more probable that the fact exists than that it does not. The actual number of witnesses involved is not material nor is the fact that the margin of probability is very slight.
**prescription**: the acquisition of a right to use the land of another. as an easement, through the making of hostile, visible and notorious use of the land, continuing for the period specified by the local law.
**presumption**: a rule of proof which permits the existence of a fact to be assumed from the proof that another fact exists when there is a logical relationship between the two or when the means of disproving the assumed fact are more readily within the control or knowledge of the adverse party against whom the presumption operates.
**presumption of death**: the rebuttable presumption which arises that a person has died when he has been continuously absent and unheard of for a period of 7 years.
**presumption of innocence**: the presumption of fact that a person accused of crime is innocent until it is shown that he in fact is guilty of the offense charged.

**presumption of payment**: a rebuttable presumption that one performing continuing services which would normally be paid periodically, as weekly or monthly, has in fact been paid when a number of years have passed without any objection or demand for payment having been made.
**presumptive heir**: a person who would be the heir if the ancestor should die at that moment.
**pretrial conference**: a conference held prior to the trial at which the court and the attorneys seek to simplify the issues in controversy and eliminate matters not in dispute.
**price**: the consideration for a sale of goods.
**prima facie**: such evidence as by itself would establish the claim or defense of the party if the evidence were believed.
**primary beneficiary**: the person designated as the first one to receive the proceeds of a life insurance policy, as distinguished from a contingent beneficiary who will receive the proceeds only if the primary beneficiary dies before the insured.
**primary liability**: the liability of a person whose act or omission gave rise to the cause of action and who in all fairness should therefore be the one to pay the victim of his wrong, even though others may also be liable for his misconduct.
**principal**: one who employs an agent to act on his behalf; the person who as between himself and the surety is primarily liable to the third person or creditor.
**principal in the first degree**: one who actually engages in the commission or perpetration of a crime.
**principal in the second degree**: one who is actually or constructivey present at the commission of the crime and who aids and abets in its commission.
**private carrier**: a carrier owned by the shipper, such as a company's own fleet of trucks.
**privileged communication**: information which the witness may refuse to testify to because of the relationship with the person furnishing the information, as husband-wife, attorney-client.
**privilege from arrest**: the immunity from arrest of parties, witnesses, and attorneys while present within the jurisdiction for the purpose of taking part in other litigation.
**privity**: a succession or chain of relationship to the same thing or right, as a privity of contract, privity of estate, privity of possession.
**probate**: the procedure for formally establishing or proving that a given writing is the last will and testament of the person purporting to have signed it.
**process**: a writ or order of court generally used as a means of acquiring jurisdiction over the person of the defendant by serving him with process.
**profit a prendre**: the right to take a part of the soil or produce of the land of another, such as to take timber or water.
**promissory estoppel**: the doctrine that a promise will be enforced although not supported by consideration when the promisor should have reasonably expected that his promise would induce action or forebearance of a definite and substantial character on the part of the promisee, and injustice can only be avoided by enforcement of the promise.
**promissory note**: an unconditional promise in writing made by one person to another, signed by the maker, engaging to pay on demand, or at a definite time, a sum certain in money to order or to bearer. (Parties-maker, payee)
**promissory representation**: a representation made by the applicant to the insurer as to what is to occur in the future.
**promissory warranty**: a representation made by the applicant to the insurer as to what is to occur in the future which the applicant warrants will occur.
**promoters**: the persons who plan the formation of the corporation and sell or promote the idea to others.
**proof**: the probative effect of the evidence: the conclusion drawn from the evidence as to the existence of particular facts.
**property**: the rights and interests one has in anything subject to ownership.
**pro rata**: proportionately, or divided according to a rate or standard.
**protest**: the formal certification by a notary public or other authorized person that proper presentment of a commercial paper was made to the primary party and that he defaulted, the certificate commonly also including a recital that notice was given to secondary parties.

**proximate cause:** the act which is the natural and reasonably foreseeable cause of the harm or event which occurs and injures the plaintiff.

**proximate damages:** damages which in the ordinary course of events are the natural and reasonably foreseeable result of the defendant's violation of the plaintiff's rights.

**proxy:** a written authorization by a stockholder to another person to vote the stock owned by the stockholder; the person who is the holder of such a written authorization.

**public charge:** a person who because of a personal disability or lack of means of support is dependent upon public charity or relief for sustenance.

**public domain:** public or government owned lands.

**public easement:** a right of way for use by members of the public at large.

**public policy:** certain objectives relating to health, morals, and integrity of government that the law seeks to advance by declaring invalid any contract which conflicts with those objectives even though there is no statute expressly declaring such contract illegal.

**punitive damages:** damages in excess of those required to compensate the plaintiff for the wrong done, which are imposed in order to punish the defendant because of the particularly wanton or willful character of his wrongdoing.

**purchase-money mortgage:** a mortgage given by the purchaser of land to the seller to secure the seller for the payment of the unpaid balance of the purchase price, which the seller purports to lend the purchaser.

**purchaser in good faith:** a person who purchases without any notice or knowledge of any defect of title, misconduct, or defense.

# Q

**qualified acceptance:** an acceptance of a draft that varies the order of the bill in some way.

**qualified indorsement:** an indorsement that includes words such as "without recourse" evidencing the intent of the indorser that he shall not be held liable for the failure of the primary party to pay the instrument.

**quantum meruit:** an action brought for the value of the services rendered the defentant when there was no express contract as to the payment to be made.

**quantum valebant:** an action brought for the value of goods sold the defendant when there was no express contract as to the purchase price.

**quasi:** as if, as though it were, having the characteristics of; a modifier employed to indicate that the subject is to be treated as though it were in fact the noun which follows the word "quasi:" as in quasi contract, quasi corporation, quasi public corporation.

**quid pro quo:** literally "what for what." An early form of the concept of consideration by which an action for debt could not be brought unless the defendant had obtained something in return for his obligation.

**quitclaim deed:** a deed by which the grantor purports only to give up whatever right or title he may have in the property without specifying or warranting that he is transferring any particular interest.

**quorum:** the minimum number of persons, shares represented, or directors who must be present at a meeting in order that business may be lawfully transacted.

# R

**ratification by minor:** the approval of a contract given by a minor after attaining majority.

**ratification of agency:** the approval of the unauthorized act of an agent or of a person who is not an agent for any purpose after the act has been done, which has the same effect as though the act had been authorized before it was done.

**ratio decidendi:** the reason or basis for deciding the case in a particular way.

**ratio legis:** the reason for a principle or rule of law.

**real defenses**: certain defenses (universal) that are available against any holder of a negotiable instrument regardless of his character, although this term is not expressly used by the Uniform Commercial Code.

**real evidence**: tangible objects that are presented in the courtroom for the observation of the trier of fact as proof of the facts in dispute or in support of the theory of a party.

**real property**: land and all rights in land.

**reasonable care**: the degree of care that a reasonable man would take under all the circumstances then known.

**rebate**: a refund made by the seller or the carrier of part of the purchase price or freight bill. Generally illegal as an unfair method of competition.

**rebuttable presumption**: a presumption which may be overcome or rebutted by proof that the actual facts were different than those presumed.

**receiver**: an impartial person appointed by a court to take possession of and manage property for the protection of all concerned.

**recognizance**: an obligation entered into before a court to do some act, such as to appear at a later date for a hearing. Also called a contract of record.

**redemption**: the buying back of one's property, which has been sold because of a default, upon paying the amount which had been originally due together with interest and costs.

**referee**: an impartial person selected by the parties or appointed by a court to determine facts or decide matters in dispute.

**referee in bankruptcy**: a referee appointed by a bankruptcy court to hear and determine various matters relating to bankruptcy proceedings.

**reformation**: a remedy by which a written instrument is corrected when it fails to express the actual intent of both parties because of fraud, accident, or mistake.

**registration of titles**: a system generally known as the Torrens system of permanent registration of title to all land within the state.

**reimbursement**: the right of one paying money on behalf of another which such other person should have himself paid to recover the amount of the payment from him.

**release of liens**: an agreement or instrument by which the holder of a lien on property, such as a **mortgage lien**, releases the property from the lien although the debt itself is not released.

**remedy**: the action or procedure that is followed in order to enforce a right or to obtain damages for injury to a right.

**remote damages**: damages which were in fact caused by the defendant's act but the possibility that such damages should occur seemed so improbable and unlikely to a reasonable man that the law does not impose liability for such damages.

**renunciation of duty**: the repudiation of one's contractual duty in advance of the time for performance, which repudiation may be accepted by the adverse party as an anticipatory breach.

**renunciation of right**: the surrender of a right or privilege as the right to act as administrator or the right to receive a legacy under the will of a decedent.

**reorganization of corporation**: procedure devised to restore insolvent corporations to financial stability through readjustment of debt and capital structure either under the supervision of a court of equity or of bankruptcy.

**repossession**: any taking again of possession although generally used in connection with the act of a conditional vendor in taking back the property upon the default of the conditional vendee.

**representations**: statements, whether oral or written, made to give the insurer the information which it needs in writing the insurance, and which if false and relating to a material fact will entitle the insurer to avoid the contract.

**representative capacity**: action taken by one not on his own behalf but on behalf of another, as an executor acting on behalf of the decedent's estate, or action taken both on one's behalf and on behalf of others, as a stockholder bringing a representative action.

**resale price maintenance agreement**: an agreement that the buyer will not resell a trademark or brand name article below a stated minimum price which agreement, by virtue of fair trade laws, is valid not only as between the contracting parties but may also bind other persons in the trade who know of the agreement although they did not sign it.

**rescission upon agreement**: the setting aside of a contract by the action of the parties as though the contract had never been made.

**rescission upon breach**: the action of one party to a contract to set the contract aside when the other party is guilty of a breach of the contract.

**reservation**: the creation by the grantor of a right that did not exist before, which he reserves or keeps for himself upon making a conveyance of property.

**residuary estate**: the balance of the testator's estate available for distribution after all administrative expenses, exemptions, debts, taxes, and specific, pecuniary, and demonstrative legacies have been paid.

**res inter alios acta**: the rule that transactions and declarations between strangers having no connection with the pending action are not admissible in evidence.

**res ipsa loquitur**: the rebuttable presumption that the thing speaks for itself when the circumstances are such that ordinarily the plaintiff could not have been injured had the defendant not been at fault.

**res judicata**: the principle that once a final judgment is entered in an action between the parties, it is binding upon them and the matters cannot be litigated again by bringing a second action.

**respondeat superior**: the doctrine that the principal or employer is vicariously liable for the unauthorized torts committed by his agent or employee while acting with the scope of his agency or the course of his employment, respectively.

**restraints on alienation**: limitations on the ability of the owner to convey freely as he chooses. Such limitations are generally regarded as invalid.

**restrictive covenants**: covenants in a deed by which the grantee agrees to refrain from doing specified acts.

**restrictive indorsement**: an indorsement that prohibits the further transfer, constitutes the indorsee the agent of the indorser, vests the title in the indorsee in trust for or to the use of some other person, is conditional, or is for collection or deposit.

**resulting trust**: a trust that is created by implication of law when the purpose of the original trust fails or is fully performed and the cy pres doctrine is inapplicable, the effect of the resulting trust being to revert the remaining property to the settlor or his heirs.

**retaliatory statute**: a statute that provides that when a corporation of another state enters the state it shall be subject to the same taxes and restrictions as would be imposed upon a corporation from the retaliating state if it had entered the other state. Also called reciprocity statutes.

**reversible error**: an error or defect in court proceedings of so serious a nature that on appeal the appellate court will set aside the proceedings of the lower court.

**reversionary interest**: the interest that a lessor has in property which is subject to an outstanding lease.

**revival of judgment**: the taking of appropriate action to preserve a judgment, in most instances to continue the lien of the judgment that would otherwise expire after a specified number of years.

**revival of will**: the restoration by the testator of a will which he had previously revoked.

**rider**: a slip of paper executed by the insurer and intended to be attached to the insurance policy for the purpose of changing it in some respect.

**riparian rights**: the right of a person through whose land runs a natural watercourse to use the water free from unreasonable pollution or diversion by the upper riparian owners and from blocking by lower riparian owners.

**risk**: the peril or contingency against which the insured is protected by the contract of insurance.

**Robinson-Patman Act**: a federal statute designed to eliminate price discrimination in interstate commerce.

**run with the land**: the concept that certain covenants in a deed to land are deemed to "run" or pass with the land so that whoever owns the land is bound by or entitled to the benefit of the covenants.

## S

**sale or return**: a sale in which the title to the property passes to the buyer at the time of the transaction but he is given the option of returning the property and restoring the title to the seller.

**scienter**: knowledge, referring to those wrongs or crimes which require a knowledge of wrong in order to constitute the offense.

**scope of employment**: the area within which the employee is authorized to act with the consequence that a tort committed while so acting imposes liability upon the employer.

**seal**: at common law an impression on wax or other tenacious material attached to the instrument. Under modern law, any mark not ordinarily part of the signature is a seal when so intended, including the letters "L. S." and the word "seal," or a pictorial representation of a seal, without regard to whether they had been printed or typed on the instrument before its signing.

**sealed verdict**: a verdict that is rendered when the jury returns to the courtroom during an adjournment of the court, the verdict then being written down and sealed and later affirmed before the court when the court is in session.

**seaman's will**: an oral or informal written will made by a seaman to dispose of his personal property.

**secondary evidence**: copies of original writings or testimony as to the contents of such writings which are admissible when the original cannot be produced and the inability to do so is reasonably explained.

**secret partner**: a partner who takes an active part in the management of the partnership but is not known to the public as a partner.

**secured transaction**: a sale of goods on credit that provides some form of special protection for the seller.

**settlor**: one who settles property in trust or creates a trust estate.

**severable contract**: a contract the terms of which are such that one part may be separated or severed from the other, so that a default as to one part is not necessarily a default as to the entire contract.

**several contracts**: separate or independent contracts made by different persons undertaking to perform the same obligation.

**severalty**: sole ownership of property by one person.

**severed realty**: real property that has been cut off and made moveable, as by cutting down a tree, and which thereby loses its character as real property and becomes personal property.

**shareholder's action**: an action brought by one or more shareholders on behalf of the shareholders generally and of the corporation to enforce a cause of action of the corporation against third persons.

**sheriff's deed**: the deed executed and delivered by the sheriff to the purchaser at a sale conducted by the sheriff in his official capacity.

**Sherman Antitrust Act**: a federal statute prohibiting combinations and contracts in restraint of interstate trade, now generally inapplicable to labor union activity.

**shop right**: the right of an employer to use in his business without charge an invention discovered by an employee during working hours and with the employer's material and equipment.

**sight draft**: a draft or bill of exchange payable on sight or when presented for payment.

**silent partner**: a partner who takes no active part in the business without regard to whether he is known to the public as a partner.

**sitdown strike**: a strike in which the employees remain in the plant and refuse to allow the employer to operate it.

**slander**: defamation of character by spoken words or gestures.

**slander of title**: the malicious making of false statements as to a seller's title.

**slander per se**: certain words deemed slanderous without requiring proof of damages to the victim, as words charging a crime involving moral turpitude and an infamous punishment, a disease which would exclude from society, or which tend to injure the victim in his business, profession, or occupation.

**slowdown**: a slowing down of production by employees without actual stopping of work.

**social security acts**: statutes providing for assistance for the aged, blind, unemployed, and similar classes of persons in need.

**soldier's will**: an oral or informal written will made by a soldier to dispose of his personal estate.

**special agent**: an agent authorized to transact a specific transaction or to do a specific act.

**special damages**: damages that do not necessarily result from the injury to the plaintiff but at the same time are not so remote that the defendant should not be held liable therefore provided that the claim for special damages is properly made in the action.
**special indorsement**: an indorsement that specifies the person to whom the instrument is indorsed.
**special jurisdiction**: a court with power to hear and determine cases within certain restricted categories.
**specific (identified) goods**: goods which are so identified to the contract that no other goods may be delivered in performance of the contract.
**specific lien**: the right of a creditor to hold particular property or assert a lien on any particular property of the debtor because of the creditor's having done work on or having some other association with the property, as distinguished from having a lien generally against the assets of the debtor merely because the debtor is indebted to him.
**specific performance**: an action brought to compel the adverse party to perform his contract on the theory that merely suing him for damages for its breach will not be an adequate remedy.
**spendthrift trust**: a trust, which to varying degrees, provides that creditors of the beneficiary shall not be able to reach the principal of income held by the trustee and that the beneficiary shall not be able to assign his interest in the trust.
**spoliation**: an alteration or change made to a written instrument by a person who has no relationship to or interest in the writing. It has no effect as long as the terms of the instrument can still be ascertained.
**stare decisis**: the principle that the decision of a court should serve as a guide or precedent and control the decision of a similar case in the future.
**status quo**: the requirement that before a contract may be rescinded, the status quo must be restored, that is, the parties must be placed in their original positions prior to the making of the contract.
**Statute of Frauds**: a statute, which in order to prevent fraud through the use of perjured testimony, requires that certain types of transactions be evidenced in writing in order to be binding or enforceable.
**Statute of limitations**: a statute that restricts the period of time within which an action may be brought.
**stoppage in transitu**: the right of the unpaid seller to stop goods being shipped to the buyer while they are still in transit and to recover them when the buyer becomes insolvent.
**stop payment**: an order by a depositor to his bank to refuse to make payment of his check when presented for payment.
**sublease**: a transfer of the premises by the lessee to a third person. The sublessee or subtenant, for a period less than the term of the original lease.
**subpoena**: a court order directing a person to appear as a witness. In some states also it is the original process that is to be served on the defendant in order to give the court jurisdiction over his person.
**subpoena duces tecum**: a court order directing a person to appear as a witness and to bring with him specified relevant papers.
**subrogation**: the right of a party secondarily liable to stand in the place of the creditor after he has made payment to the creditor and to enforce the creditor's right against the party primarily liable in order to obtain indemnity from him.
**subsidiary corporation**: a corporation that is controlled by another corporation through the ownership by the latter of a controlling amount of the voting stock of the former.
**subsidiary term**: a provision of a contract that is not fundamental or does not go to the root of the contract.
**substantial performance**: the equitable doctrine that a contractor substantially performing a contract in good faith is entitled to recover the contract price less damages for noncompletion or defective work.
**substantive law**: the law that defines rights and liabilities.
**substitution**: discharge of contracts by substituting another in its place.
**subtenant**: one who rents the leased premises from the original tenant for a period of time less than the balance of the lease to the original tenant.
**sui generis**: in a class by itself, or its own kind.
**sui juris**: legally competent, possessing capacity.
**summary judgment**: a judgment entered by the court when no substantial dispute of fact is present, the court acting on the basis of affidavits which show that the claim or defense of a party is a sham.
**summons**: a writ by which an action was commenced under the common law.

**superior servant rule**: an exception to the fellow-servant rule that is made when the injured servant is under the control of the servant whose conduct caused him injury.

**supersedeas**: a stay of proceedings pending the taking of an appeal or an order entered for the purpose of effecting such a stay.

**surcharge**: a money judgment entered against a fiduciary for the amount of loss which his negligence or misconduct has caused the estate under his control.

**suretyship**: an undertaking to pay the debt or be liable for the default of another.

**surrender**: the yielding up of the tenant's leasehold estate to the lessor in consequence of which the lease terminates.

**survival acts**: statutes which provide that causes of action shall not terminate on death but shall survive and may be enforced by or against a decedent's estate.

**survivorship**: the right by which a surviving joint tenant or tenant by the entireties acquires the interest of the predeceasing tenant automatically upon his death.

**symbolic delivery**: the delivery of goods by delivery of the means of control, as a key or relevant document of title, as a negotiable bill of lading.

**syndicate**: an association of individuals formed to conduct a particular business transaction, generally of a financial nature.

# T

**tacking**: the adding together of successive periods of adverse possession of persons in privity with each other in order to constitute a sufficient period of continuous adverse possession to vest title thereby.

**Taft-Hartley Act**: popular name for the National Labor Management Relations Act of 1947,

**tenancy at sufferance**: the holding over by a tenant after his lease has expired of the rented land without the permission of the landlord and prior to the time that the landlord has elected to treat him as a trespasser or a tenant.

**tenancy at will**: the holding of land for an indefinite period that may be terminated at any time by the landlord or by the landlord and tenant acting together.

**tenancy for years**: a tenancy for a fixed period of time, even though the time is less than a year.

**tenancy from year to year**: a tenancy which continues indefinitely from year to year until terminated.

**tenancy in common**: the relation that exists when two or more persons own undivided interests in property.

**tenancy in partnership**: the ownership relation that exists between partners under the Uniform Partnership Act.

**tender of payment**: an unconditional offer to pay the exact amount of money due at the time and place specified by the contract.

**tender of performance**: an unconditional offer to perform at the time and in the manner specified by the contract.

**tentative trust**: a trust which arises when money is deposited in a bank account in the name of the depositor "in trust for" a named person.

**terminable fee**: an estate that terminates upon the happening of a contingency without any entry by the grantor or his heirs, as a conveyance for "so long as" the land is used for a specified purpose.

**testamentary**: designed to take effect at death, as by disposing of property or appointing an executor.

**testate**: the condition of leaving a will upon death.

**testate succession**: the distribution of an estate in accordance with the will of the decedent.

**testator-testatrix**: a man-woman who makes a will.

**testimonium clause**: a concluding paragraph in a deed, contract, or other instrument, reciting that the instrument has been executed on a specified date by the parties.

**testimony**: the answers of witnesses under oath to questions given at the time of the trial in the presence of the trier of fact.

**theory of the case**: the rule that when a case is tried on the basis of one theory, the appellant in taking an appeal cannot argue a different theory to the appellate court.

**third-party beneficiary**: a third person whom the parties to a contract intend to benefit by the making of the contract and to confer upon him the right to sue for breach of the contract.

**tie-in sale**: the requirement imposed by the seller that the buyer of particular goods or equipment also purchase certain other goods from the seller in order to obtain the original property desired.

**time draft**: a bill of exchange payable at a stated time after sight or a stated time after a certain date.

**title insurance**: a form of insurance by which the insurer insures the buyer of real property against the risk of loss should the title acquired from the seller be defective in any way.

**toll the statute**: stop the running of the period of the Statute of Limitations by the doing of some act by the debtor.

**Torrens System**: see registration of titles.

**tort**: a private injury or wrong arising from a breach of a duty created by law.

**trade acceptance**: a draft or bill of exchange drawn by the seller of goods on the purchaser at the time of sale and accepted by the purchaser.

**trade fixtures**: articles of personal property which have been attached to the freehold by a tenant and which are used for or are necessary to the carrying on of the tenant's trade.

**trade-mark**: a name, device, or symbol used by a manufacturer or seller to distinguish his goods from those of other persons.

**trade name**: a name under which a business is carried on and, if fictitious, it must be registered.

**trade secrets**: secrets of any character peculiar and important to the business of the employer that have been communicated to the employee in the course of confidential employment.

**treason**: an attempt to overthrow or betray the government to which one owes allegiance.

**treasury stock**: stock of the corporation which the corporation has reacquired.

**trier of fact**: in most cases a jury, although it may be the judge alone in certain classes of cases, as in equity, or in any case when jury trial is waived, or an administrative agency or commission.

**trust**: a transfer of property by one person to another with the understanding or declaration that such property be held for the benefit of another, or the holding of property by the owner in trust for another, upon his declaration of trust, without a transfer to another person. (Parties—settlor, trustee, beneficiary.)

**trust corpus**: the fund or property that is transferred to the trustee as the body or subject matter of the trust.

**trust deed**: a form of deed which transfers the trust property to the trustee for the purposes therein stated, particularly used as a form of mortgage when the trustee is to hold the title to the mortgagor's land in trust for the benefit of the mortgage bondholders.

**trustee de son tort**: a person who is not a trustee but who has wrongly intermeddled with property of another and rather than proceed against him for the tort, the law will require him to account for the property as though he were such a trustee.

**trustee in bankruptcy**: an impartial person elected to administer the bankrupt's estate.

**trust receipt**: a credit security device under which the wholesale buyer executes a receipt stating that he holds the purchased goods in trust for the person financing the purchase by lending him money. The trust receipt is replaced by the secured transaction under the Uniform Commercial Code.

# U

**uberrima fides**: utmost good faith, a duty to exercise the utmost good faith which arises in certain relationships, as that between an insurer and the applicant for insurance.

**ultra vires**: an act or contract which the corporation does not have authority to do or make.    Glossary

**underwriter**: an insurer.

**undisclosed principal**: a principal on whose behalf an agent acts without disclosing to the third person the fact that he is an agent nor the identity of the principal.

**undue influence**: the influence that is asserted upon another person by one who dominates that person.

**unfair competition**: the wrong of employing competitive methods that have been declared unfair by statute or an administrative agency.

**unfair labor practice acts**: statutes that prohibit certain labor practices and declare them to be unfair labor practices.

**unincorporated association**: a combination of two or more persons for the furtherance of a common nonprofit purpose.

**union contract**: a contract between a labor union and an employer or group of employers prescribing the general terms of employment of workers by the latter.

**union shop**: under present unfair labor practice statutes, a place of employment where nonunion men may be employed for a trial period of not more than 30 days after which the nonunion worker must join the union or be discharged.

**universal agent**: an agent authorized by the principal to do all acts that can lawfully be delegated to a representative.

**usury**: the lending of money at greater than the maximum rate allowed by law.

# V

**vacation of judgment**: the setting aside of a judgment.

**valid**: legal.

**verdict**: the decision of the trial or petty jury.

**vice-principal rule**: the rule that persons performing supervisory functions or acting as vice employers are not to be regarded as fellow servants of those under their authority for the purpose of determining the liability of the employer for the injuries of the employee at common law.

**void**: no legal effect and not binding on anyone.

**voidable**: a transaction that may be set aside by one party thereto because of fraud or similar reason but which is binding on the other party until the injured party elects to avoid the contract.

**voidable preference**: a preference given by the bankrupt to one of his creditors, but which may be set aside by the trustee in bankruptcy.

**voir dire examination**: the preliminary examination of a juror or a witness to ascertain that he is qualified to act as such.

**volenti non fit injuria**: the maxim that the defendant's act cannot constitute a tort if the plaintiff had consented thereto.

**voluntary nonsuit**: a means of the plaintiff's stopping a trial at any time by moving for a voluntary nonsuit.

**voting trust**: the transfer by two or more persons of their shares of stock of a corporation to a trustee who is to vote the shares and act for such shareholders.

# W

**waiver**: the release or relinquishment of a known right or objection.

**warehouse receipt**: a receipt issued by the warehouseman for goods stored with him. Regulated generally by the Uniform Warehouse Receipts Act or the Uniform Commercial Code, which clothe the receipt with some degree of negotiability.

**warehouseman**: a person regularly engaged in the business of storing the goods of others for compensation. If he holds himself out to serve the public without discrimination, he is a public warehouseman.

**warranties of indorser of negotiable instrument**: the implied covenants made by an indorser of a negotiable instrument distinct from any undertaking to pay upon the default of the primary party.

**warranties of insured**: statements or promises made by the applicant for insurance which he guarantees to be as stated and which if false will entitle the insurer to avoid the contract of insurance in many jurisdictions.

**warranties of seller of goods**: warranties consisting of express warranties that relate to matters forming part of the basis of the bargain; warranties as to title and right to sell; and the implied warranties which the law adds to a sale depending upon the nature of the transaction.

**warranty deed**: a deed by which the grantor conveys a specific estate or interest to the grantee and covenants that he has transferred the estate or interest by making one or more of the covenants of title.

**warranty of authority:** an implied warranty of an agent that he has the authority which he purports to possess.

**warranty of principal:** an implied warranty of an agent that he is acting for an existing principal who has capacity to contract.

**watered stock**: stock issued by a corporation as fully paid when in fact it is not.

**way**: an easement to pass over the land of another.

**will**: an instrument executed with the formality required by law, by which a person makes a disposition of his property to take effect upon his death or appoints an executor.

**willful**: intentional as distinguished from accidental or involuntary. In penal statutes, with evil intent or legal malice, or without reasonable ground for believing one's act to be lawful.

**witness**: a person who has observed the facts to which he testifies or an expert witness who may testify on the basis of observation, the testimony presented in the court, or hypothetical questions put to him by the attorneys in the case.

**Wool Products Labeling Act**: a federal statute prohibiting the misbranding of woolen fabrics.

**workmen's compensation**: a system providing for payments to workmen because they have been injured from a risk arising out of the course of their employment while they were employed at their employment or have contracted an occupational disease in that manner, payment being made without consideration of the negligence of any party.

**works of charity**: in connection with Sunday laws, acts involved in religious worship or aiding persons in distress.

**works of necessity**: in connection with Sunday laws, acts that must be done at the particular time in order to be effective in saving life, health, or property.

# Y

**year and a day**: the common-law requirement that death result within a year and a day in order to impose criminal liability for homicide.

# Z

**zoning restrictions**: restrictions imposed by government on the use of property for the advancement of the general welfare.

www.ingramcontent.com/pod-product-compliance
Lightning Source LLC
Chambersburg PA
CBHW082038300426
44117CB00015B/2521